Beyond Behavior Management

Other Redleaf Press Publications by Jenna Bilmes

*Common Psychological Disorders in Young Children: A Handbook
for Early Childhood Professionals* (with Tara Welker)

The Six Life Skills Children Need (family companion to *Beyond
Behavior Management*)

Beyond Behavior Management

SECOND EDITION

The Six Life Skills Children Need

Jenna Bilmes

Redleaf Press®
www.redleafpress.org
800-423-8309

Published by Redleaf Press
10 Yorkton Court
St. Paul, MN 55117
www.redleafpress.org

First edition published 2004. Second edition 2012.
Cover design by Jim Handrigan
Cover photograph © iStockphoto.com/Alex Slobodkin
Interior design by 4 Seasons Book Design/Michelle Cook
Typeset in Formata and Adobe Garamond Pro
Printed in the United States of America

Library of Congress Cataloging-in-Publication Data
Bilmes, Jenna, 1948-
   Beyond behavior management : the six life skills children need / Jenna Bilmes. —
2nd ed.
     p. cm.
   Summary: "Developed and tested in the classroom, *Beyond Behavior Management*
helps you guide young children's behavior by helping them build essential life skills:
collaboration, adaptability, attachment, self-regulation, contribution, and belonging" —
Provided by publisher.
   Includes bibliographical references and index.
   ISBN 978-1-60554-073-3 (pbk.)
   1. Classroom management. 2. Social skills in children—Study and teaching.   I. Title.
LB3013.B54 2012
371.102'4—dc23
                                        2011039610

                                                                              U17-02

Printed on acid-free paper

For the children and those entrusted with their care.

And for my parents who, as we know, were my first and most important teachers.

Contents

Preface

Until Lizbeth entered my life, I had believed I was a wonderful teacher. But it turned out that years of experience and my college degree were no match for this five-year-old. She threw paint on the windows and turned a favorite tape into a twisted mass of ribbon. She was fluent in the vilest profanity. During a tantrum, she head-butted me hard enough to crack my rib. Lizbeth was first to arrive in the morning, last to leave in the afternoon, and the only one who never came down with chicken pox.

That year with Lizbeth was painful and challenging. But more importantly, that year I started on a journey that was to change the way I taught forever.

Lizbeth crossed my path after I had a few years of experience with children. By then I had learned classroom management from teachers with far more experience than I had. I gave my kids clear limits and time-outs. They received praise when they behaved and stern words combined with "the look" when they did not. I saw, I tried, I conquered. It was the year of stickers, a student-of-the-week phase, and gold tokens for good nappers. With each management technique, I gained more and more control over the children in my care.

To me, Lizbeth appeared to be a stubborn, spoiled, headstrong girl who needed to learn that she wasn't the boss of the universe. And I was determined to be the one to teach her that lesson. I reached deep into my bag of tricks and techniques in an effort to control and manage her. When she crashed a bike, I took away her outside time. She demolished the class gingerbread house, so I forced her to sit in the time-out chair until she apologized to the other children. When she bombarded an innocent boy with her infamous profanity, I took away her right to go on the zoo trip. As she escalated her behavior, I escalated the consequences. But Lizbeth only became more disruptive and defiant.

When my bag of tricks was exhausted, I looked for others to blame. How could I be expected to fix a child whose mother wasn't willing to work with us? Look at the neighborhood she was free to roam at all hours of the day and night! Yet every time I sent her to the office, the director would give her a hug and a chat and would promptly return her to my room. I didn't send her down there for a hug! I wanted that girl to have the fear of God put into her. I wanted blood!

This child brought out the worst in me, time and time again. I became consumed with mean-spirited battles of will with a five-year-old that left me frustrated and discouraged. I had allowed Lizbeth's behavior to turn me into somebody I didn't like very much. It was time to look within myself, not only to examine my relationship with Lizbeth but also to rethink my entire approach to discipline and guidance. What were my overriding goals for children anyhow? And did my current strategies help them reach those goals?

I had a pretty good idea of the beliefs and skills I wanted the children in my care to have. They should know how to have a friend and be a friend, and they should be able to solve conflicts with words rather than force. I wanted them to know right from wrong and to "be good" because that is what people do, rather than behave so they could get a reward or avoid a punishment.

But if that is what I believed, then why was I doing what I was doing? How were children to learn compassion when I told them to ignore their friend in the time-out chair who wept for his mommy? How could they practice conflict resolution when I was so quick to jump in as both judge and jury to solve all their problems? How were children learning to "be good" for goodness' sake when I was bribing them with rewards? Why did I make it my job to manage children's behavior? Shouldn't I focus instead on ways to give them the guidance and practice they needed to manage their own behavior?

One day in a workshop, a group of teachers listed all the strategies we used to teach children language and literacy. Lo and behold, time-out wasn't on the list. Neither was the loss of recess, exclusion from the group, or guilt. Instead, we teamed reading-challenged children with other children in the class who could read. We gave them extra one-on-one practice, and we made sure they never felt inadequate. We gave them messages that there was nothing wrong with them and that we would all work together as a team to support them. Punishment was out of the question! If we punished them, wouldn't the child avoid reading or feel stupid and different from the rest of the children?

If we didn't make children feel bad to help them learn how to read, why then did we try to make children feel bad to help them act good?

The clouds cleared and the sun rose and I had my epiphany. I heard the BIG MESSAGE: the way most of us instinctively react to misbehavior is the least effective way to help children develop good behavior.

I probably should have felt good about this revelation, but I didn't. I knew I had to change my old practices, but I had no idea what to put in their place. I had to figure out all over again what my role was supposed to be in a child's life.

When I first taught two-year-olds, one of the more experienced teachers told me to try to distract children who cried when their parents left them. "Bring them to the window to watch the birds," she said. "If that doesn't work, just ignore them. They'll stop after a few minutes."

And then I had the privilege of working with Sharon. British, with long, wild hair and a tattered Laura Ashley dress, she was a combination of the Pied Piper and Mary Poppins to the fourteen kids in her care. I watched as she knelt down by a distressed child. "Oh you poor dear," she cooed. "You miss your mommy, don't you?" I expected the child to scream even louder, but instead the child began to calm down. "I sometimes miss my mommy too," Sharon continued. "Me too," the child said as the sobs stopped. "I like to look out the window when I feel sad," Sharon said. "Come, let's look together."

What a lesson for me! What a lesson to the child! And what a lesson to the other children in the class. In one brief moment, Sharon modeled compassion, empathy, and emotional management skills to all of us. In all of her interactions with children, she made herself the child's ally, not the child's enemy.

I began to think of different supervisors I had worked for. Florence was a nightmare. As soon as she came near me, my stomach would tighten and I avoided all eye contact in the hope that she would pass me by. Her exchanges with me were inevitably a list of things I was doing wrong and how she wanted them changed. Now and then she threw me a bone with a "good job" comment, which rolled off my back as I awaited the ax to fall.

Sienna, on the other hand, was a born motivator. She worked with each of us as a mentor and a colleague. She shared her observations and solicited our input as we worked together, strategizing how to make our school a better place.

I began to wonder how the children in my class saw me. Was I Florence, micromanaging their every move and pushing them to think of themselves as part of a problem? Or was I Sienna, respecting children and empowering them to be part of the solution?

I began to incorporate new techniques I observed from my gifted mentors, often with no understanding of the theory behind the practice. All I cared about was that these new practices worked better than the management techniques I had learned before. Not only did the children with challenges improve, but the entire atmosphere of community, acceptance, and cooperation flourished for all children in the classroom as well.

It has been fourteen years since I put a child in time-out or handed out a sticker. Still a classroom teacher, I have also led workshops for hundreds of fellow teachers in the theory and practice of effective and humane guidance for young children. These generous educators have shared their own experiences and discoveries with me, and I pass along the wisdom I have collected.

I invite you to explore the theories and practices that can turn you and your children around. Help an unreachable, unteachable Lizbeth begin to connect with and care about others. Model compassion and caring for children so they know your classroom is a safe place. Allow children to see you as their guide and ally as they learn to develop friendships, manage emotions, and resolve problems. Transform your classroom into the place you always imagined it could be.

I wish I could tell you that this journey is a simple one, but I can't. If guiding young children's behavior was an easy procedure, principals' offices would not be hosting a steady stream of children who were sent by teachers for being unmanageable. Parents, teachers, and the court systems would not be pulling out their hair trying to figure it all out. You probably wouldn't be picking up this book today. The truth is there simply isn't a step-by-step method that fits all situations or all children.

The good news is that each of us has a wealth of life experiences and wisdom within us. We can draw on that knowledge to guide our thinking in effective ways to help kids on the path to becoming responsible, happy, and productive citizens.

As you tap into your personal wisdom, you will find yourself validating many of your current practices. Your effective strategies will become much clearer. At the same time, you'll start to understand why other strategies have not produced the results you were seeking. You won't find a cookbook approach to discipline here. Instead, you will gain new understandings and some fresh approaches to weave into the art of your teaching.

Acknowledgments
for the Second Edition

I'd like to express my deeply felt appreciation to the following people who helped this idea of a second edition become a reality:

- Again, the folks at Redleaf Press, especially my tireless editors, Beth Wallace and David Heath, who make the magic happen.

- My generous readers, whose e-mails and messages pushed me to think harder and deeper about some of the ideas in the original book.

- Participants in sessions around the country, who asked the right questions at the right moments to keep me on my toes and push me to continue my own education.

- A big thanks to my kids for gifting me with three grandkids to love and learn from.

- A belated thanks to my daughter, Tatiana, who when reading the first draft of the first edition said, "Don't you think the content would be easier for people to understand if you used some charts?"

- And finally, I'd like to give a special acknowledgment to my colleague Isela Garcia, who for the last twenty years co-developed and co-tested many of the strategies you'll find in this volume.

Thank you to all.

Acknowledgments for the First Edition

As I typed out this manuscript, so many names and faces passed before me—the children who taught me to look beneath the surface and the teachers who taught me their art, new understanding from one training session and the new connection made at another. The book that you now hold is the collected wisdom of hundreds of folks and dozens of presenters who have crossed my path and left their mark on my personal and professional life. I feel so honored to have been given the opportunity to gather that wisdom in this one volume, which I now pass on to you in their names.

A number of individuals, however, have altered my life path over the past thirty years, and this book never would have happened without them. Y'all know who you are, but just for the record, I'd like to thank you one more time here:

- Sharon, who first got me to wonder how her one hug worked better than my ten time-outs.

- Isela and Lori, who hung in there for better and for worse and made possible the impossible.

- Susan, who taught me that if you watch carefully enough and listen quietly enough, children will let you know what's in their hearts.

- Mindy, Bev, Jen, Keith, Tyler, and John, who gave me unbelievable opportunities to learn because they trusted that I had something to teach.

- Dr. Tara and Dr. Marcy, who brought their own knowledge and wisdom to the table and were never too busy to teach me what they knew.

- The incredibly gifted and dedicated staff at FACES of Crisis Nursery, who have tried, fine-tuned, and endorsed virtually every idea in this book.

- Those of you who asked for this book to be written: Redleaf Press, which made this book possible, and my editor, Beth, who did her magic to make it right.

- The kids I work with every day, who amaze me with their complexity, diversity, and hope.

- My ever-tolerant family, who put up with my unavailability and all-nighters.

- My buddy MR, who pushed me page by page, never doubting that I could do this.

Introduction

I'm often asked how I came up with these six life skills, and I must admit that I can't take credit for discovering them. For ten years or so I worked with challenging kids alongside a handful of exceptional colleagues. We would chat for hours trying to figure out what was really going on underneath the surface of these children. We noticed some of the children who seemed to have the most trouble didn't get along with adults. Others couldn't get along with other kids. Some of them seemed to think of themselves as failures—even before they'd reached their fifth birthday!

The aha moment came when we decided to step back from reacting to behaviors and instead began to help these kids develop relationships and hope. Our strategy worked, and over the years we tried out and perfected a book full of strategies that seemed to work magic with these children. We felt we had invented something totally new and wonderful. Then an excellent child psychologist joined our staff and told us how she loved the way we were implementing resiliency theory. We had no idea there was actually a research-based theory that underlaid our practices.

In the 1970s, decades before our discovery, researchers such as Emmy Werner began identifying what they called "protective factors" or "resiliency factors." These early researchers found that children who had these protective factors were able to overcome adversities in their lives to become successful students and productive adults. As we combed through the various lists of protective factors that these researchers had developed, they were the very things we had discovered in our own work with kids! Just like us, these researchers had identified relationships, optimism, emotional skills, collaboration, adaptability, and purpose as forming the base of happy and successful lives. With the growing trend to ensure that early childhood practices are research and evidence based, we were excited to see how this research validated what we were already doing to help our children.

Changes in Early Childhood Education

Since the first edition of this book was published, there have been a number of significant changes in early childhood education. Two of the most important are (1) the creation of state early learning standards and (2) an increased focus on culture and its impact on child development. In preparing the second edition of the book, I wanted to make it easier for early childhood educators to take into account these big changes as they think about children and life skills.

Early Learning Standards

More and more researchers are finding evidence of a link between the strength of children's strong social and emotional development and how well they demonstrate cognitive skills such as literacy and mathematics. In fact, the major complaint kindergarten teachers have about children who are not ready for school *isn't* that kids don't know the alphabet or can't count; it's the one in ten kids who lack key social and emotional skills. Children's misbehavior often interferes with their and their classmates' learning.

Recognizing this, most states have developed social and emotional standards as part of their early learning standards. To make it easier for you to add social and emotional supports to your own lesson planning, this new edition has been reorganized using the most common structure of national social and emotional standards. The strategies in this book and state standards share the same research base and a similar strength-based approach to considering children's development. Although the structure of social and emotional standards varies some from state to state, I think you'll find it easy to find a variety of teaching strategies to address the social and emotional standards in your own state.

Culture and Diversity

The National Association for the Education of Young Children (NAEYC) and other organizations have come out with new information to help teachers understand and be sensitive to the wide range of values and expectations families bring to their programs. Throughout this book, you will find reminders and cautions about diversity in families and their values. This information can sometimes be the key in understanding a child's behaviors and selecting the best strategy to help the child develop the skills she needs in school while still respecting her family's beliefs.

Let me give you an example from my own experience. One of the preschoolers in our school was nicknamed Gordo by his family. *Gordo* in Spanish translates to "fat" in English. I suggested to our program director that we use the child's given name at school instead of what I considered to be a derogatory nickname. A Latina herself, my director explained to me that this child's uncle was also called Gordo and that in the family it was an honor for the child to be called by the same name. What I saw as an insult was in fact a matter of pride for this child and a strong connection to his family and community! What might have happened if I hadn't checked first and just told the teacher to call him by his given name? The child might have felt that the teachers didn't like him very much, and the family might have felt alienated and disrespected. Lesson learned: ask questions before jumping to conclusions.

The Six Life Skills, Revised

In addition to taking account of early childhood learning standards and new information about cultural differences, this second edition presents the life skills in a slightly different way. Have children changed so much in ten years? Of course not. But my understanding has grown as I've watched how teachers use the first edition of the book. I think reorganizing the skills makes them easier for teachers to think about and use. Here are the six life skills as I think about them now:

1. **Attachment:** Attachment is a child's warm and genuine relationship with adults, both within the family and without.

2. **Belonging:** In the first edition, this life skill was called "affiliation." In this edition, it has been expanded from only looking at a child's friendships and sense of belonging in the classroom community to also include a child's sense of belonging to his family and to their community.

3. **Self-regulation:** Self-regulation includes emotional skills such as labeling feelings and managing emotions. In this edition, I also write about the importance of empathy as one of the building blocks toward self-regulation.

4. **Collaboration:** Collaboration is the ability to work and play with others. It includes the life skill of conflict resolution, from the first edition of the book, as well as other social skills such as sharing and waiting for a turn that used to be found in the old affiliation chapter.

5. **Contribution:** Contribution is an expansion of initiative and respect from the first edition. Now, instead of just looking at a child's desire to grow and learn new things, I am also examining her desire to *use* those skills and talents for the benefit of herself, her family, and others.

6. **Adaptability:** Adaptability is the ability to move from situation to situation and to modify behavior based on the norms of where you are and whom you are with, without compromising principles and core values. As adults, we do this all the time. For example, we might yell and cheer at a sporting event but be much more subdued at a funeral. Adaptable children begin to figure out when to be noisy and when to be quiet, where it's okay to wrestle on the floor with friends and where it's not okay.

I'm very excited about the changes in this new edition. Aligning the chapters with the way state standards address social and emotional development makes this edition easier to use for planning and for explaining strategies to others. In addition, pieces on family and community will fill in some gaps that I found in the first edition. One of the things I love so much about working with young children is that we are never done with growing and learning new things, both from them and from one another. If you have read the first edition, I invite you now to take a second look at the six life skills through fresh eyes. If this is your first time reading this book, I'm happy to have you join me as we continue our journey together.

ONE

The Six Life Skills

The journey from childhood to adulthood is a long one. There are many paths a child might take, each one leading to a unique future. As a teacher, you have the opportunity to guide children along their path for a short distance. To be successful as a guide, however, you need a clear vision of your destination. Only when you know where you are going can you make wise decisions about which roads to take.

Take an imaginary trip into the future for a few moments. Imagine that you are meeting up with children in your care again when they are in their early twenties. What do you hope to see?

Think for a moment or two about your hopes for the children you work with. Jot down a list of what you'd wish for them when they are young adults.

Your work with children helps to guide them into the future. This is especially true when we consider children's behavior. How we behave with children today models skills and teaches them social and emotional choices they will use for the rest of their lives. Once you have a clear vision of where you are heading, it's far easier to find the road that will lead you to your destination. As we continue to explore the factors that influence children's behavior, keep your destination map in mind. Begin by envisioning the road that leads to your goals. What will your road look like?

I invite you to join me in a little experiment. So if you would, please find the "This Way or That Way" form on page 27. You might want to make a copy of the form so you can use it as you read along. There are six lines on this form, each one labeled with one of the six life skills that enable children to be successful in school and in life: attachment, belonging, self-regulation, collaboration, contribution, and adaptability. As you read through the next few pages, I'd like for you to think of two children with whom you have worked, either now or in the past. One of these children should be what we might call an easy child, and the other should be a child who struggles to get through the day peacefully. Be ready with a pencil—I'll be asking you to make some marks on the "This Way or That Way" form as we go along. Let's get started.

Attachment

The first and most important life skill is that children are "attached" to one or more significant adults in their lives. In this book, I use the term *attachment* to mean any close, ongoing relationship that the child has with one or more adults inside and outside the home. In an early childhood program, we would expect an attached child to have a warm and mutually respectful relationship with one or more adults in the program. We can tell a child is attached when she seeks out her adult to share news of a new puppy at home or to get help tying her shoes. An attached child would respond with a smile when the teacher says good morning and will usually be compliant with teacher requests. When a child is not attached to one of the adults at school, we might see him flinch and look away when a teacher touches his shoulder. Sometimes you will see that child avoid sitting near the teacher at circle time or during a small-group activity. It's not that these children are unsociable; in fact, they might be very popular with some of the other children. It just seems that they have no use for the grown-up people in their worlds or at least those outside their immediate families.

Let's look now at the first scale on the form. This is the scale called "Attachment." You'll see on the right side it says "Likes and gets along well with adults," and the left side says "Avoids and has little use for adults." Thinking again of the two children you picked at the start of this activity, put an X somewhere along the line to represent how you remember your "easy" child. If you notice the child has a good relationship with teachers, you might put the X closer to the right side of the line. If the child tries to avoid adults or usually doesn't seem to cooperate with teachers, you might put the X closer to the left side of the line. Switch your thinking now to the more "difficult" child you identified and do the same exercise, but this time use an O so you can keep track of your ratings for each child.

Belonging

As children grow from infancy, their social worlds become larger and larger. Most children's earliest social lives are centered on their families—parents, grandparents, aunts, uncles, brothers, sisters, and close family friends. These relationships form their first experiences in *belonging*. A child who has a strong sense of belonging might seek out a younger or older sibling or cousin from another classroom during the day. You might hear a young toddler say something like "*my* mama" when another child tries to interact with his mother, or a preschool child might talk excitedly about visiting her grandparents. These early experiences of belonging to a family form the basis for later friendships and group identity outside the home. We know a child feels he belongs in the classroom community when he forms relationships with one or more children, when he is happy to arrive at school in the morning, and when he moves comfortably through the classroom environment. A child who doesn't feel a sense of belonging will often say things such as "Nobody likes me" or "I don't have friends" or "Nobody lets me play." She may constantly ask if it's time to go home yet.

Look now at the second scale on the form—the one labeled "Belonging." On the right side you'll see the words "Is a part of the group," and on the left you'll see "Is apart from the group." Thinking again about the easy and difficult children, mark the scale with an *X* for the easier child, and mark the scale with an *O* for the more challenging child. The more evidence you see of the child having friends and feeling like a part of the classroom community, the farther to the right you will place the mark. The less evidence you see, mark farther to the left.

Self-Regulation

I use the term *self-regulation* to mean the ability for a child to understand and safely manage strong emotions when they occur. For example, a child who is learning to self-regulate might "use her words" instead of hitting back when somebody takes a toy she was playing with. A child also has to learn how to stay in control when he gets very excited or overstimulated, such as can happen around his birthday or during the holiday season. For young children in a group setting, there are many stepping stones to self-regulation. To manage emotions, children need to first notice that they even *have* emotions. They need to learn how to put a moment between their feelings and their reactions. Children also have to understand that other people have feelings too, and those feelings matter. Even then, it takes a lot of practice and adult support for a child to be able to avoid letting her emotions rule her behavior when she is angry or overexcited.

Move down now to the third scale on the form, called "Self-Regulation." On the right side of the scale, you'll see the words "Can safely manage emotions," and on the left, the words "Emotions rule behaviors." Mark this scale with an *X* and *O* as you did for the first two life skills for your easy and difficult children.

Collaboration

Collaboration might seem to be a very grown-up term to use when talking about young children. You might be more familiar with this concept for older children or for adults in the workplace. But the roots of collaboration begin in early childhood. In little-kid terms, *collaboration* is more commonly called "gets along well with others." When you see a young child demonstrating the ability to collaborate, you might see her working in the sandbox with two other children to dig a hole to the other side of the world. Maybe you'll see him take turns using a spray bottle of water to mist seedlings potted and placed on the windowsill. A child who is good at collaboration can join a group playing mommies and babies without causing meltdowns and total chaos. A child who is poor at collaboration seems to get into constant disputes with other children over space and stuff. She appears to lack basic friendship skills.

When you move down to the fourth scale for "Collaboration" on the form, you'll see that the right side is labeled "Works and plays well with others," and the left side says "Struggles to cooperate with other children." Mark the *X* and *O* on this scale for your easy and difficult children as you did for other scales.

Contribution

The life skill of *contribution* includes the belief in one's own gifts and talents and the desire to use those gifts to better oneself, one's family, one's community, as well as the world at large. Consider the persistence of a baby learning to stand and take her first steps. This is a great example of the belief in one's own abilities and the persistence of working through the challenges to perfect a skill. Think of the two-year-old trying to help mommy clean up the table after lunch by carrying his own dishes to the sink. Or the preschooler who just learned how to tie her shoes and is now patiently teaching her friend. Sometimes, however, something happens during a child's early years that dampens this spark of excitement and enthusiasm. These children might become easily defeated in learning new things, such as pumping on swings or folding up their nap blankets. You might often hear these children say things such as "I can't do it" or "I don't want to help." They may act like passive players who seem to let life happen around them.

Look now at the next-to-last scale on your form for "Contribution." The right side of the scale has the words "Eager to learn and help others," and the left side says "Acts hopeless and helpless." Thinking again of your two example children, put the *X* and *O* where you believe they would be along that scale.

Adaptability

The final life skill I write about in this book is *adaptability*. Children (and adults) are adaptable when they can figure out how to be successful in different places and with different people. As adults, we know that while we might wear a swimsuit to the beach, we won't wear one to a formal wedding. The way we talk and act at home with family and close friends might be quite different from the way we are at a staff meeting at work. For most of us, adaptability is so ingrained that we are probably not even conscious of it. Young children, however, need many cues and adult reminders to change their behavior as they move from one situation to another. Early on, adults begin to teach children the skill that different places and different people might call for different behaviors. For example, some parents might be fine with their child marching around the house loudly singing "Happy Birthday to You," but remind the child to be quiet during a religious service. A teacher might tell a child to "use your walking feet" in the school hallway but encourage that same child to run around the play yard during outside time. A child who is adaptable will most often at least *try* to comply with adult prompting and will begin to internalize the rules and norms of different environments. Other children, however, may find it much more challenging to change their behaviors to go with the flow of a new setting. For example, a child who has been told at home to slap anyone who calls her a derogatory name might have trouble complying with a school guideline to "use your words." Another child who sleeps with a sibling at home might have trouble settling in on his own nap mat and may consistently try to pull his mat over so he can sleep cuddled with a friend. And, yet another child totally falls apart on field trips when she is out of her own predictable routines.

We are now at the final scale on the form for "Adaptability." The right side of the scale says "Adapts easily to new situations," and the left says "Struggles to adapt." Mark your final *X* and *O* on this scale for the two example children, as you have for the other scales for life skills.

So What Does This All Mean?

If you haven't done so already, please go back and mark your *X*s and *O*s on the "This Way or That Way" form. Then look at the form as a whole and see if you can find some sort of pattern.

Do most of your *X*s, or the mark for the easier child, fall closer to the right side of the page? And do most of your *O*s, or the mark for the more challenging child, fall closer to the left side? Most people who do this exercise find this to be the trend for at least four of the six scales. It's not surprising, is it? Our own observations tell us that easier children tend to be stronger in these skills and more difficult children tend to be weaker in these skills.

So, if easier children have stronger life skills and difficult children's skills are weaker, wouldn't helping the challenging children to build these skills lead to them doing better in school and in life? In fact, that is what we see in practice. As we help children move from the left to the right side of the form they do better! And that is the purpose of this book: to provide a multitude of easy-to-implement strategies that help all children strengthen these six life skills, which is reflected as they move closer to the right side of the form.

Helping Children Build Life Skills

When we think of how to react with our most challenging children, here is the first question we should ask ourselves:

> Will this move a child farther to the left on the "This Way or That Way" form or farther to the right?

If the response or intervention moves a child farther away from building the six underlying strengths, how can we expect behavior that is more positive? Many popular behavior management techniques, such as time-out, red-yellow-green charts ("traffic lights"), or losing privileges are attempts to change children's negative behaviors for the better. But as you have seen from filling out the "This Way or That Way" form, challenging behaviors are actually symptoms of a deeper issue: the lack of one or more basic life skills children need to do well in school and life. The most effective way to help a child change a problem behavior is not to address the behavior itself but, instead, to find ways to strengthen the weak skills that underlie the behavior.

Consider for a moment one common behavior management technique: sending a child away from the group to "think about it." This technique is used when a child is doing something like grabbing a toy away from another child. Think of the six scales on the "This Way or That Way" form you just completed. Do you think the "think about it" strategy might move a child farther to the right side of the form, the left side of the form, or neither? For some children, being sent away from the group to be alone can feel very isolating. A child may wonder if the teacher still loves her. She may not understand why everyone else is in one area while she is banished to another area to be alone. For children like this, sending them away from the group might move them to the left side of the form on the Attachment and Belonging scales. It surely won't move them to the right side. What about the Self-Regulation and Collaboration scales? Being sent away from the group probably won't help a child develop the skills he needs to manage emotions, nor does it help him develop the friendship skills that are part of Collaboration. In many ways, the "think about it" strategy is a punishment for the child because she doesn't have those skills.

How about the next scale, Contribution? What message does it give a child to be sent away for not behaving the way an adult wished he would? Do you think it helps or hurts his self-image? Do you think it sends a message that we are all here to support each other or does it say, "Figure it out by yourself"?

If you have trouble answering that question, think for a moment about being at a staff meeting. Maybe you just got an urgent text message from your daughter that you need to respond to right away. How would you feel if the director stopped what she was explaining and said to you, "Please leave the room and stand in the hallway to think about the importance of paying attention during meeting time." How would that work for you? Do you think it would move you farther to the right or left side of the Contribution scale?

Finally, look at the scale for Adaptability. Much like Self-Regulation and Collaboration, being sent away from the group to sit alone doesn't help a child practice and learn school expectations. It punishes the child for not having the skill.

It doesn't make sense to expect children to do better when our interactions with them are getting in the way of them acquiring the basic life skills. When you have questions about interventions or strategies you are using or thinking of using, ask yourself, "Will using this strategy help build or weaken the six life skills this child needs to thrive in today's world?" This is so important. Let's look at the question in terms of each of the life skills.

- **Attachment:** Will the strategy move the child to see you as a supportive and loving ally or as an opponent who works against her? Will the strategy help the child feel safe and secure or add a layer of fear and apprehension?

- **Belonging:** Will the strategy build ties, friendships, bonds, and a team or family feeling? Or will the strategy single this child out as somewhat unappealing, unacceptable, and deficient? Will the strategy move the child to be more a part of the group or will the child feel more apart from the group?

- **Self-regulation:** Does the strategy validate the child's feelings and reassure him that the whole range of human emotions is acceptable? Will the strategy help the child develop the skills he needs to manage strong emotions? Does the strategy model self-regulation on the part of the adult? Does the strategy model empathy?

- **Collaboration:** Does the strategy model how to get along well with others? Does the intervention help the child build self-respect and strengthen her respect for others? Was the child demeaned in the eyes of peers? Does the strategy promote the belief that "might makes right" or does it encourage working to find the best solution for all parties involved?

- **Contribution:** Does the intervention promote the idea that we are all growing, changing, and learning new things? Or, does it leave the child feeling like a failure before he's even five years old? Does it leave the child feeling hopeful or hopeless, empowered or powerless? Does the strategy isolate the child to figure things out on her own, or does it encourage the classroom community to work together to support the growth and development of all the children in the group?

- **Adaptability:** Does the intervention help the child learn the cultural norms of school or does it punish him for not already knowing those norms? Does the intervention support values taught at home while teaching new behaviors for school? Or does the intervention push the child into choosing between home and school values and behaviors?

As you guide and redirect children throughout the day, think about these questions. Try as often as you can to help all the children in your care develop the six life skills every day.

Rewards and Punishment

Rewards and punishment are specific methods of correcting behavior. These methods are used by many teachers in many programs. They are a way teachers attempt to control a child's behavior, the way the famous researcher B. F. Skinner tried to control a pigeon's behavior in the lab. Let's think, though, about whether we *can* actually control the behavior of another person.

While we would love to be able to control the behavior of children in our care, the reality is that compliance is voluntary. While we might be able to influence Little Johnny, ultimately he is the only one who can directly control his behavior, just as we are the only ones who can control ours. The image below demonstrates what I mean by this.

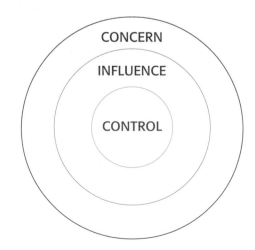

There are many things in the world that would fit into our circle of concern. For example, you might be concerned about hurricanes, about how Little Johnny runs away from you in the play yard when it's time to go inside, or about locking your keys in the car. Let's look at these three concerns and sort them into three piles: things we can directly control, things we can influence, and things we can't control at all. I think we can agree that none of us can control hurricanes. They would go in the outer circle, the circle of concern. What about your car keys? Maybe you'll call someone and ask for the spare set from home. You might decide to call a professional to come in and break into the car for you. Maybe you'll take a friend up on an offer to pop your door open with a hanger. This would go in the center circle, your circle of control. One hint that something would go into this center circle is that you can begin your solution sentence with "I can . . ." For example, "I can call a car service" or "I can let Amanda try to pop open the car door."

Let's look now at Little Johnny in the play yard. When the signal rings to go inside, Little Johnny runs the other way more often than not. Where would getting Johnny to come inside go in our diagram? We can eliminate putting this issue in the outside circle because in the end it's our responsibility to make sure that Little Johnny *does* in fact stay under adult supervision and eventually get inside with the rest of the group. Can we *control* whether Little Johnny runs or comes with us? Remember, when we control something, we have to be able to start the sentence with "I can . . ." Maybe you decide to use your control by deciding "I can chase him when he runs, catch him, and carry him inside." While it's true that you can catch Little Johnny and carry him inside, it's also true that Little Johnny can still run away from you. Running is in his control.

Attempts to control Little Johnny will only be an exercise in frustration. The only person you can control is *you*. Since we need to get Little Johnny inside and since Little Johnny is the only one who can control his behavior choices, the question facing us is how to *influence* Little Johnny to make the choice to come with us rather than run away. The better question is how to expand our sphere of influence so we can help the class function better and help Little Johnny develop his skills. One way we can expand our spheres of influence with children is by nurturing healthy and respectful relationships and generating mutual respect. Other ways to expand our sphere of influence are to

- develop a community based on mutual respect;
- establish yourself as each child's strongest ally and most loyal cheerleader;
- focus on maintaining healthy relationships while avoiding judgment; and
- concentrate on relationships and the social and emotional climate of the classroom.

All these strategies are within your control. While you can't *control* Little Johnny's behavior choices, you can control your own interactions and the classroom environment so that you gradually have more and more influence over Johnny's choices.

Be clear about those things over which you have direct control, those you might influence, and those about which you may have concerns but no control. Remembering the limits of your control will help you invest your time and energies wisely when you make plans about how best to approach children's behavior and social-emotional growth.

Punishment

"But what if I have taught the right behavior and I know they have learned it, and they still purposely misbehave? Isn't punishment appropriate then?" Many, many teachers have questions like this. The first question I always ask myself before responding to a child is: "Will this strategy or response move the child farther to the left or farther to the right on the 'This Way or That Way' form?" Here is the second question I ask:

> Will this punish a child for not having a skill, or will it help teach a child one of the six life skills?

You should think of social-emotional skills no differently than you think of skills in reading or math. I think we can all agree that if a child doesn't have the skill to count, we would never think of putting him in time-out to "think about it." How absurd would that be? Instead, we think of ways to help the child learn the skills needed to be able to count better next time. Social and emotional skills are no different. Children depend on the adults in their world to teach them the skills to do better next time, not blame or punish them for not being skilled already.

Why might children not use the skills we are pretty sure they have, and what might be effective to help them? Have you ever made a New Year's resolution? Have you ever kept one? You're an adult, and you're highly motivated. You know exactly what you are supposed to do, yet by Valentine's Day you find yourself slipping into old patterns. Think of a child who has learned at home to print his name in all uppercase letters. We invest a lot of time teaching children how to print their names in uppercase and lowercase letters. Do they still print their names in all caps frequently? Many do. They know the new behavior, and they know what is expected. They are highly motivated to be successful, yet they still revert to old habits. The same thing happens with social and emotional skills. We teach children how to stand in line and practice it many times. Yet when they are excited or under stress, children go back to their old behavior of pushing and hitting. For all of us, it takes lots of practice to change old patterns until the new behavior becomes so automatic that it is part of who we are. The more we practice, the more we strengthen neurological connections in our brains that lead to long-term memory. That's why we see professional athletes, dancers, and gymnasts practicing routines over and over again. It is the constant repetition that makes their movements almost automatic.

So often we teach the child a skill and then immediately throw him back into the problem situation and expect him to perform. Maybe he is splashing others at the water table where we have used a kind but firm technique to teach that splashing others is out of bounds at school. The child seems to have clearly understood our guidance and has agreed to keep the others dry from now on. A minute later, there he is again splashing his buddy. What is happening?

Here is an example from an adult's life experience: Imagine for a moment that your best friend is a recovering alcoholic, celebrating her third week sober. You have gone with her to a holiday party where alcohol is being served. Would you leave your best friend alone at the beckoning champagne table for half an hour while you make a phone call? When our friends or relatives are struggling to break an addiction or a sweet tooth, we stay sensitive to their vulnerability as they work to establish new habits. We support them in situations when temptation hovers. We surely don't intentionally put temptation in their path.

We need to extend the same care and courtesy to the children in our care. When a child is struggling to learn not to push in line, have her be your partner so you can support her early attempts. If a child is learning to share toys, stay close by him in the block area and at the water table. When a child is practicing the new skill of conflict resolution, gently reinforce the process rather than sending the child back alone with the direction to "use your words." Don't expect more from a young child than you would expect from yourself.

"But won't punishing children help them pay attention? Won't knowing there's a consequence for misbehavior motivate them to remember the behavior we have spent so much energy to teach them?" The punishment debate is a sticky issue for many adults. In adult society, there are consequences for misbehavior. If adults speed, they get speeding tickets. Shouldn't children learn early on that bad behavior gets punished? On the surface, it seems to make a lot of sense to punish children in order to prepare them for the adult world. Shift your thinking for a moment to literacy. What are some of the consequences in the adult world for being functionally illiterate? Less income? Fewer choices about work opportunities? Lower standards of living? If functionally illiterate adults suffer those consequences, wouldn't it make sense to give negative consequences to a child who never pays attention at book time? Should we give that child the old broken desk in the drafty dark corner of the classroom? Should we give the child half portions at lunch and explain, "Here you go. Illiterate people don't earn enough money for a lot of food. And no more desserts at school, since only people who read can afford them."

Most teachers would read the above paragraph with horror that I even suggested such treatment of a child who is not interested in books. It seems absurd to punish a young child for not liking to read. It is just as crazy to punish children for being socially or emotionally illiterate. We should do everything in our power to give them skills while these children are still young so they can avoid having that kind of life later.

Responding to troubling behavior is difficult, and we would like such behavior to stop immediately. When individual children do things to hurt others or to disrupt the peace of the classroom, we sometimes feel like striking back and making that child pay for the pain and chaos she has created. We have the mistaken belief that making the child feel bad is the fastest road to making her act good.

Punishing children doesn't help them develop the strengths they'll need to thrive when they are older. Punishment and other negative and hurtful strategies do nothing to move children along the road to learning life skills. In fact, they knock children off the road to social and emotional competency. Teachers should do their best to teach children the skills they need and help children build the strengths they require for success in school and in life. Teachers who follow this path will be instrumental in guiding children to reach their social and emotional goals.

Rewards

When we give a child a reward for doing what we want them to do, what effect might it have on some of the scales on the "This Way or That Way" form? As the adults in charge, teachers have the power to give or withhold the goodies. The downside of these techniques is that we are not modeling the kinds of behavior we want to see the children imitate. On the contrary, the use of rewards models the very behavior we want children to stop! Instead of helping children appreciate that success in life depends on maintaining healthy relationships, we model for children the promise of bribes and the threat of pain to navigate relationships. How many times have you shuddered to hear such manipulations as "If you don't give me the bike, you can't come to my birthday party," or "If you give me the truck, I'll be your best friend." Where do children learn such things? It is no different for a teacher to give a child a sticker for helping to clean up the paint area. Rewards don't help children build respectful relationships with adults or with one another.

Rewards change behavior in the short term, but the long-term cost of using such a strategy is too high. Most teachers and parents do not want to raise kids who behave only when they think they will be rewarded. Instead, we want children to be motivated to do the right thing because it feels good. We want them to make good choices for themselves, their families, and the world around them, even when they aren't rewarded. We want them to stand their own ground and stand up for what's right, even if it's difficult or painful. We certainly don't want them to make destructive choices for external rewards.

Teachers have a wealth of goodies—stickers, praise, recess, tokens, and more—they can use to get their way. Surely we don't want to model this kind of manipulation during a child's most vulnerable years. Instead, we need to help children build their own internal motivations and moral compasses by teaching them how to develop the six life skills so they can make positive choices in life.

Would I Want to Work for Me?

So now you know the first two questions I always ask myself:

1. Will this move a child farther to the left on the "This Way or That Way" form or farther to the right?

2. Will this punish a child for not having a skill, or will it help teach a child one of the six life skills?

Here is the third and final question I ask: If I needed correction or redirection, how would I feel if my supervisor used a strategy like this with me? I use a shorthand version of this question, as follows, when I am thinking of using a strategy:

Would I want to work for me?

Try this little exercise to better understand what I'm talking about. Think for a few minutes about the best job you ever had. And then think about the worst job you ever had. Think about the workplace atmosphere for both jobs. Think about your supervisors for both jobs. Make a chart like this and fill it with words and phrases that come to mind.

Worst job/Worst supervisor	Best job/Best supervisor

After you have filled the chart with your initial thoughts, ask yourself these follow-up questions:

- How did you feel in each situation when you made a mistake?
- How did you feel in each situation when you did a good job?
- How did you feel about going to work each day?
- When you reflect back to each of these situations, which emotions come to the surface?

Add your reflections to the bottom of each of the columns, and then review both lists when they are completed. Think again of what each job brought out in you, how you felt, and how well you worked. Now take a deep breath and try to figure out how your lists relate to working with young children.

When we reflect on our own histories, it becomes clear what kinds of leaders and what kinds of environments bring out the best in people. A quick reflection on what kind of leaders we are and what kinds of environments we have established for children often reveals cause for celebration as well as startling and disturbing revelations.

You may realize that you have many of the qualities you have admired in your own best supervisors. You may suddenly understand why many of your practices have been so successful. But you may also begin to understand why you struggle in other areas. This is not meant to be an exercise in guilt. It is meant to be a paradigm shift—a new way to look at an old situation. This new view may reveal many things that were hidden before. The first step in change is to be able to see the current situation objectively and to identify any problem areas. To paraphrase author and poet Maya Angelou, it is only when we know better that we can do better.

When I first did this exercise, I ran the gamut of emotions. Initially I was shocked. I had always viewed myself as an excellent and conscientious teacher. Suddenly, though, I saw many of my practices in a different light. Would I want to work for me? The answer was a firm no. Justification came next. I rationalized my practices by saying that adults are different than children, that in the workplace some of these children would be fired, and that jobs and school are two different things. Even though a part of me understood changes needed to be made, I felt defensive about my practices. I had learned and modeled my guidance practices from the best of the best. I have always tried to be a good and moral person who only wants the best for children. It took me a while to accept the clear revelation that some things I was saying and doing were harmful to them.

Understanding your definitions of quality leaders and environments will help you learn how to become the teacher you dream of being. Children respond to different leadership styles in the same ways we do. The same things that motivate us in the workplace motivate children in the school environment. The same qualities we respond to in leaders in our own lives are the qualities children respond to in the classroom community. Become a leader who fosters positive attitudes, behavior, and responses.

Here is the key question to ask yourself: Would I want to work for me? The immutable law of nature is that we will reap what we sow. If your supervisor's behavior motivated you to grow and change, if that supervisor's practice excited you about doing your best work, if that environment felt good and kept you coming back for more, then it will probably do the same for the children in your care.

What we teach children is directly linked to *how* we teach children. The values a leader establishes for her organization become an integral part of the institutional culture itself. Leaders who model and practice honesty create institutions with honesty as a part of their culture. When leaders reward competition, the organizational atmosphere becomes competitive rather than cooperative. As we begin to think about our best approach to this monumental leadership role, stay aware that what we teach is directly linked to how we teach. I urge you to regularly ask yourself my three questions before responding to a child's behavior.

1. Will this move a child farther to the left on the "This Way or That Way" form or farther to the right?
2. Will this punish a child for not having a skill, or will it help teach a child one of the six life skills?
3. Would I want to work for me?

How This Book Is Organized

Children come to early childhood classrooms with a whole range of skills and personalities. Some children are beginning to read, whereas others have no previous experience with books. Some children are social butterflies who draw peers to them like bees to a flower. Other children are content to play alone. Some children are well on their way to developing the six life skills, whereas others have barely begun.

What steps can a teacher take to help individual children reach their destination of social and emotional competency? What role does a teacher play in guiding children along that path?

As you read through the six life skills, specific children may have popped into your mind. As we have seen, our own evidence shows that children who have these six skills tend to do well in life, while those who don't have them tend to struggle more.

Throughout the rest of this book, you will find strategies you can easily implement in your classroom to begin to move your most challenging children from the left side of the "This Way or That Way" form to the right side, while strengthening the life skills of all the children in your group.

Supportive Interactions, Classroom Culture, and Special Activities

Each of the next six chapters of this book focuses on building one of the six life skills. At the beginning of each chapter, there are samples of state early learning standards from around the country which represent various facets of that skill. Within each chapter, activities and strategies are broken down into three categories: supportive interactions, classroom culture, and special activities. The order of activities and strategies is deliberate. The most powerful impact we can have on children's behavior is through our daily, personal, supportive interactions. A classroom culture that supports and upholds children's strengths is the next most powerful intervention. In this book, classroom culture includes the physical environment, daily schedule, rituals, routines, values, and norms promoted by the teaching staff. Special activities are those things you might include in your lesson plans, such as making a class book all about feelings or playing a game of Simon Says to help children practice self-control. Our interactions and the classroom culture exist from the moment children walk in the door until they leave at the end of the day. While special activities are a valuable supplement to the curriculum, it is important to invest the bulk of your energy in modifying interactions and the classroom culture.

Supportive Interactions

Who we are and what we live—what we model for children—has the most powerful impact on children of any strategy. Our talk to children becomes their self-talk. Our expectations become their expectations. As an adult, you have the wisdom and experience needed to be a powerful influence on a child's life. Your interactions and interventions can help children become empowered citizens, committed to solving problems and making purposeful choices in the best interest of themselves and others.

Your daily interactions with children not only affect your personal relationships but also model and set community norms for the entire classroom. The significance of adult modeling was brought home to me when my daughter, Tati, was a four-year-old in preschool. One of her favorite games to play at home with her dolls was something she called Christopher Vedra. She would set out a dozen dolls on the floor, each one lying on a baby blanket. Then she would announce, "Naptime! Everybody get quiet now." A moment later, she would begin to drag one of the baby blankets with baby across the floor, saying sternly, "I told you to be quiet, Christopher Vedra. Now I have to move your mat." Another moment would pass and once again she would drag Christopher's mat to another area of the floor. This reprimand-and-move sequence would be repeated ten or fifteen times, each time more severely. Need I say that Christopher Vedra was a very active and challenging child in her class at school?

How often have you seen children playing teacher at school and heard your words come from their mouths? How many times have you watched children replay last night's domestic squabbles in the dramatic play area?

Sometimes at school we are inadvertently modeling exactly the behavior we are trying to stop. For instance, many teachers say to a crying child, "As soon as you are done crying, I will be happy to listen to your words." I learned that line from other teachers when I began working, and I must have used it a thousand times or more before I examined my behavior a bit more closely. When we say these words, what messages are we sending to the child in distress? And what messages are we sending to the rest of the class about socially appropriate ways to respond to people in distress? Twenty minutes later, when Isabel hits Jarred and Jarred is crying, we attempt to employ Standard Teacher Script Number Two, which goes something like this: "Isabel, look at Jarred's face. How do you think he is feeling?" Isabel is most likely thinking, "As soon as he is done with that crying, I'll listen to what he has to say."

As we guide, support, and live with children, we can never lose sight that they are watching and listening to everything we do. To get children to say thank you, make sure you say thank you. To teach children to solve problems, make sure they see and hear you solve problems. To help children learn how to manage frustration, make sure you demonstrate your own anger-management skills.

Look back again at the lists of qualities of your most and least favorite jobs on page 17. How many of the factors had to do with relationships and daily interactions? Was there an atmosphere of trust and respect? Was collegiality promoted, or was there dog-eat-dog competition? Did administration establish an environment of all work and no play, or did the workplace include an element of joy and playfulness? Did you feel alone, or did you feel like a part of a team?

As the leader of the classroom, you establish the standards for everyone in the room. The actions you take, the beliefs you have about individual children, and the learning environment you establish will be directly reflected in children's behavior and beliefs about themselves and each other.

Next to home, school is the biggest influence on young children. So next to the family, teachers are the biggest single influence on children. You have it within your power to make a significant impact on the beliefs and skills of the children in your care. And affecting beliefs in the right direction will result in the internal growth and development children need to thrive in the classroom and in the larger world.

Classroom Culture

The rituals and routines—the classroom culture you establish in your classroom—are a reflection of your philosophy and your leadership. Are there jobs for everyone in the classroom? Do you have a consistent daily schedule and a clear room arrangement? Do you have a routine to welcome new children and say good-bye to children who leave the program? The best way to help children learn the skills they need is to introduce and weave the skills regularly into many situations throughout the year.

Think about how you would like the children in your classroom to talk to each other. How would you like them to ask each other if they can play? How do you want them to share supplies at the cooking table? What words would you like them to say if they accidentally hurt someone? Children learn what they live. Plan carefully how you will ask for a turn when you sit to work on a puzzle with a child or what you will say when you must interrupt a child's conversation. Establish a classroom culture that supports the social and emotional lessons you want to pass on to the children in your care.

Special Activities

Special activities help reinforce the lessons children get from your supportive interactions and the classroom culture. Many games and classroom projects can be added to your weekly lesson plans to support children's social and emotional development. Playing Freeze Dance, for example, helps children learn how to regulate their behavior. Helping children put together a classroom book about their families supports the development of attachment. Activities such as these are a nice supplement to your work with children, but by no means do they do the job on their own. Most of what children learn socially and emotionally still comes from interactions with significant adults in their lives and from the environments in which they live.

Children Who Need Extra Support

The strategies in the six life skills chapters will help most children develop the underlying skills they need to move easily through their days. Yet there is always that small handful of more challenging children who need extra support to reach that goal. Since the publication of the first edition, I have gotten many questions about how to support these children without reverting to a typical behavior plan using rewards and punishments. A new final chapter has been added to talk about just this challenge. It will help you figure out ways to support that child who is still struggling to make it happily through the day.

One Step at a Time

As you read the rest of this book, remember that growth and change involve a series of baby steps. Gradually, learn one new technique at a time and try it out. Then begin to weave it into your daily practice until you feel comfortable with it before you try another. Changing belief systems may be a revolution, but changing practice is an evolution. And similarly, it is important to remember that growth and change in children are also an evolution, not a revolution. Certainly, some strategic changes in practice have an impact on children and their behavior in immediate and dramatic ways. But true growth and change happen slowly over time for us and for them.

The number one factor in children's development of positive beliefs and skills is the quality of the relationship between the child and the teaching staff.

Children with easygoing temperaments, a quick smile, and well-developed social skills generally know how to engage adults and draw them close. On the other hand, children with difficult and challenging behavior do not bring out the best in most adults. It is very easy for our relationships to deteriorate quickly with these children. The result, unfortunately, is that the children who most need us to be emotionally attached are the very children who are most skilled at driving us away.

Learning a multitude of professional strategies, techniques, and interventions will help strengthen relationships with each of the unique personalities in your classrooms. When personal relationships have been damaged, you can use these strategies to begin repairing attachment, which is so necessary for the development of healthy beliefs and skills.

What is the destination of your journey, then? As you reflect on children you know, you will begin to see that those who are not armed with the six strengths struggle to survive from day to day. Their destination is mere survival. Your goal is for children to thrive. In your frustration or disappointment with a child's behavior, you need to learn to keep your focus on your long-term goals for the child rather than on the quick fix. Reward and punishment produce fast, yet temporary, results.

Focus your efforts on building relationships with children and help them develop friendship skills, emotional skills, and a sense of purpose. Teach them what they need to know about how to succeed in the school environment. Make it your mission to help children develop the strengths they will need to thrive in school and in life.

As teachers of young children, it is important to keep our eye on the goal so we don't get lost along the way. Help children learn to make good choices for themselves, for their communities, and for society as a whole. Many children are unable to reach that destination alone. They need compassionate and clear-minded adults to lead them along the path. Be that adult.

Our Strength-Based Behavior Plan

Our plan is to help all children develop positive beliefs about how the world works and learn the social and emotional skills they will need to succeed in school and in life.

- We will provide supportive and nurturing interactions that meet each child's needs physically, emotionally, socially, and cognitively so he or she feels cherished and safe.

- We will commit to providing interactions and experiences that help each child develop the strengths of attachment, belonging, self-regulation, collaboration, contribution, and adaptability.

- We will design specific intervention programs and support for children who need additional help in developing the strengths they need for success in today's world. We will bring in outside resources as necessary to help all children in our program reach social and emotional competency when we have exhausted our own resources.

Discussion/Reflection Questions

1. What are your long-term goals for the children in your class?

   _____

   _____

   _____

2. Twenty years from now, what kind of personal qualities would you like to see in the children you are teaching?

   _____

   _____

   _____

3. Are there any connections between the six life skills and what you want for children? Describe them.

   _____

   _____

   _____

4. Discuss the quote "What we teach children is directly linked to how we teach children."

   _____

   _____

   _____

Exercises

1. Take a closer look at a challenging child in your group. Which of the six life skills is the child lacking? What is the relationship between the behavior that is driving you crazy and the child's strength or strengths?

   _____

   _____

   _____

   _____

   _____

2. Is the child already developing strengths? Which ones?

   _____

   _____

   _____

   _____

3. Increase your awareness of your personal interactions with children over the course of a day. What are some ways your current practices are helping children build the six life skills? What is one practice you are thinking of changing?

   _____

   _____

   _____

   _____

Reflection/Journal Assignment

1. Think of yourself in relation to the six life skills. How have these strengths helped you to get where you are today? Are you still working to develop one or more of these strengths? If so, how has the lack of a strength made an impact on your life?

   _____

   _____

   _____

   _____

   _____

   _____

   _____

   _____

2. Reflect on your favorite job or favorite supervisor, and describe your vision of the kind of classroom you would like to lead. What would the classroom feel like when you walked in the door each day? How would everyone in the classroom community interact with each other? How would successes be recognized? How would problems be solved? As the children's supervisor, how would you like them to see you?

   _____

   _____

   _____

   _____

   _____

   _____

   _____

   _____

This Way or That Way Form

Attachment

Avoids and has
little use for adults

Likes and gets
along well with adults

←——————————————————————————→

Belonging

Is apart from the group

Is a part of the group

←——————————————————————————→

Self-Regulation

Emotions rule behaviors

Can safely
manage emotions

←——————————————————————————→

Collaboration

Struggles to cooperate
with other children

Works and plays well
with others

←——————————————————————————→

Contribution

Acts hopeless
and helpless

Eager to learn
and help others

←——————————————————————————→

Adaptability

Struggles to adapt

Adapts easily
to new situations

←——————————————————————————→

Chapter 1 Resources

Brooks, Robert, and Sam Goldstein. 2001. *Raising Resilient Children: Fostering Strength, Hope, and Optimism in Your Child*. Lincolnwood, IL: Contemporary Books.

Bruce, Nefertiti, and Karen B. Cairone with the Devereux Center for Resilient Children. 2010. *Socially Strong, Emotionally Secure: 50 Activities to Promote Resilience in Young Children*. Silver Spring, MD: Gryphon House.

Center on the Social and Emotional Foundations for Early Learning. http://csefel .vanderbilt.edu.

Cesarone, Bernard, ed. 1999. *Resilience Guide: A Collection of Resources on Resilience in Children and Families*. ERIC Publications. ED436307. www.eric.ed.gov:80 /PDFS/ED436307.pdf.

Covey, Stephen R. 2004. *The 7 Habits of Highly Effective People: Powerful Lessons in Personal Change*. Rev. ed. New York: Free Press.

———. 1991. *Principle-Centered Leadership*. New York: Summit Books.

Dodge, Diane Trister, Laura J. Colker, and Cate Heroman. 2009. *The Creative Curriculum for Preschool*. 4th ed. Washington, DC: Teaching Strategies.

Katz, Lilian G., and Diane E. McClellan. 1997. *Fostering Children's Social Competence: The Teacher's Role*. NAEYC Research into Practice, vol. 8. Washington, DC: National Association for the Education of Young Children.

Koralek, Derry. 1999. *Classroom Strategies to Promote Children's Social and Emotional Development*. Lewisville, NC: Kaplan Press.

Marshall, Hermine H. 2001. "Cultural Influences on the Development of Self-Concept: Updating Our Thinking." *Young Children* 56 (6): 19–22.

Nelson, Jane, Lynn Lott, and H. Stephen Glenn. 2000. *Positive Discipline in the Classroom: Developing Mutual Respect, Cooperation, and Responsibility in Your Classroom*. 3rd ed. Roseville, CA: Prima Publishing.

Perry, Bruce Duncan. 2011. "Keep the Cool in School: Promoting Non-Violent Behavior in Children." Accessed September 29. http://teacher.scholastic.com /professional/bruceperry/cool.htm.

Peters, Tom, and Nancy Austin. 1985. *A Passion for Excellence: The Leadership Difference*. New York: Random House.

Swift, Madelyn. 1999. *Discipline for Life: Getting It Right with Children*. 3rd ed. Southlake, TX: Childright.

Trumbull, Elise, Carrie Rothstein-Fisch, Patricia M. Greenfield, and Blanca Quiroz. 2001. *Bridging Cultures between Home and School: A Guide for Teachers*. Mahwah, NJ: Lawrence Erlbaum Associates.

Weinstein, Carol, Mary Curran, and Saundra Tomlinson-Clarke. 2003. "Culturally Responsive Classroom Management: Awareness into Action." *Theory into Practice* 42 (4): 269–76.

Werner, Emmy. 1993. "Risk, Resilience, and Recovery: Perspectives from the Kauai Longitudinal Study." *Development and Psychopathology* 5 (Fall): 503–15.

York, Stacey. 2003. *Roots and Wings: Affirming Culture in Early Childhood Programs*. Rev. ed. St. Paul, MN: Redleaf Press.

TWO

Attachment

I have grown-ups in my life who cherish and guide me.

Because of overwhelming evidence that relationships underlie school achievement and life success, there are references to *attachment* in state standards throughout the country. The below examples come from Idaho and Texas, and you will probably find something similar in your own state standards. This chapter will help you meet those standards.

- "Children trust, interact with, and seek assistance from adults." *Idaho Early Learning Guidelines, 2008*

- "Child forms warm relationships with teachers." *Revised Texas Prekindergarten Guidelines, 2008*

Juan Carlos held his shoe up to his teacher. "Did you need help?" she asked.

He nodded yes, and Ms. G sat down to help him put on the shoe. "There you go," she said. He ran off with a big grin on his face.

When the librarian came into the room to read a book to the children, Juan Carlos hid behind Ms. G's leg. "Hey, baby," she said to him. "That's the Story Lady. Remember? We saw her before. Come sit by me, and we'll listen to the book."

Later in the day, Mrs. Morales came in to pick up her son. "Mama, mama, mama," Juan Carlos shouted as he ran up to her.

"Let's get your things," she said.

"Come," he answered, pulling her by her hand to fetch his things from his cubby.

What Does Attachment Look Like?

In the story, Juan Carlos shows many signs of a child who has healthy relationships with significant adults. He sees adults as potentially supportive and helpful. He is wary of strangers and goes to an adult he trusts to stay safe. And he is excited to be reunited with his primary caregiver at the end of the day.

Young children need much more from adults than a peer playmate can provide. Don't confuse forming relationships with becoming a child's best friend. For children to relax and learn, they first need to know there will be an adult around who will take care of their basic needs. They need to feel sure they will be fed, cleaned, and kept warm. They have to know they will be kept safe and secure. They need to feel loved and cherished, and they need to feel like they belong. They need to feel confident that their adults will teach them the expectations and rules of the world. When children have healthy relationships with significant adults, they do the following:

- Look to them for love and affection.

- Depend on them for safety and security.

- Count on them for knowledge, wisdom, and guidance.

- Accept their help and comfort.

When Things Go Wrong

Children are survivors. When they don't have consistent, strong, caring, and guiding adult figures in their lives, they learn to be very self-sufficient. On the surface, teachers might appreciate the lack of neediness in these children, but the flip side of this independence is that these children often view adults as useless, irritants, or peers. They are unresponsive to adults, often ignore adult requests, and show no emotional response to adult praise or displeasure. They don't care to join in play or conversation with adults, and almost never go to an adult for help, comfort, or guidance. They might slap at an adult when they are annoyed or say "You can't make me" when they are redirected.

What are some signs that you may be working with a child like this? Read the following stories. Do these children remind you of any children in your program?

> Sullivan's mother picked him up after school. "Hi, Donna," the teacher greeted her and then announced, "Sullivan, your mom is here."
>
> Sullivan looked up briefly, glanced at his mother, and then returned to his play.
>
> "Sullivan, let's get going. I'm in a hurry," called Donna.

Sullivan shuffled over to his cubby, grabbed his backpack, and followed his mother down the hallway.

If this behavior is consistent, Sullivan's lack of response to reuniting with his mother at the end of the day might be a sign of a problem in his relationships with primary caregivers.

Keylon had scratches on his legs from climbing a tree in the park and a scab on his knee from falling off the scooter at school. He was a constant whirlwind who loved to roughhouse. His favorite activity during outside time was to challenge his buddies with feats of strength and speed. Emily, his teacher, had been having many challenges with Keylon. He ran up the climbing structure when she called the children to come inside, he clowned around at group time, and he often responded to her requests with, "You're not the boss of me."

"He rarely even says hello to me. This kid is a boy's boy. All he cares about are his friends," Emily said. "He's been in time-out more times than I can count for sassing me, but he only seems to get worse. The kid just wants nothing to do with me."

Children like Sullivan and Keylon who don't have strong relationships with significant adults might ignore adults. Oddly, though, these same children might seem very comfortable and friendly with total strangers who do not have a guiding role in the child's life.

"Frieda is such a friendly child," said Ms. Hernandez. "She just jumps onto anyone who comes into the classroom. She gloms right on to the volunteers, the substitutes, visiting parents—it doesn't matter who walks into the room. Right away they become her best friend."

Frieda's behavior looks friendly and healthy, but it is anything but. Healthy preschool children become very close to trusted and familiar adults. Children who do not have strong relationships with one or more caregivers sometimes demonstrate this by becoming overly affectionate with many adults without discrimination. Children with strong adult relationships in their lives take the time to get to know people first. Children without these strong relationships may not discriminate between adults they know and trust and total strangers.

"Hey, Case, what's up? You look really angry about something," Ms. F asked.

"I didn't do nothing," Case answered, looking down at the floor.

"I didn't say you did anything wrong. I just saw your face, and I wondered if I could help you with something," Ms. F replied.

"I didn't do nothing, I said," Case repeated, and he moved off to the loft to be alone.

Children like Case don't expect a supportive response from adults for their strong emotions, and Case has learned to keep his feelings to himself, dealing with them the best he can.

Mahika took a tumble in the yard and skinned her knee. She hid under the play structure to poke at the wound in privacy. It wasn't until naptime that Ms. Li saw the hole in Mahika's pants and blood on her knee. Ms. Li gently cleaned the injury and put a bandage over it.

Mahika didn't think of going to Ms. Li or any other adult for comfort or support. Both Case and Mahika both need help to see adults as a source of comfort and guidance. They try their best to handle life by themselves, but children don't have the skills, knowledge, and wisdom to take care of themselves in the many challenging situations they will face. Help children like these understand early on that you are someone they can come to for help, support, guidance, and comfort.

Sometimes a problem in bonding between a teacher and a child can be traced back to a difference in the teacher's and the child's family's expectations about how to interact with adults in authority. Maybe you expect a child to make eye contact with you when you are redirecting his behavior. However, the family may be teaching the child that eye contact during redirection is disrespectful and defiant.

You might find a child's frequent requests for assistance to be clingy behavior. However, the child's family might encourage their children to ask for help with minor things they can do themselves as one way to establish helping bonds between adults and children. You might expect children to obey you without question because you are the authority figure in the classroom. However, the child's family might encourage their children to ask why and negotiate with adults.

Don't be too quick to jump to conclusions about children's behavior, especially when teaching a diverse population or a group of children where many are culturally different from you. (Remember, too, that in this sense, cultural differences include such things as socioeconomic class, coming from a rural or urban background, and even coming from a different region of the country.) Young children reflect the culture in which they were raised. When you are surprised by children's behavior in the classroom, don't assume right away that there's a problem with the child. Dig a bit deeper and communicate with families to uncover any differences in child-rearing beliefs that may exist. Often it is fine to do things differently at home and at school. In that case, you can help both the children and their families understand what the expectations at school will be without invalidating a child's home culture.

Supportive Interactions to Promote Attachment

When all goes well in a child's early development, he will identify one or more adults who will nurture and guide him. The language and daily interactions you have with children set the tone for the kind of relationship you have with them. Your careful choice of language can help children view you as a valuable mentor rather than an opponent. Language that helps children feel safe and supported promotes positive emotional growth and development.

Three strategies to help strengthen your attachment to children are:

1. Get to know children well.

2. Interact with affection.

3. Recognize "insides."

Get to Know Children Well

It's one thing to have civil and kind interactions with children, but quite another to develop genuine relationships with individual children. Relationships grow over time as you learn to accept and trust one another. Some kids have personalities that are easy and quick to know. Other children may be more private or may have personality qualities that rub you the wrong way. Discover their more endearing characteristics before you get overwhelmed by their challenges and fall into unhealthy relationships.

Learn about children by talking to families and by observing children both at home and in the classroom. What are the family's expectations for their child? What do they see as their child's strengths and challenges? Who is this child?

Just as you might do with a friend or coworker, include personal bits in your conversations with children.

You might say to a coworker . . .	When talking with a child . . .
"Hi, is Alvie over his cold yet?"	"Good morning. Is your nana still visiting you at your house?"
"I saw there was a gem show in town last week. Did you go?"	"You're such a good ball kicker. Do you play soccer with your cousins?"
"You know how to use this new computer program, don't you? Can you help me with a problem I'm having?"	"Your mom told me she is teaching you how to cook at your house. No wonder you are always first to sign up for a cooking project!"

Not only does this casual, personal conversation help you and the child build a relationship, it's also a great strategy for helping children develop language skills. Researchers have found that the vast majority of *teacher talk* in the classroom is actually *housekeeping talk,* such as "Five more minutes until cleanup" or "Use your walking feet." While we need to provide these directions and redirections, this kind of talk does little to support language development. On the other hand, back-and-forth conversation with individual children is one of the best strategies for supporting language development.

Be Affectionate

What teachers do when they respond to children is important, but *how* we do it is often what makes the difference between helpful and hurtful technique. For example, what message is Kataryn getting from the teacher in the following scene?

Early in the day, Kataryn hit Stormasia when Stormy wouldn't let her use the red swing. Mrs. Galen helped the girls solve the problem, and things seemed to go fine until they went inside and Kataryn purposely got paint on Yvonne's dress.

"Kataryn, that's enough. If you keep on bothering other kids, you'll work at the round table by yourself. Kids who can't play nice play alone," said Mrs. Galen.

Not five minutes passed before Kataryn pushed Marquis into the wall. Mrs. Galen responded right away. "That's it, Kataryn. I've had enough of you this morning. You just sit yourself at that round table and think about being nice to your friends."

"Kataryn's always bad," Adrian told a visitor later in the day. "Mrs. Galen always makes her sit by herself 'cause she's not nobody's friend."

Now compare the story above about Kataryn and Mrs. Galen to this version. What message are Kataryn and the other children getting in this scene?

Early in the day, Kataryn hit Stormasia when Stormy wouldn't let her use the red swing. Mrs. Galen helped the girls problem solve and things seemed to go fine until they went inside and Kataryn purposely got paint on Yvonne's dress.

"Kataryn, something seems to be bothering you today. Do you want to talk to me about what's wrong this morning?" Mrs. Galen asked.

"Nothin' is wrong. Yvonne got in my way," Kataryn answered.

Not five minutes passed before Kataryn pushed Marquis into the wall. Mrs. Galen responded right away. "Oh, sweetie. You're having a hard time managing yourself this morning. I need to keep you and the other kids safe. I'm afraid you're hurting others today, and I'm also scared somebody might hurt you back," Ms. Galen said, getting down to Kataryn's level and pulling her in for a hug. "Come stay over here by me now, so we can all stay safe here. Maybe later we'll find some time to talk more. Right now, let's find something for you to do close to me so if you feel like you need to bother somebody, I'll be right here to help you."

"Mrs. Galen helps kids here," Adrian told a visitor later in the day. "She's teaching Kataryn how to play nice with the kids."

In the second scenario, when Mrs. Galen pulled Kataryn by her side, she made it clear to everyone that she liked Kataryn. At the same time, she showed that she intended to keep the children all safe. Her attitude and language toward Kataryn during the episode did not alienate the child either from herself or from others in the classroom.

Making love and affection contingent on *good* behavior may seem to make sense on the surface. If children crave relationships with significant adults, wouldn't they behave better in order to get that love? In fact, the opposite is true. Researchers such as John Bowlby and Mary Ainsworth tell us that children learn to behave well when they have good relationships with adults. Early learning for children is relationship based. The way in which teachers go about guiding children can strengthen or undermine the relationships between the teacher and children as well as between children and their peers. Different teachers have different effects on children, even when their actions look similar on the surface. Children are more responsive to corrective guidance when they are feeling safe and secure in the relationship, rather than defensive and uneasy. Treating children with love and affection, regardless of their behavior, makes a teacher's job easier.

Healthy and productive relationships with children are based on many of the same factors you probably listed about your own favorite supervisor in chapter 1. When our language with children lets them know they are seen and understood, we begin to increase our sphere of influence.

Recognize "Insides"

During the preschool years, children start to notice differences in people by external characteristics, such as gender, skin color, and material possessions. While this is a typical development stage, it is important to help children become aware that people are more than what is on their outsides.

Emphasize character traits in your dialogue with children, especially when you first greet them in the morning.

Instead of saying . . .	Try saying . . .
"Good morning. I like your new tennis shoes."	"Good morning. I feel happy when I see your big smile."
"What pretty hair ribbons."	"Tell me about your visit with your grandma."
"Aren't you a handsome boy today."	"I'm so happy to see you this morning."

Keep Children Safe

Children seek out and need reliable adults who keep them emotionally and physically safe and set predictable and clear limits. Safety is fundamental to attachment.

Be a Pillar of Safety

Children who feel unsafe often behave in unsafe ways. Safety and security are not "normal" for them; their status quo is risk and insecurity. Because they don't feel safe and secure, they have trouble recognizing when they do things that cause others to feel unsafe and insecure. What seems dangerous and scary to other children or even to adults just seems normal to these children. Help children begin to identify you as their pillar of safety and security in the classroom.

When . . .	Instead of saying . . .	Try . . .
Tyesha cries to you because Jaylyn hit her back.	"That's what happens when you hurt. You get hurt back. See?"	"This is a safe place. Let's find a way to keep you safe and a way to keep Jaylyn safe."
Mazen uses profanity and directs it toward you.	"Do you want to get kicked out of this school like you got kicked out of your last school?"	"Let's figure out words you can use here at school to tell me when you are angry with me."
Sovannary gets anxious during transitions and starts to toss things around the classroom.	"Go sit over there by yourself in the thinking chair. I'm tired of you breaking our things."	"Sovannary, come on over here with me so I can help you feel safe."
Matthew bites Amina.	"Nobody likes bad boys, Matthew."	"Let's get ice for Amina, and then you can stay by me so everyone stays safe here this morning."

Mean What You Say and Say What You Mean

Have you ever heard yourself saying something like this? "Mitchell never listens to me the first time I give him a warning. I always have to give him three chances before he stops."

It's not a kindness to give children three chances. It's confusing. Some children hear the first warning the way you intend it. They hear, "Stop going down the slide headfirst." Other children like Mitchell hear, "You can go down the slide three times headfirst. Then you will have to stop."

Sometimes what we say and what children hear are two different things. In some families, elders redirect children by suggestion and by letting children experience natural consequences. In other families, elders are more direct in their communication. Guiding children with a different style than what they hear at home can be confusing and lead to miscommunication. For example, Esme comes from a family that is direct when they want Esme to do something. Read what happens when her teacher uses a less direct style.

What the teacher said	What Esme heard	How Esme responded	What the teacher thought
"It's time to find a book and go to circle, Esme."	"You can get a book if you want."	"I don't want to read a book," Esme answered. She wandered off to the home-living center to get a baby doll instead.	"I wish she would obey me. Maybe I could coax her with an animal book."
"It's reading time, Esme. Wouldn't you like to look at one of the new baby animals books?"	"Would you like to read an animal book?"	"No," Esme answered. She sat down at the little housekeeping table to feed her baby doll.	"I need to keep smiling so she can't tell I'm getting annoyed."
"If you don't hurry up and pick a book, you might not get one you like."	"You might not get a good book."	"Okay," Esme answered. She didn't want a book anyway so it didn't matter.	"That girl never listens. I give up."

At the end of this exchange, the teacher turned her back and walked off, annoyed with Esme.

Although at first glance we might think Esme feels a sense of power that she can do whatever she wants, in truth she feels unsafe and insecure. She wonders if the teacher really likes and cares for her. She knows her mother loves her, and her mother would have made her go to circle with everyone else.

Deep inside, children know that they are children. They depend on kind but firm adults to run the show and keep them safe. Children who don't have this sense of safety and security compensate by trying to take over more control and power. Without an adult to depend on, children try to become their own adult. However, they know inside that they aren't ready for that kind of power, and they are terrified by the failure of the adults around them to take it on instead.

This is especially problematic when children come from homes and communities where adults are firm and follow through and they suddenly find themselves in a classroom with a less directive teacher. From the teacher's viewpoint, she is giving children choices and allowing them to experience the consequences of their behavior choices. From the child's viewpoint, however, it can appear either that the teacher is not in control or doesn't care about the child or her behavior. This teacher-child miscommunication can lead to ever-increasing misbehavior on the child's part and ever-increasing frustration on the teacher's part. For these children, it is even more essential that we mean what we say and say what we mean. Don't leave room for children to misinterpret your intent. Earn children's respect and trust by being exquisitely consistent with your words and your actions.

Help children feel safe and secure by being a person of your word. If you don't mean it, don't say it. If you choose to say it, commit to following through. When you decide to change your mind about what you said, make sure you let the child know. If you decide that Esme can get a doll instead of a book, don't leave her guessing. Say something like, "Okay. You can get a doll instead if you like."

Leave Notes for Children When You Are Absent

For some children, finding a substitute teacher at school can be a traumatic event that can shake their sense of security and safety. Without a clear explanation, children's imaginations can run wild. For some children who have experienced the loss of a significant adult, your absence may trigger anxiety or acting out. Think of writing a generic note to the children and leave it in the classroom for such occasions. Make sure the assistant teacher or substitute knows to read this note aloud at group time. The note might say something like:

> Dear Children,
>
> I am not at school today because I had something I had to take care of at my home. But (substitute's name) is here to take care of you while I am not here. I am thinking about all of you and know you will all have a very good day today. I will be back soon.
>
> Love, (your name)

Make sure the substitute posts the note on the wall at the children's level or leaves it in the library for those children who need to revisit it later in the day.

Repair Breaks in Relationships

If a child does something to hurt a relationship with a caregiver or a peer, what kinds of strategies might you teach that child to help repair the damage? List three possibilities in the space below.

_____

_____

_____

_____

_____

The strategies we want children to use to repair weakened relationships are the very ones we should use for those times we have mistakenly damaged our relationships with children. By modeling conciliatory behavior and words, we teach children that making that first move is a sign of strength, not weakness. We demonstrate that all of us sometimes act in haste or do and say thoughtless things when we are upset or stressed. And we show them that, with caring and effort, relationships can be repaired. Make a plan now for what you might say or do if you have damaged your relationship with a child. One example of what you might say is: "I apologize for being so angry. Let's talk about it." Can you think of other examples? Write them below.

_____

_____

_____

_____

_____

Give Children Help and Comfort

Some children come to your classroom with a history of seeing adults as hurtful instead of helpful. When children see adults as enemies instead of allies, they don't think of using adults for help or comfort.

Use a Magic Word: Come

Give children the gift of your physical support. When you see a child beginning to spin out of control, move over to him and take his hand. Gently say "Come sit by me" or "Come hold my hand." Using *come* instead of *go* is particularly effective for children from home cultures in which parents emphasize doing things with others over developing independence.

You might also use the word *come* in place of the word *go* when asking resistant children to do something.

Instead of saying . . .	Approach the child, take her hand, and gently say . . .
"Go wash your hands."	"Come, let's wash hands."
"Go put on your shoes before we go out."	"Come, let's get your shoes."
"Sit down while you eat."	"Come, let's sit down."

Help Fix Mistakes

Being a guide and mentor has nothing to do with being bossy and punitive. Being a guide and mentor involves establishing yourself as an unconditional support system, cheerleader, and safety net who also brings years of life wisdom and experience to share.

Think about your own experiences. You goofed big time. It was the first week on the job in a new school, and you said the wrong thing to the wrong mother. By the next morning she had already called your supervisor, and now you are being called into the office. How do you feel? What words do you want to hear? What words would help you feel that your supervisor was there for you to help you learn and to help you do your job? What would your dream supervisor say and how would she say it?

When children have failed to live up to the expectations of their significant adults, they have many of the same feelings we do when we fail to live up to the expectations of others. Will the adult abandon them? Will the adult leave them feeling worse? Can the adult somehow help pull them through and motivate them to move on? Be a child's safe guide and mentor as they learn to navigate the world and recover from their mistakes. Use phrases like these to reassure children and help them move forward:

- We can fix this.
- I'll teach you what you need to know in school.
- Let's figure out a way to solve this.
- It might be helpful (friendly, thoughtful) if you . . .
- Let me show you another way to . . .
- Let's practice the school way to . . .

Our interactions with individual children show the rest of the class what our practice will be when dealing with any child who is struggling. All of us mess up sometimes. And when we mess up we need a safe and supportive environment that accepts our mistakes and supports us as we move on. It's essential to draw the child in to be a part of the group rather than push the child out to be apart from the group. If we respond in a punitive way, other children will follow suit and also behave in punitive ways. If we respond as supportive mentors, we model the classroom standard: we all help each other in this classroom.

Support Attachment in the Classroom Culture

Weave nurturing moments into the daily life of the classroom. Nurturing moments don't require the same sort of daily and weekly planning that projects and special events do. Nurturing moments are just "the way things are done here." They are part of the culture of the classroom. Teachers can consciously build nurturing time into the regular schedule. Because children have so little control over their worlds, they are dependent on their adult caregivers to provide for their other basic life needs. Even as adults, we often show others that we care by paying attention to their basic needs.

When we focus our daily practices to accommodate children's needs, we help them feel comfortable and connected. At the same time, we model essential life skills for living peacefully and in community with others.

Get Close

So much to do, so little time. Sometimes, just by tweaking things you already do, you can greatly enrich your relationships with individual children. Instead of guiding a child by calling to him across the room, move close to the child, get down to his eye level, and speak quietly enough that only you and the child hear what is being said.

Instead of . . .	Try . . .
Calling across the room, "Lavone, is this your coat on the floor?"	Bringing the coat over to Lavone, squatting down, and gently saying, "Lavone, is this your coat? Put it in your cubby to keep it clean."
Calling across the room, "Frederick, did you wash your hands after you went potty?"	Walking over to Frederick, squatting down, taking his hands in yours, and gently saying, "Frederick, your hands are dry. I think you might have forgotten to wash. Scoot back in there and clean them up quickly."

Greet Children and Families Individually

Greetings are an important time of the day. In some families, children are taught to formally greet elders as a sign of respect when they enter a room. Remind children and families of your personal connections every day by individually greeting each child and the child's family. Some teachers do this as the children enter the classroom. Others do it at morning meeting time. What words should you use?

Reflect on your own experiences of being a guest in a friend's home or greeting guests in your own home. What are some of the ways you help others feel comfortable? Record some of your personal reflections below. How might you adapt these words and gestures to greet children in your classroom?

With my friends . . .	With the children in my class . . .
"Hi. I'm so glad you could come over."	"Hi. I'm so glad you came to school today."
_____	_____
_____	_____
_____	_____
_____	_____

Say Meaningful Good-Byes

Departures are another important time of the day to connect personally with children. Good-byes help everyone feel a sense of closure and anticipation to reconnect the next day. Imagine how empty and neglected you would feel if, when you left a gathering at a friend's house, nobody acknowledged that you were leaving! In the following chart, write some things you might hear when you leave a gathering or some things you say or do when friends leave your house. Then adapt these words and gestures to be appropriate for the children in your classroom.

With my friends . . .	With the children in my class . . .
"I had fun today. Let's get together again next week."	"I had fun with you today. I can't wait for tomorrow."
"I know a wonderful place for coffee."	"We've got some fun things to do the next time you come."
_____	_____
_____	_____
_____	_____
_____	_____

Greetings and good-byes help children make easier transitions to and from the classroom. They also teach children important friendship skills for building and maintaining important relationships. Make sure to learn how to greet and say good-bye to all the children and families in their home languages.

Give Children Opportunities to Talk With, Play With, and Emulate Adults

The best environments for young children provide ample time for small-group and individual activities. Center-based classrooms provide children with learning tailored to young children's learning styles. At the same time, center-based classrooms free up adults to interact with children individually or in small groups.

Some teachers make the mistake of limiting their involvement with children to teacher-directed large-group activities. They use center time to catch up on paperwork, planning, or cleaning tasks. Nevertheless, center time is a wonderful opportunity to connect with children individually for conversation, play, or modeling desired behavior. Center time provides excellent opportunities for teachers to model social and emotional skills in small-group and individual settings.

Limit large-group time to once or twice a day for only fifteen minutes or so. Make sure you invest the bulk of your time in working and interacting in groups small enough so that you have frequent and meaningful interactions with individuals.

Play with Children

One of the best investments of time you can make with children is to play with them on a regular basis. Five minutes of one-on-one play daily can do more to improve a child's behavior in a week than most other interventions can do in a year.

Many teachers find that center time is the best opportunity to find five uninterrupted minutes to play. To make the most of the time, imagine yourself as another child in your class who has very good play skills. Remember that when children play blocks with each other, nobody ever says, "How many rectangles did you use to build that farm?" That's a teacher script. To build relationships when playing with children, let the child lead the play and allow yourself to join in.

Instead of saying . . .	Try . . .
"How many rectangles did you use to build that farm?"	"How can I play?"
"Let's match up the mommy animals and the baby animals."	"Here's some food for the cows. Eat, cows."
"Oh no. Elephants don't belong in a farm. Where do elephants go?"	"Oh no. My chicken is scared of the elephant. He's running to try to get under the fence."

Sportscasting

Some children are not ready to let anyone else join in their play. A beginning step is to keep them aware that although they won't play with you, you still see them and appreciate their play and their thoughts.

Begin to connect with these children by using a technique called "sportscasting." When you sportscast, imagine yourself as an announcer at the Olympics, reporting on an athlete at an event. Speak aloud and report what you see. Remember that sportscasters don't interview athletes during the event!

Instead of saying . . .	Try . . .
"What do you think will happen if you pour the water into the funnel?"	"Lulu is picking up the large bottle of water. It looks like she's going to pour it into the funnel."
"The boat is upside down. Turn it over and see how it works."	"Stephano has the boat upside down and is riding it in the water. He let go and the boat went right down to the bottom. Now he's picking it up. He turned it over. He let go. It is staying on top this time."
"What color is that water?"	"Tito has a pitcher of red water. He's filling little cups. Now he's filling the big cup."

There is a time and place, of course, for you to extend children's play and thinking by asking "what if" kinds of questions. Just make sure to balance those interactions with the relationship-building interactions suggested above.

Activities to Support Attachment

Integrate deliberate attachment activities into the daily programming. These activities guide all children as they learn to view adults as a source of comfort, strength, and guidance. They are especially effective with children who have not learned to rely on or connect with adults. The following story shows how powerful these games can be with the children teachers typically find most difficult.

To her astonishment, when Ms. Emily played "Tickle Bug" with Deion on his cot at rest time, Keylon called over to ask her to come do it with him. When Keylon's turn came around, the four-year-old giggled like a toddler and pleaded, "More, more." Within a few days of beginning baby games, Keylon started being more responsive to Ms. Emily and for the first time ran to greet her when he arrived at school.

Paradoxically, while kids like Keylon might shy away from playing four-year-old games such as Legos with adults, they may be very willing to play baby games like "Tickle Bug." Children who have not had warm and playful experiences with adults as infants and toddlers are often drawn to this adult-baby interaction. For some of these difficult children, this is the place to begin to rebuild relationships. Punishing kids who are not connected to adults only reinforces their belief that adults are useless. Over time, these children become more and more alienated and difficult. Instead, begin to find ways to develop relationships with children like Keylon.

Rest Time Activities

Often teachers look forward to the time of year when the children are finally able to settle themselves down for nap or rest without much adult involvement. Nevertheless, naptime or rest time is a wonderful opportunity to build attachment with children. Take advantage of this time to strengthen relationships with children, especially those with whom you need to improve your relationship.

Sit next to the child as he lies down, and pat his back rhythmically. Use a singsong voice to chant such things as "Today I saw Matthew and he was on the swing and he was having fun. And he played with Brit and they played in the water and they laughed and they laughed. Then Matthew had lunch and he ate some applesauce and he ate some macaroni and he drank some milk." The idea is to let the child hear that he is seen and that you see him in a positive light.

Another valuable naptime routine is to sing the chorus section of "You Are My Sunshine" to the child as you rub or pat her back. Children seem to universally relax and feel loved when adults sing this song to them as they drift off to sleep. If you are not familiar with the song, you can easily find the music and lyrics on the Internet.

Baby Games

Baby games are warm and simple attachment games—the kind of games that you might play with an infant or toddler. Adults naturally play baby games with tiny ones to help build reciprocal and affectionate relationships. Use these guidelines to help make the activities successful:

- Teach the child to say or sign "more" when they want the activity repeated, which helps children develop the habit of initiating interactions with adults.

- Try to do the activity over and over until the child is finished. The more we practice a new skill, the more we learn.

- Do the activity exactly the same way each time you do it. Predictability helps the child feel safe and secure.
- Baby games are particularly effective to use if a child is having a bad day or is beginning to show signs of stress or falling apart.

Here are some baby games that you can use to help connect with children.

Tickle Bug

1. Put one hand high in the air and begin to chant, "Here comes the Tickle Bug."
2. Slowly bring your hand lower and closer to the child while you continue the chant.
3. Gently tickle the child with one finger. Touch a neutral part of the child's body, such as his arm or his foot, if you are not comfortable tickling his belly.
4. When you tickle, say, "Tickle, tickle, tickle."
5. Try to do this until the child indicates that he is done.

Peekaboo

1. Put a small blanket or cloth over your head.
2. Chant over and over, "Where's (your name)?"
3. When the child pulls the blanket off, say, "Here I am!"
4. Allow the child to put the blanket on her own head if she likes. Change the chant to, "Where's (child's name)?" and "There you are!" when you uncover her.

This Little Piggy

1. Take one of the child's hands in your own.
2. Taking each finger in turn, chant, "This little piggy went to market, this little piggy stayed home, this little piggy had roast beef, this little piggy had none." On the last finger, say your line with great anticipation, "And this little piggy went . . ."
3. Put your hand high in the air and as you bring it close to the child say, "Wee, wee, wee, wee, wee."
4. Tickle the child gently with one finger while saying, "All the way home."

One, Two, Three, Jump

1. Start with the child standing on a very low box or step.

2. Stand a few feet away with your arms outstretched to catch the child.

3. Say, "One, two, three, jump," with great anticipation.

4. Catch the child in your arms and say, "Whee," while you swing or twirl her around gently.

Doubles

1. Sit on a swing, and seat the child on your lap facing you with his legs straddled around your body.

2. With one arm, hold him around his back.

3. Chant a singsong as you pump and swing together. Either sing a lullaby or make up a singsong, such as "Swing, swing, swinging together. Swing, swing, swinging together."

4. If you are not comfortable having a child on your lap, push the child on the swing from the front instead of behind. Push the child's feet. Sing and chant as above.

One, Two, Three, Whee

1. Sit in a chair and seat the child on your knees facing you.

2. Either hold the child from behind with both hands or hold the child's forearms.

3. Bounce the child on your lap while you chant, "One, two, three."

4. On three, part your legs so the child drops down a foot or two while you still hold onto her safely. Say, "Whee" in an excited tone of voice.

Nurturing Activities

Many children need predictable and structured activities to help them attach to their primary caretakers. Teachers have found the following three activities to be useful tools to help children develop attachment skills.

Follow these general tips for success:

*   Present only one activity at a time, the same activity every day for one week. Rotate the three activities, one week at a time, all year long or as long as children are still interested.

*   Initially, most children will want to participate. Over time, many children will be "done" with the activity, but a handful of children will still show interest. The interested children need the activity the most. Keep offering it as long as any children still need it.

- Some teachers set up these activities outdoors. The teacher sitting at the table with the child also supervises a section of the play yard.

- Set up a waiting list for children who want to participate. That way they can play someplace else while waiting for their turn.

- Allow children to watch if they wish. But make sure to teach the guideline that the teacher will only be talking to the child at the activity table.

- Boys and girls both love all of these activities.

- Some teachers like to have these activities available for children to use independently or with each other. Remember, though, that when they are being used for attachment, they are teacher-child activities.

- Some children have trouble defining their body boundaries. Use universal precautions and clearly define that you will only put lotion or "nail paint" where you have said you will (lotion goes on hands; nail paint only on nails). Some children will beg for lotion or paint on arms, faces, or other body parts. To help children better define boundaries, make sure you stick to your predefined limit. This is particularly important for children who have been violated or who invade the body space of others.

- Teach families how to do these activities during parent meetings or in newsletters, and explain to families how these activities help children feel safe and secure.

Lotion Table

1. Fill a basket with three or four small plastic bottles of lotion.

2. Invite the child to sit across from you to have lotion rubbed into her hands.

3. Open each bottle in turn, holding it up for the child to smell. Let the child choose the lotion she would like to use.

4. Pour a small portion of lotion onto your own hand, and rub it gently into the child's hand.

5. Either quietly sing a song to the child or carry on a soft and gentle conversation.

Tips to remember:

1. White lotion can be disturbing for children who have been victims of sexual abuse. Use universal precautions and shake a drop of food coloring into any bottles of white lotion you may have.

2. When rubbing lotion into the child's hands, some teachers find it useful to think to themselves something such as, "This is such a precious baby." This self-talk helps to set a mood where attachment can flourish.

3. Invite family participation by asking families to donate extra bottles of lotion they are not using at home.

Nail Painting

1. Use a regular, inexpensive watercolor paint set with a fine brush and a cup of water.

2. Invite the child to choose a paint color.

3. Engage the child in one-on-one conversation while you paint his nails.

Tips to remember:

1. If you use the term *nail painting* rather than *nail polish*, some boys feel more freedom to participate.

2. When painting children's nails, some teachers find it useful to imagine they are manicurists in a nail salon. This helps them to carry on respectful and interested chat with their "client." Most children, like adults, love the combination of physical grooming and casual, respectful chatting.

3. Some teachers have children wash the nail paint off during the next transition. The paint comes off easily with regular soap and water.

Owie Table

1. Gather a supply of plain, inexpensive adhesive bandages, cotton balls, a washable red marking pen, an eyedropper and a cup of clear water, disposable rubber gloves, and a small plastic container for waste.

2. Invite the child over for you to attend to his pretend owie.

3. Ask the child where on his hand the owie is.

4. Put on the rubber gloves. Dab a small red dot with the washable marker on the "injury." Using the eyedropper with water, drop a bit of water on the marker dot. The ink will dissolve and will look like blood.

5. Use the cotton ball to dab up the red water, and dispose of the cotton in the waste container.

6. Put an adhesive bandage on the "injury."

7. During the care of the owie, say something such as, "Sometimes kids get hurt here at school. Some hurts are on the inside and some are on the outside. When a child gets hurt, he can come to a grown-up for help."

Tips to remember:

1. For children to feel safe and secure at school, they need to know that adults will be in charge and will be responsive to their feelings of hurt, fear, and anxiety. This activity is very helpful for children who have had to take care of themselves and who haven't used adults much as helpers.

2. Some teachers find it useful to limit children to one "owie" session a day. If some children want to repeat the play over and over, teachers can repeat the activity every day until children are done with it.

Discussion/Reflection Questions

1. In twenty years, when a child from your class reflects back, how would you like him to remember you?

   _____

   _____

   _____

2. What is the difference between teaching preschool and teaching twenty unique preschool-age children?

   _____

   _____

   _____

3. Consider a traditional, one-size-fits-all school- or centerwide discipline policy (for example, first offense gets a verbal warning, second offense pulls a card, third offense triggers a note sent to parents, and so on). How do you think this would work for teaching social and emotional skills to young children?

   _____

   _____

   _____

4. Do you think it's important for children's development that their teachers respond exactly the same way to the same behavior, regardless of the situation or the underlying need of the children involved? Why or why not?

    _____

    _____

    _____

Exercises

1. Spend five minutes playing with one of your more challenging children in the block area or the dramatic play area. Make an effort to avoid "teacher talk" during this play session. Instead, try to interact as a well-adjusted child might do. Did you find it difficult to avoid teacher talk? How did the child react during the play? Did you see any change in your relationship with the child after the play session?

    _____

    _____

    _____

    _____

    _____

2. Think of a child who has a behavior that irritates you. Explore whether the behavior that bothers you might be a cultural difference in expectations between school and home. Might your goal be that a child learns to be independent while the parent's goal is that children learn to accept and give help? Might you be emphasizing teamwork and mutual support while the family stresses the importance of competition and being the best? How can you find out what the family's expectations are?

    _____

    _____

    _____

    _____

3. Choose one or two baby games and introduce them to one of your challenging children every day for a week. Did anything change?

_____

_____

_____

_____

_____

Reflection/Journal Assignment

Nurturing moments help children feel safe and secure. They should be designed to meet the basic needs of children to send the message that adults take responsibility for the child's well-being and that adults will maintain predictability and order. How do you already meet the basic needs of children in your class? What other ideas might you try? As you read through the rest of this book, make sure to add to your chart any new ideas that come to you.

Children's needs	How can I meet children's needs throughout the day?
Physical needs: food, rest, exercise, toileting, grooming	
Safety needs: physical safety, emotional safety	
Belonging needs: love, affection, connections to others	
Self-esteem needs: I matter, I am seen, I am valued, I am accepted, I know what grown-ups expect of me	
Cognitive needs: materials and activities that are accessible to each individual child	

Special Moments

According to noted child psychiatrist Dr. Bruce Perry, children who have one or more trusted and loving adults in their lives have a huge advantage over children who don't. Having a strong relationship with an adult such as a parent, grandparent, or aunt encourages children to succeed and helps them survive the bumps they experience in the world outside their home. In our own busy and complex lives, it's good to find out that it's often the small efforts we make with children that can send them the message that we are there for them.

Think About It

Think back to your childhood. Who do you remember as a key adult in your life? What fond memories pop into your mind when you think about that adult? For me, it was one of my grandmothers. I remember her taking me grocery shopping with her, letting me use her cold cream on my hands after my bath, and teaching me how to make mashed potatoes. In all these things, the message was that she wanted me around and wanted to share her life with me. Remember your own special moments and try to pass them on to the important child in your life.

Some Ideas

- Rock and sing to your baby or young child. Smooth lotion on each other's hands.

- Cook a meal together. Fix a broken item together. Fold laundry together.

- Spend five minutes with your child at bedtime. Turn off the TV and the cell phone. Just chat together.

- Plan a weekly lunch date with older children when you can sit together and chat as friends.

From *Beyond Behavior Management: The Six Life Skills Children Need*, second edition, by Jenna Bilmes, © 2012. Published by Redleaf Press, www.redleafpress.org. This page may be reproduced for teacher–family communication.

Chapter 2 Resources

Bailey, Becky. 1996. *I Love You Rituals: Activities to Build Bonds and Strengthen Relationships with Children.* Oviedo, FL: Loving Guidance.

Brooks, Robert, and Sam Goldstein. 2001. *Raising Resilient Children: Fostering Strength, Hope, and Optimism in Your Child.* Lincolnwood, IL: Contemporary Books.

Bruce, Nefertiti, and Karen B. Cairone with the Devereux Center for Resilient Children. 2010. *Socially Strong, Emotionally Secure: 50 Activities to Promote Resilience in Young Children.* Silver Spring, MD: Gryphon House.

Covey, Stephen R. 1997. *The 7 Habits of Highly Effective Families: Building a Beautiful Family Culture in a Turbulent World.* New York: Golden Books.

Dinkmeyer, Don, and Gary D. McKay. 1973. *Raising a Responsible Child: Practical Steps to Successful Family Relationships.* New York: Simon and Schuster.

Gordon, Thomas. 1970. *Parent Effectiveness Training: The Tested New Way to Raise Responsible Children.* New York: P. Wyden.

Greenspan, Stanley I., and Serena Wieder. 1998. *The Child with Special Needs: Encouraging Intellectual and Emotional Growth.* Reading, MA: Addison-Wesley.

Kohl, Herbert. 1998. *The Discipline of Hope: Learning from a Lifetime of Teaching.* New York: The New Press.

Koplow, Lesley, ed. 2007. *Unsmiling Faces: How Preschools Can Heal.* New York: Teachers College Press.

Koralek, Derry. 1999. *Classroom Strategies to Promote Children's Social and Emotional Development.* Lewisville, NC: Kaplan Press.

Marston, Stephanie. 1990. *The Magic of Encouragement: Nurturing Your Child's Self-Esteem.* New York: W. Morrow.

McClellan, Diane E., and Lilian G. Katz. 2001. "Assessing Young Children's Social Competence." ERIC Publications. ED 450953. http://www.eric.ed.gov:80/PDFS/ED450953.pdf.

Mulligan, Sarah A., Kathleen Miller Green, Sandra L. Morris, Ted J. Maloney, Dana McMurray, and Tamara Kittelson-Alfred. 1992. "Welcoming All Children: A Closer Look at Inclusive Child Care." In *Integrated Child Care: Meeting the Challenge.* Tucson, AZ: Communication Skill Builders.

Pollack, William. 1998. *Real Boys: Rescuing Our Sons from the Myths of Boyhood.* New York: Random House.

Tobin, Larry. 1991. *What Do You Do with a Child Like This? Inside the Lives of Troubled Children.* Duluth, MN: Whole Person Associates.

York, Stacey. 2003. *Roots and Wings: Affirming Culture in Early Childhood Programs.* Rev. ed. St. Paul, MN: Redleaf Press.

THREE

Belonging

I am a part of the group, not apart from the group.

We early childhood folks have always known that parents and families are a child's first teacher and that two of the big tasks in preschool are to help children make friends and become a part of the classroom community. Now there are research-based early learning standards to reinforce our evidence-based beliefs. The examples below come from North Dakota, Ohio, and Colorado, and there is probably something similar in your own state standards either in the social-emotional or social studies/citizenship domains. This chapter will help you meet those standards.

- "[Children] begin to develop friendships with peers." *North Dakota Early Learning Guidelines*

- "[Children] develop a sense of belonging to different groups (e.g., family, group of friends, preschool class, boys or girls)." *Ohio Early Learning Content Standards*

- "Children have an increasing awareness of belonging to the program, family, and community." *Colorado Building Blocks*

"My buddies, my buddies," Ryker called out as soon as his grandmother dropped him off at his classroom. He ran into the room airplane style, with his arms wide out and a huge smile on his face, soaring around the other children.

"Weekends are so hard for him," his grandmother said to the teacher. "There are no other kids around, and he keeps asking me when it will be school again. All he can talk about are his friends Mikey and David."

Ryker ran back to kiss his grandmother good-bye.

"Miss Stephanie, can we play the farmer game again today, and can I be the dog again and David be the cheese again?" he asked his teacher.

What Does Belonging Look Like?

A child's family is the first and most important place where a feeling of identity and belonging start. It is in the family that a child gets his or her name. A child wakes up each morning and goes to sleep each night with her family. These are the first people most children get to know well. In the family, a child learns the role of son or daughter, sister or brother, grandson or granddaughter, niece or nephew. It is in the family that a child begins to discover his cultural identity. According to Dr. Hiram Fitzgerald from Michigan State University, by the age of five a child's cultural self is already established. The child knows whether children sleep with their parents or in a different room. He knows whether his family eats meat or not, how and when it is appropriate to talk with adults, and what to do if a sibling wants to use one of his toys. He may not always do what his family elders expect of him, but he knows the expectations.

For some children more than others, a first introduction to the culture of an early childhood classroom can be confusing and uncomfortable. Perhaps chicken legs are served at lunch to a child who has been raised as a vegetarian. Maybe a child who has grown up in a house where she is expected to share a toy she is using is shocked when a child tells her "No, don't touch that. I'm using it." Nevertheless, with the right support, most children begin to regard the classroom as sort of a home away from home, even though the rules and customs may be different from their family traditions. When you think about it, an early childhood classroom does resemble a home structure in a number of ways. Like at home, there are one or more adults in charge of all the children. Adults both at home and at school provide food, take care of bumps and bruises, and schedule the child's day. In fact, I think most of us have had the experience of having children feel so at home when they are at school that they accidentally call us "Mommy"—usually surprising themselves as much as us!

When Things Go Wrong

Out of the corner of her eye, Ms. Davis saw Olivia and Noah sitting under the climber, using small twigs to pretend "smoke." She immediately went over, got down to their level, and gently said, "Oh no. We don't smoke here. Even pretending. Smoking is bad for you. Only nasty people smoke. Put the sticks down and come with me to get some of the giant balls from the shed." Olivia, whose mother smoked, wondered why her teacher thought that her mother was nasty.

Alicia, the teacher in the four-year-old room, thought it would be fun to make a guessing game for children from their baby pictures. She planned to make cards with a copy of their baby picture on one side and a current photo on the other. All of the children except for Alexander brought in their baby photos. When Alicia explained to him that he needed to bring in the picture or he would be the only one without a photo card, he began to cry. "I can't play that game." Alexander had been living in his current foster home for a few months and had never even seen a baby picture of himself.

Sometimes it's easy to forget that the children in our care have rich lives outside of our four walls. They have a wide diversity of family histories, traditions, living conditions, and relationships. Take care to respect children's home lives and connections in your interactions and activities. Support this first and most important relationship as a starting point for children's development of relationships outside the home.

Most preschool classrooms have children who span the developmental stages of friendships. Some may work alone, some work next to others, some have a special friend, and some may play well in small groups. Sometimes children's play stages are at the heart of what look like behavior problems in the classroom.

Tatiana and Clay were given the buddy job of washing paintbrushes at the sink. Immediately conflict broke out. Clay was trying hard to get Tatiana to share space at the sink, but Tatiana kept elbowing him out of the way and finally pushed him off the stepstool he was trying to share with her.

"Teacher," Clay complained. "Tatiana pushed me off the steps."

"Tatiana, be nice to your friend. Move over and share the steps," the teacher instructed her.

As soon as the teacher moved away, trouble broke out again. Tatiana grabbed the brushes out of Clay's hands. "Teacher," he yelled.

This time the teacher said, "Tatiana, pushing and grabbing are not nice. You've lost your chance to wash paintbrushes now. I want you to go sit down until the rest of us are done with our jobs."

Tatiana threw herself on the floor crying and began to kick the stepstool Clay was standing on. Eventually, the teacher carried her away to the time-out area to cool off.

The teacher in the story wasn't aware that Tatiana didn't have the skills she needed to work with a partner without adult support. She wasn't being mean or naughty; she was just put in a situation she couldn't manage alone. If the teacher had had this information, she might have either given Tatiana the job to do alone or could have stayed with the children to help them work together. She might also have worked with Tatiana at other times during the day to teach her sharing and taking turns—skills she was still missing. Before long, Tatiana would be able to do partner work without constant conflict and needing so much intervention from the teachers.

Even after children learn to play with another child, small-group areas like blocks or dramatic play can be a challenge for them. Because they don't know how to play easily with more than one child at a time, conflict can break out. Consider the following story.

Zack and Adrian had been building together peacefully for ten minutes when Sean and Amy came over to join them. Zack said, "Adrian, don't play with those stupid kids. Let's hide so they can't find us."

"I wanna keep doing blocks," Adrian said.

Zack kicked down the structure they had been building and started tossing blocks around the area. A flying block hit Sean, Adrian began to suck his fingers and weep, and Amy struck Zack in the head saying, "You're the one who's stupid."

"That's enough," Mr. F said, approaching the children. "The four of you pick up the mess and find another area to play where you won't fight."

Amy immediately went to the water table and Adrian followed. Sean intentionally stepped on Zack's hand in response to being struck with the block. Mr. F returned just in time to prevent Zack from pummeling Sean with another block.

"I hate that block area," Mr. F complained to his co-teacher later that day. "I think we need to close it down for a few months."

While closing down areas, such as dramatic play and blocks, might lead to a quieter room, that strategy also denies children the practice they need to work together in small groups. A closer observation would have revealed that Zack didn't have the skills he needed to play in a group of three to five children. When Sean and Amy tried to enter the play, Zack's anxiety rose, and he began a fight-or-flight strategy. Instead of closing down the block center, the teachers might have chosen to make sure an adult was always nearby to help less-skilled children negotiate the area. As small-group skills increased, bickering, name-calling, conflict, and aggression would decrease.

"Kirsten is a loner child," Miss Felicia reported to the girl's mother. "She'll either play alone or sometimes just with Maria. If Maria is playing doctor with the other girls, Kirsten complains there's nobody to play with. I try to get her to join the other girls, but she just runs to hide behind the sofa." Miss Felicia and her mother decided to stop pushing her to play with others and just let her be.

In fact, Kirsten was interested in playing with others, but had trouble understanding the play. She couldn't figure out what the kids were doing or how she could join in to be part of the group. Instead, she opted to be apart from the group. At the end of the year, Kirsten was no closer to being able to work in small groups than she had been in September. Closer observation might have revealed Kirsten's problem to her teachers. They might have joined Kirsten in small-group activities and helped her figure out what the children were doing. They might have modeled language for her such as, "How can I play?" Gradually, Kirsten would have developed the skills she needed to figure out how to play in small groups without adult support.

One of the most frustrating times of the day in many classrooms is large-group time, whether the activity is a story, music and movement, or a class meeting or discussion. You might hear "Move," or "Stop touching me," or "You can't sit here," as children struggle to negotiate space. As they vie for your attention, some children will call out of turn or fight over who gets to sit next to you. Other children who can't yet control their impulses in large-group settings will leave when they get bored, play with neighbors, talk during a story, or ignore directions. Some children will be so hungry for your interaction during large group that they cause continual disruption just so they can get your attention! It's frustrating for teachers and children alike to have half of large-group time focused on redirecting, reprimanding, and otherwise disciplining unruly children.

The helpful strategies you might use for these children might not be much different from those you would use with a toddler in the same situation. What strategies might you use if you had a toddler for the day? You might expect her to have a lot of trouble sitting still and paying attention quietly for the whole book. She would probably get up and down many times, chatter to others, and try to come up and touch the book or turn the pages. Maybe she would just get bored after a few minutes and leave the group. You might try to hold that child on your lap or let her turn the pages. You might want to let her point to pictures in the book or act out pieces of the story.

Some children move through these stages of play with little adult assistance. Through inborn temperaments, social-observational skills, or watching others who are modeling behavior, they appear to effortlessly move from one stage to another. Others have more difficulty. Careful observation of children with challenges might reveal surprising insights. You might suddenly realize that rather than a discipline issue, you are seeing a developmental issue. These children need a great deal more help to move from one stage of play skills to the next. Once you understand the developmental play level of each child and the ~~difficulty he is having transitioning to the next stage, you can accommodate~~ ~~children at each of the play levels, model and teach the language and behaviors~~ ~~of friendship, and make plans to scaffold children from one level to the next~~ ~~by using supportive interactions, an inclusive classroom culture, and special~~ ~~activities.~~

Support Family Belonging

It is a big step for children when they first leave the known life of home and venture into the strangeness of the larger world. Help children reinforce their identity as members of their families while learning how to navigate the outside world by becoming familiar with the worlds from which they come.

Preschools have a culture all their own. The culture might be influenced by documents such as state early learning standards, an adopted curriculum, and accreditation standards. You can often see this part of the culture in parent handbooks or new teacher orientation materials. Just as important to the culture are the values and beliefs that teachers and the director bring to the program. This part of the culture may be invisible to outsiders or to teachers who are new to the program. Some pieces of the invisible culture might be the way conflicts are addressed among teachers, how common areas are maintained, and how staff birthdays are handled.

Learn about Family Culture

Some families may share the same goals and beliefs as your preschool program. Other families, however, may have different goals for their young children and different beliefs about families' roles in the education of their children (Trumbull et al. 2011).

Common preschool early learning standards and practices	Contrasting beliefs and values of some families
Children develop independence in personal-care routines and performance of tasks.	Children accept help from and assist others in personal-care routines and tasks.
Children take pride in individual achievement.	Children use their talents to contribute to the welfare of the group.
Children learn to regulate their own behaviors.	It is an adult responsibility to regulate young children's behavior.

(continued on next page)

Common preschool early learning standards and practices	Contrasting beliefs and values of some families
Emphasis on cognitive skills such as language, literacy, and mathematics.	Emphasis on social skills such as helping, sharing, and obeying adults.
Emphasis on promoting a child's self-esteem with praise and positive reinforcement.	Emphasis on promoting appropriate social behavior with correction and criticism.
Emphasis on children learning to distinguish between personal and community space and things.	Emphasis on children sharing space and things.
Teachers and parents should be partners in a child's education.	It is a teacher's job to teach children academic subjects. It is a parent's role to teach children morals and how to behave.

As you looked at this chart, you may have said to yourself that you do things from *both* sides of it. For example, you may have private cubbies where children can keep things they brought from home and, at the same time, teach children that all of the materials in the classroom are meant to be shared. Still, most of us find that over the course of a day, we tend to lean more toward one approach than the other. None of the approaches is better or worse than the others. Children can grow up to be happy, productive members of society whether they are raised by parents to favor one set of values or the other. Just remember that when they are taught a different approach from that used at school, children can find it difficult to adapt. They might be misunderstood as being disobedient or immature.

Some schools have policies that expect teachers to make home visits early in the year. Home visits are a good opportunity to learn about children, their families, and their neighborhoods. At the home, you will have a chance to watch the interactions between the elders and the child. If you focus on some of the beliefs and values in the chart, you may get some valuable insight on family values. If you have the chance, ask the child to show you what she likes to do at home. Make sure to take notes to refer to later for lesson plans and progress reports. If your school doesn't make home visits, gather information from the families at other times. Talk to families during enrollment to find out information they would like to share about their child. Chat with families briefly at drop-off and pickup times to fill in your picture of each child. Make sure you discover the answer to questions such as these:

- What does the family call the child?
- Who lives in the household? How does the child refer to each of these people?

- What are the family's goals for their child this year? What are their goals for the child's future?

- How does the family teach their children how to behave? What are the important rules the family wants the child to follow?

- What is the child interested in? What are the child's talents?

You may find that families have very different beliefs about child rearing than your own. Your own cultural background might lead you to believe that the parents are babying their four-year-old. Perhaps you believe the parents are too harsh or too sarcastic when dealing with their child. Maybe when you ask the parents what the child is good at, they appear uncomfortable with the question. Make these conversations with families a time to explore differences in cultural expectations and beliefs about children. Approach these differences with an "aha!" as you gain insight into a child's behavior. What you might have seen as passive might really be respecting authority. What you might have perceived as low self-esteem might really be a family emphasis on community instead of individual glory.

Review the exercise you did in chapter 1 in which you defined long-term goals for children. Compare your goals with the family's goals for their child. Do your goals lean more toward fostering the child's individualism? Do the family's goals lean more toward collectivism? Is it vice versa? Or are you coming from a similar orientation? As you work with other people's children, stay conscious that your strategies must respect and support the family's goals for their child at the same time you prepare children to be successful in a mainstream school setting.

Share with families your program's goals for children in their preschool years, and listen to their perspectives on what they would like their children to get out of the school experience. Be sensitive to possible differences between your program goals and family values. Take note of these differences in philosophy as you guide children through their daily routines, and communicate with families when you have questions about your expectations or classroom practices.

Learn about Family Structure

The stereotypic notion of a family consisting of a mother, father, and one or more children is just one of many family variations you might discover in your classroom. The children in your group may come from single-parent families, blended families, families with same-sex parents, or foster families. They may live with relatives other than their biological parents, either on a temporary or permanent basis, or they may have extended family living in the same household. They may be separated from one or both parents because of incarceration, military deployment, or divorce. Their parents may be married, living together, or living apart. They may come from homes with immigrant parents or adoptive parents. They may refer to family friends as aunts, uncles, and cousins.

Take time at the beginning of the year to become familiar with each child's family and find out how they would like their child to understand their family situation. Take note of unique characteristics of each child's family so you can avoid sending confusing or troubling messages to a child. For example, if the children are making photo frames as holiday gifts for their families, make sure to make provision for children who have two families. If you choose to do Mother's Day or Father's Day activities, consider how you will make them work for children who have single parents, two moms or dads, or who live with other significant adults or foster parents. Think about substituting Family Day activities and circumventing the problem altogether. If families are being invited to a spring potluck, have a clear understanding of who should receive invitations. At parent conference time, ensure that you conference with the key decision makers in the child's life.

Supportive Interactions to Reinforce Family Belonging

It is important for us to recognize and support children's family connections in our daily interactions. Talk to children about what they do with family members when they are not at school. Share family traditions and routines. Help children begin to define for themselves who their family is, what their family values, and what their family believes. Developing a strong sense of family is essential as children explore the diverse world outside their homes. Work closely with families who have complicated relationship structures to make sure you are not sending contradictory messages to the child.

- Begin to use the child's family name(s) when talking about their home lives. For example, you might say, "Brandon, does your Robinson family have any pets?" or "Isabella, does your Garcia-Johnson family live in a mobile home like the family in our story?"

- From time to time, refer to children by both their given and family names. You might sometimes do this when you have two children with the same first name, but think about doing this for all the children in your group. For example, you might say, "Let's see, I think it's Jacob Fry's turn to feed the mouse today."

- For fun, sometimes refer to the children as Mr. (last name) or Miss (last name). For example, say, "After Mr. Wang is done at the easel, it will be Miss Popov's turn."

How else might you tweak your interactions with children and families to meet the needs of the program as well as the needs of the family? Let's look, for example, at how you might promote the early learning standard of independence while at the same time reinforcing a family's value of helpfulness.

Strategies to promote independence	Strategies to promote helpfulness
"Look at you! You got your shoes on all by yourself!"	"Arturo, thank you for helping David put his shoes on. Now we can all go outside."
Job board with tasks for each child.	Buddy jobs for children to do in pairs.
"Who was playing in the block area this morning? Please go back and put the blocks away so we can do story time."	"There are lots of blocks still out in the block area. Can we get some helpers to put them away so we can do story time?"

As early childhood educators, it is our task to respect the goals and cultural traditions children bring from their homes, while at the same time introducing children and their families to the skills and knowledge that children will need to be successful in our schools. You will find additional examples throughout this book of how you might vary your interactions, activities, and routines to meet both the goals of your program and the families' goals for their children.

Support Family Belonging through the Classroom Culture

Children do not enter the classroom as an empty slate. They bring with them their home language, traditions, preferences, and culture. Just as adults might keep mementos of home at their workplace, encourage children to bring similar items into the classroom.

Family pictures, familiar bedtime music, and special foods from home help reinforce for children that they belong to their family. It also sends a message that school is their place and that their whole being is honored and respected.

- Display photos of children and their families on a family photo wall, in picture albums, or in individual or collage frames around the classroom. Have families bring in family pictures or take pictures at drop-off time, pickup time, or home visits. Make sure that all children are represented with at least one family member. Some teachers have made a family photo album to keep in their home-living areas. Others have framed photos and have hung or placed them in various areas around the room.

- Ask families to donate extra household items to the room. Some items you might request are small rugs, place mats, pitchers, rolling pins, curtains, tapestries, vases, picture frames, cookbooks, hats, and baskets. Use these items throughout the classroom to bring a homelike atmosphere that reflects children's lives and experiences.

- Ask families to donate old magazines, picture books, and cookbooks that reflect their cultures and traditions. Add these materials to the class library as well as to the dramatic play areas and other appropriate areas of the classroom.

- Include books and recordings in all languages spoken by the children in the class. Invite family members to come in to read books or tell stories in their home language to small groups of children.

- Encourage families to teach the class nursery rhymes, chants, and fingerplays that they use at home. Weave this rich variety of family cultural traditions into the classroom repertoire.

- Ask families to lend you CDs or tapes of lullaby music used at home, and use this music for rest times and quiet times in the classroom.

- Discover families' skills and talents. Ask these experts to enrich the curriculum and environment of the classroom. Look for talents such as playing musical instruments or singing, cooking, painting, woodworking, beading, sewing, working with clay, storytelling, and collecting (shells, rocks, dolls, bones, or snow globes).

Activities to Support Family Belonging

When children see us connecting with their families, they become increasingly comfortable with the transitions back and forth from home and school. School becomes for them almost an extended family. Try one or more of the suggestions below to help you in this effort.

All About Us Book

When we help children learn about each other, we open the door to forging new friendships. Children will learn about each other in informal ways throughout the year. But teachers can also help everyone get to know each other early in the year by sharing some of the information they get during home visits or enrollment interviews. Put the results of a survey into a Big Book for the children and their families to share.

1. Print out children's answers to questions such as: Who lives in your house? What is your favorite food? What is your favorite thing to play? What are you good at?

2. Have children illustrate their page by drawing a picture.

3. Bind the pages together as a Big Book with poster board front and back covers.

4. Read the book to children at group time.

5. On the top of the back page, write "Family Response Page." Circulate the book to a different family each night and invite families to write comments.

Keep the book in the classroom library for children to look at and for adults to use as a reference and reminder.

While I Am at School

Some children are distressed at school because they have trouble understanding that people still exist even though you can't see them. For some children, the distress can be so great that they try to act out enough to get sent home from school! Help children learn to visually imagine what home or family looks like while they are away at school. Children who learn to visualize often show much less anxiety when they are away from home. Children can practice this skill in large or small groups.

1. Model the skill yourself first. Say something like, "I am thinking of my mom. I bet right now she is cooking supper at her house."

2. Ask the children if they can guess what their grown-up from home is doing right then. For children who have trouble with this skill, encourage families to share something of their daily plan with their child during the good-bye ritual.

3. Children can draw or paste pictures of their images to make a class Big Book called "While I Am at School."

Cooking Projects

Ask families about favorite foods they cook at home for their children, both every day and for celebrations. Invite family members to make simple recipes with children as a cooking project or to share at snacktime. Don't be disappointed if the Garcias tell you that pizza is the family favorite and the Johnsons tell you that their family always eats homemade tacos for birthday celebrations. The goal of this activity is not to introduce stereotypical ethnic food to the classroom. The goal is for children to bring a bit of the familiarity of daily home life into the classroom.

Promote Belonging to the Group

We focus so much on helping young children develop independence that we sometimes forget about interdependence. We want to encourage children to zip their own pants and clean up after themselves. But at the same time, success in school and in life requires that children also learn to develop community skills. They need to learn to work in pairs and in groups. They need to develop empathy and helping skills. They need to begin to understand how to figure out a group's culture and expectations.

Balancing self and community, or independence and teamwork, is a tricky proposition for children and adults alike. It is not nearly as simple as it might sound. As adults, we may be asked to work on a committee with people we would not choose as friends. We may be neighbors with families who are quite different from ourselves. We may have to work on a large project with a variety of people. It takes years of practice to figure out how to work well with others without losing the best of ourselves.

One area of the room might be used for a teacher-directed, large-group activity once or twice a day. You could conduct large-group morning meetings or large-group music or story times. Often furniture is moved for these times of the day so all the children can fit comfortably in the space.

Support Belonging to the Group through the Classroom Culture

"I'm a Jumping Cactus kid," Efrain proudly announced to his father after the first day of school.

"What's that?" asked his dad.

"That means that we all yell 'Go, go, go' at the end of circle," Efrain explained.

From the very first day, Efrain begins to identify himself as part of a community that has a distinct set of rituals and customs. Create rituals and daily routines to help everyone in the class feel a sense of connection and belonging.

We Wish You Well

Help children identify all of the members of the group. A simple way to practice this in the daily classroom routine is to acknowledge children who are absent each day. One teacher developed the following daily routine for her children:

1. During group time, look around to see who is absent that day.

2. As a group, sing "We Wish You Well" by Becky Bailey (sung to the tune of "Farmer in the Dell": "We wish you well, we wish you well, all through the day today, we wish you well").

3. For each absent adult or child, have one child "write" a "Wish You Well" note to that person and put it in the person's cubby.

Morning Meetings

Personal greetings and good-byes are important bridge builders with individual children, and so are group meeting times. Meetings are useful for the whole group to use rituals to symbolically reconnect as a community, to greet those who are present and to think of those who are absent, or to pass on information about the day.

Have a regular routine for morning meetings to help children feel safe and secure. Here is one possible routine:

1. Sing a greeting song that includes the name of each child who is present.

2. Conduct the "We Wish You Well" routine.

3. Preview special activities for the day.

4. Play a transition game.

Some teachers read a story in the morning; other teachers talk about an ongoing project or unit of study. Some teachers use the same schedule all year, and others begin with a shorter schedule early in the year and add more topics as the year goes on. However you choose to do your meeting, it is most important to follow the same routine day after day. This helps children anticipate what will happen in a meeting. The meeting itself is apt to be challenging to many of the children in the class. Knowing what will happen and about how long it will last helps everyone be less anxious. Think of yourself in an unfamiliar situation you know will challenge you and surrounded by other people. Knowing what is coming and how long you have to endure it would help, wouldn't it? It's the same for children.

Welcome New Community Members

The more you have worked to establish community norms and common language, the more important it is to work with the children to establish a routine for welcoming new members. Think about what new children and adults would need to know. Where would they keep their things? How would they learn the routines? How would they be introduced to others?

Who will show them where things are, how to enter play, and how to play games like Shoe Store? Here are some ideas:

• Make sure to visually include new children right away. Have a labeled cubby ready for them. Add their name cards and photos to appropriate areas of the room such as the sign-in sheets and job boards.

• Pair the child up with different partners throughout the day. Guide the child-mentors to explain traditional routines, rituals, and scripts to the new child. Make sure the new child has a partner for any transition times, since these moments can be most confusing to new members.

• At group time, have children review standard classroom procedures. For example, say, "Gordon is new to our class and he probably doesn't know about cleanup time. Who here can tell Gordon one of our cleanup time rules?"

Classroom Jobs

Community members all pitch in to support the community. There are many jobs to do and each member is needed to make sure everything gets done to support the group. Help children take group ownership of the classroom by having jobs for everyone. Think about using sophisticated titles for your class jobs. These terms help children make the connection between what they do in the classroom and job functions in the adult world. Here are twenty-three suggestions put together by teachers at a recent conference:

1. Paramedic (helps with first aid)
2. Door holder (holds door open while class walks through)
3. Banker (collects lunch money, book orders)
4. Toy detective (finds homes for stray toy pieces)
5. Housekeeper (sweeps or uses carpet sweeper)
6. Gardener (waters plants)
7. Audio-visual technician (turns CD player on and off)
8. Transition person (rings chime to get children's attention)
9. Zookeeper (feeds pets)
10. Usher (puts out sit-upons or cushions)
11. Host (puts out name cards for lunch)
12. Wish You Well Kid (writes "We Wish You Well" notes for absent children)
13. Back rubber (rubs backs at rest time)
14. Computer technician (turns computer on and off)
15. Coat zipper (zips coats)
16. Busboy or busgirl (cleans tables after meals and snacks)
17. Room inspector (checks all centers after cleanup)
18. Story reader ("reads" a favorite book to other children)
19. Mail sorter (puts out notes that go home in cubbies)
20. Greeter (greets guests)
21. Librarian (keeps library in order)
22. Lightbulb keeper (turns lights on and off)
23. Hygienist (hands out toothbrushes)

If you have more than twenty-three children in the group, make some of the jobs two-person jobs or use the buddy job system described earlier.

Transitional Objects

Young children are still learning the concept of object permanence—things exist even when they are out of sight. Before children fully understand this concept, they can become anxious when transitioning from home to school. These children are not sure home and family exist when they aren't visible.

Concrete transitional objects help them know that home and family exist, even though they are far away. Suggest to families that they allow their children to bring a significant transitional object with them to school, such as a family photo, a set of old keys, or a piece of a parent's clothing.

In the same way, some children fear that school will disappear when they go home. You might find these children with their pockets stuffed with small school items at the end of the day. To support these children, find a school token they can take home at the end of each day. You might want to send home their name card from the attendance pocket chart or from the job board. Children know that this item is important to the classroom and will feel comfort in bringing it back and forth from school to home. Some children may have trouble bringing objects back to school for various reasons. Rather than continuing to send items home, you might want to explore a different strategy. One teacher gave the child the essential job of turning on the lights in the classroom every morning. This important job helped the child look forward to coming to school in the morning in the same way that returning a school book might help another child.

Activities to Support Belonging to the Group

Oftentimes teachers are overwhelmed by the scope of all the content they need to address during the preschool years. It's easy to push activities to support social and emotional development aside in order to make time for language and literacy or mathematics. Many social and emotional activities, though, can do double duty. Not only do they help children develop the six life skills they need, but many of the activity suggestions that follow can also be woven into your lesson planning for language and literacy or mathematics. To help you see these connections, look for some suggestions at the end of each of the following activities.

Scrapbook

Shared history is one of the basic building blocks of community. Reflect often on common experiences to draw individuals together. Shared memories might encompass a whole range of emotionally charged moments. These moments might include celebrations, struggles, a joyful day at the park, or a sad day working through the death of a classroom pet. Scrapbooking these moments is one way to create a shared history. Help children record these moments and pull them out from time to time for reflection and revisiting. If you are planning to go through NAEYC accreditation, think of using this scrapbook as a basis for your classroom portfolio.

1. Get a photo album or three-ring binder.

2. Collect photos of special events, field trips, visitors, interesting projects, and so on.

3. Periodically, help children organize the pictures in the album and take dictation of their memories.

4. Keep the album in the class library or home-living area.

Here is a powerful example of how one classroom teacher used her memory album.

> Jazma had just finished reading the story *The Dead Bird* at morning meeting. "I remember when our worms died," said Jessica. "Yeah, they got too hot, didn't they?" added David. "They did get too hot, David. You're right," Jazma said. "At center time, if you like, you can come to the library corner with me and we'll look at the worm book we made." When the meeting was over and the children were settled in for the morning, Jazma took out the class-made worm book and shared it with the children who flowed in and out of the library center. They remembered the day they bought the worms and when they made a house for them. And they reflected on the Monday morning when they discovered the worms had died. They looked at the photos of the worm funeral and of the memorial worm sculptures they made that week. While many of the memories were sad, the children were drawn together by the many "remember whens."

This activity can be used to support such language and literacy curriculum goals as concepts of print and expressive and receptive language development.

Highlight of the Day

Help your children reflect on and record experiences they have had, places they have visited together, and funny things that have happened. Don't only focus on special activities such as going on a field trip or having a snow play day. Help children recognize that every day is full of gifts and memories.

1. Assign a rotating job of deciding on the "Highlight of the Day."

2. Help the child find materials to illustrate the highlight and take dictation to describe the activity. In the beginning, you might have to help children notice that something special occurred during the day. Guide them to remember simple pleasures such as the bug they found outside, the new program for the computer, or a child's new haircut.

3. Post the highlight on the door for parents to see at pickup.

4. Next morning, add the highlight to a binder collection that has all the highlights of the year. You can also post the highlights along the ceiling as a timeline.

This activity can be used to support such language and literacy curriculum goals as expressive language development and an understanding that print carries meaning. If you add step 4, you can use the activity for your social studies curriculum to illustrate the concept of the passage of time, and for your mathematics curriculum to demonstrate the concept of ordering.

Photo Wall

Another strategy to build community and shared memories is to use your camera to record class history. Photos can be posted in centers or on a single designated wall.

1. Collect photos of memorable events.

2. Help children mount photos on colored paper.

3. Take dictation from the children about their memories.

4. Post on a memory board or throughout the room.

This activity can be used to support such language and literacy curriculum goals as expressive language.

Name the Class

Cohesive communities must establish common language, behaviors, and practices. Remember that children will have one set of norms and expectations at home and another set at school. Help children identify themselves as community members by giving the class a name and by using this name often as you refer to routines and expectations. For example, say, "Sinker Dragons, come on inside and get ready for lunch," or "It's time for the Superstars to clean up the room to get ready for story." By using the group name, you will be cuing the children that they are expected to follow the group norm now rather than their individual desires.

1. Have the children suggest three or four names for the class.

2. Hold a group discussion on the names.

3. Help the children agree on a name. Sometimes it is helpful to suggest a combination of the two most popular names. One class came to agreement on Ballerina Dinosaurs.

4. Sometimes it may take three or four meetings before you can agree, but the time is worth it.

This activity can be used to support social studies goals such as coming to consensus.

Class Pledge

Children need hundreds of repetitions and reminders to establish new habits and behaviors. One way to remind children of group values is to design a class pledge that gets recited every morning during the first group meeting of the day. Some classrooms have used their class name and their classroom guiding principles to make a simple pledge or chant.

One teacher designed the following chant as her class pledge:

> Superstars take care of themselves.
> Superstars take care of others.
> Superstars take care of the world.

This activity can be used to support social studies goals, such as independence and empathy.

Class-Made Big Books

Young children have trouble classifying objects two ways at once. For example, when they sort, they can often sort by size or by color but not by size and color at the same time. Likewise, young children often have trouble seeing themselves simultaneously as an individual and as a member of the classroom community. Sometimes a child may be so fearful of losing his sense of self that he resists blending in with others. This child might express anxiety by singing the loudest or throwing the tambourine at music time. Assign each child one page to make for a class Big Book. Books like these act as visual symbols that one can be an individual and still be a part of a group effort.

1. Gather large sheets of paper, one for each child in the group.
2. Have each child illustrate a page. Take dictation to narrate the contribution.
3. Bind the pages together with a front and back cover.
4. Print the name of the class somewhere on the front cover.
5. Use some of these ideas to make Big Books: What We Do at School, My Family, When I Grow Up, I Can Help.

This activity can be used to support such language and literacy curriculum goals as concepts of print.

Class Puzzle

A class puzzle can help children visualize the community as a collection of individuals. For young children, the act of putting together a puzzle with a picture of the class gives them a symbolic way to understand how the community is made up of individuals.

1. Take a photo of the class, including adults and children.
2. Enlarge the photo to at least 8½ by 11, and mount on poster board.
3. Cover with contact paper on both sides.
4. Cut into puzzle pieces using a template or freehand.
5. Store the pieces in a plastic sandwich bag or a small container, and add the puzzle to your collection.
6. Update your puzzle anytime new children join the group.

This activity can be used to support such physical development skills as eye-hand coordination.

Class Flag

A class flag, like a class name, is a concrete symbol of unity. The more visual and tangible cues and symbols we provide for children, the easier it is for children to grasp such intangible concepts as community. Kids need to see it and touch it in order to understand it . . . whatever "it" may be.

1. Use a piece of plain fabric or large poster board.
2. Print the name of the class somewhere on the flag.
3. Have each child decorate the flag. You can use fabric paint to help each child put her handprint on the flag. Children can attach small photos of themselves or their family on the flag.
4. Adults are also part of the classroom community and should be represented the same way as the children.
5. Make sure the flag is updated when new children join the group.

This activity can be used to support such social studies curriculum goals as understanding communities.

Who's Missing?

Another visual tool to help children focus on the entire community is the large-group game Who's Missing?

1. Have all the children close their eyes.

2. Quietly select one child and have him move to an area of the room where the others can't see him.

3. When the rest of the children open their eyes, have them try to figure out who is missing by looking to see who is still in the group.

This activity can be used to support such math curriculum goals as recognizing sets.

Who Am I?

A variation on Who's Missing is Who Am I? This can be played in either a small or large group.

1. Have one child close her eyes.

2. Select another child to sit in a chair in the middle of the group. Put a sheet or light blanket over the child in the middle.

3. When the child opens her eyes, have her guess who is hidden under the sheet.

4. Have the child under the sheet say "hello" or some other words if the child has trouble guessing who is under the sheet.

5. When the child has guessed, the one who was under the sheet will be the next one to guess.

This activity can be used to support critical-thinking and observation skills, such as making predictions.

Yearbooks

Help children reflect on the wonderful experiences and people they have met during the year. Just as bringing a toy for naptime was comforting to children early in the school year, taking home photos of their preschool year at the end of the year is comforting as they step out into new adventures.

1. Staple together some blank pages to make individual small books.

2. Gather photos that were taken of the class during the year. Add extra pictures if needed to make sure everyone is pictured multiple times.

3. Allow children to select pictures to glue in their books.

4. Some children might want to have friends "sign" their yearbooks.

This activity can be used to support language and curriculum goals, such as learning concepts of print and developing expressive and receptive language skills.

Play Inclusive Versions of Traditional Games

Many traditional games for young children involve competition and elimination rather than cooperation and inclusion. When choosing games with the goal of encouraging connection, try to select cooperative and inclusive games. *Everybody Wins* by Jeffrey Sobel is a good resource for these games. Modify other games to make them cooperative and inclusive as well.

Farmer in the Dell: Tweak the game so all of the children are chosen and the cheese has lots of friends for the ending rather than standing alone. Modify the song characters of the male farmer, his wife, their children, and their pets to reflect the family structures of the children in your classroom to reinforce belonging and acceptance. Think of expanding your farm family to include grandparents and cousins. Or begin with a girl farmer and have her pick a husband. Maybe your farmer can pick some helpers and they can all pick a variety of children and pets. On the last verse, after the rat takes the cheese, sing, "The cheese stands with friends, the cheese stands with friends. Hi-ho, the derry-o, the cheese stands with friends."

Musical Chairs: Eliminate chairs, not kids. At first, children will scoot over to share chairs. As more chairs are eliminated, children will begin to sit on each other's laps. Remind the children during the game that "we only win when everyone wins." Instead of the typical sounds of "I was here first" and "Ha-ha, you're out," you will hear "Come here and share with me" and "You can sit on my lap." Remember to have a celebratory cheer at the end of the game.

Support the Development of Friendships

It is as much the teacher's responsibility to facilitate children's friendships and belonging to the group as it is to teach them colors or numbers. Let's look first at the stages children go through as they develop friendships with other children.

1. **Solo play**—Although infants and toddlers are very tuned in and show curiosity about one another, they lack the skills they need to sustain meaningful peer play for more than a moment or two. Most of their play and exploration is done alone, even when they are in the middle of a room full of other children.

2. **Adult-child play**—As infants mature and develop relationships with their significant adults, they begin to also develop play skills with those adults. They may attempt to "talk" to their adults, will giggle at patty-cake, and will repeatedly toss a toy down from a stroller to have their grown-up fetch it for them.

3. **Parallel play**—When young children are first introduced to other children, they are very curious. They may observe the other child for long periods of time and will often try to touch and feel the other's face or clothing. They seem to regard each other more as playthings to explore than as potential friends. Very young children still lack the language and skills needed for meaningful interactive play with peers, so while they will be happy to play side by side, they may have very little actual interaction.

4. **Dyad play**—Next, children will begin to play interactively with others and will identify somebody as their friend. For example, two children might race their bikes or build a zoo together from blocks.

5. **Small-group play**—When three to five children are role-playing in the home-living area or when they are working together at the art table sharing materials, they are demonstrating that they can do small-group work. To be successful at small-group play, children must learn how to be included in play, how to take turns and share, and how to play common themes such as babies or building roads in the sand.

6. **Large-group play**—Although most preschool children are unable to function in large groups without significant adult support and guidance, they can take the first step of identifying themselves as an important member of the classroom community.

Most preschool classrooms have children who span the developmental stages of friendships regardless of their chronological ages. Some are still working alone. Some are working next to, although not with, other children. Some have developed a special relationship with a friend, while others can be found in the dramatic play or block areas working cooperatively in small groups. You may even see a child who shows some skills with large groups. Sometimes we notice a child with this skill playing teacher with a group of his pretend students, looking and sounding a bit too much like ourselves!

Supportive Interactions to Promote Friendships

Children first learn play skills and a vocabulary for friendship by the way adults speak to and play with them. Children learn what they live. "Do what I say, not what I do" does not work with young children.

Help children learn to play by joining in the play yourself. Model and coach how to speak to and play with others. What you say is what you'll hear. What you do is what you'll see. When you play alongside children who are not yet interacting with other children, emphasize basic friendship concepts. Help them develop an understanding of what friendly behavior looks and sounds like. Focus their attention on the friendly overtures of others. Teach them the value of friendship and the basic friendship skills of taking turns, sharing, and using friendly language.

Comment on Friendly Behavior

Many teachers tell children, "We are all friends in our class." This is a myth, and children know it. Even young children have preferred playmates and friends. However, you can establish a more honest (and achievable) classroom norm by saying, "We all have friendly behavior in our classroom." When you enforce friendly behavior, rather than artificial friendships, children develop skills that will serve them for life. So many times we are required to interact with people we would not choose as friends—maybe on a church committee or as a member of the school council or at work. Whether we are friends or not, we are still expected to maintain civil and friendly behavior toward each other.

Telling children to "be nice" or "be friends" is akin to you being told that tomorrow you should "speak Turkish." Instead of those vague directions, help children develop an understanding of friendly behavior with your daily language, commenting when you see it. For example, you might say:

"I see two kids working together."

"You guys look like you are having fun playing superheroes together."

"Did the two of you set that table together?"

Notice and Recognize Friendly Overtures

Some children are not aware that others are making friendly overtures. They need some help to recognize the friendly behavior of others. Support these children by giving them descriptive feedback when you see someone acting in a friendly manner toward them. Use a pattern such as "I saw (child's name and action). He was being friendly to you." For example:

"I saw Raymond share his cookie with you. He was being friendly to you."

"I saw CJ give you a turn with the easel. She was being friendly to you."

We All Have Something in Common

Young children find the familiar comforting. They often don't want to try an unfamiliar food or a new babysitter, and they love to hear the same favorite book over and over. They might shy away from playing with kids who appear different from themselves.

Help children notice how they share similarities with other children, particularly with children of a different gender or with different physical characteristics. Focus your observations of commonalities on internal rather than surface qualities.

"You have a dog at home just like Iris has."

"I see two kids who both like to do linker cubes."

"Did you know that Leticia says that *The Hungry Caterpillar* is her favorite book too?"

We Are Each Unique

Children can shock adults by the very frank observations they make about unusual features of others, such as, "Look how fat that man is." Instinctively, we want to shush children and tell them, "That's not nice to say." However, young children aren't commenting on others to be rude. They are genuinely interested. Sometimes, these observations can also cause them to be a bit anxious, and their tone of voice might sound aggressive or defensive. Regardless, try to respond in a matter-of-fact way that validates the child's observation of the diversity of humanity.

To avoid being caught off-guard, take some time to practice supportive responses to children's observations of differences. Try a simple response that first validates the child's observation of a difference, followed by generalization of commonality.

When a child says . . .	Acknowledge the difference	Generalize the sameness
"Dharma's lunch looks yucky."	"Dharma's lunch is different than yours."	"But everybody's lunch is yummy food."
"Karen's skin is all pasty white."	"Karen has light skin, and you have dark skin."	"All people have skin on the outside of their bodies."
"Passion don't have no mama."	"Passion lives with her grandma, and you live with your mama."	"All kids live with grown-ups who take care of them."

We're Different and We're Friends

Children have some things in common with others and some things that are unique, and they can be friends regardless. Focus children's attention on how two children can have differences and still be very good friends.

Be careful to use benign surface differences when you do this activity. The safest one to use is a difference in preferences. Look for differences in what foods they like, what activities they like to do, or what colors they are choosing for their paint project.

"You like to use the tire swing best, and Becka likes to use the rope swing best. You like different things, and you can still be friends."

"You ate two servings of carrots, and Marcia doesn't even like to eat one carrot! You like different things, and you can still be friends."

Use Peers as Resources

Help children learn that friendship is something worth working for. As you interact and speak with children throughout the day, help them view their peers as valuable resources for help and for pleasure.

When you say . . .	The child learns . . .
"____ knows how to____. Go ask him/her." For example, "Brandon knows how to open the jar. Go ask him for help."	Peers are valuable resources.
"That was a heavy table. It was good to have two kids work together to move it."	Sometimes it takes more than one person to reach a goal.
"I saw you guys playing catch outside. It's good to have another kid to play with."	Interacting with others can be fun.

Support Friendships through the Classroom Culture

Because children develop at their own pace, classrooms are likely to have children at all stages of play development, from solo through large-group skill levels. Supportive classrooms will have spaces and places that support each level of play and include opportunities for children to grow to the next. The classroom culture will also have established rituals and routines, a common social language, and an atmosphere of respect for developmental differences.

Support Solo and Parallel Play

Help children feel comfortable during the program day by providing time, space, and activities for a child who chooses to work alone or with one special friend. These opportunities allow children to practice friendship skills at their own pace. Consider setting up a few cozy areas that are set off to the side of more busy and active areas. Plan a few simple and predictable activities specifically for partners. These simple partner activities can be risk-free opportunities to practice working with others. Remember that even when children work alone or with one special partner, they will observe and learn from nearby children at work and at play in small groups.

One-Person Play Areas: All the people and action in a preschool room can easily overwhelm children who are still playing alone or next to others. Make sure to include options for them throughout the classroom in which they can participate and still be alone. For example, if you offer a collage art activity at a table set with four spaces, you might want to invite a child to use the same materials at a smaller table off to the side a bit.

In the block area, you might want to put a hula hoop on the floor to define a child's space. Masking tape can be used in the same way to define space. Make sure all of the children in the room understand that when a child chooses to use one of these one-person areas that her space and privacy should be respected.

You might say something like, "Sometimes children like to play all by themselves and that's okay. When a child plays in our one-person play spots, remember that we don't talk to them and we don't touch their stuff. That's called private time." These one-person play areas should be an open option for any child in the room who feels a need or desire for some solitary time.

Side-by-Side Play Areas: When children are at the stage of parallel play, they don't actually interact with each other during the activity. It's important then to make sure each child has his own set of supplies to work with. For example, give each child her own blob of playdough and her own set of playdough tools. When children move on to dyad play, they will be able to begin to negotiate sharing materials. Trying to get children to share materials when they are still at parallel play might result in grabbing and hurting.

Set up some areas where children can work side by side with the same materials. For example, you can put two tubs in the water table or set two easels side by side in the art area. Just as with one-person activity spots, you might want to set up a smaller table for two children for special activities such as collages or cooking.

Support Dyad Play

Some of the children in your group will be ready for dyad play, or playing with one other child. Dyad play is very different from being able to play peacefully in a group of three to five children. In dyad play, there is only one relationship to manage and a minimum of negotiation over space and materials. Giving children plenty of opportunity for dyad play will prepare them for the more hectic and involved play with three to five children, which will come later. Help children develop an understanding that some activities need two people. For children who are just beginning dyad work, consider having one of the adults in the room be the child's partner. However, as children become more skilled at working with others, your role will become the facilitator instead of participant.

Two-Person Play Areas: Encourage children to practice dyad play by making sure there are some materials and centers that are more fun to do with two people than alone.

- Include big blocks, rocking boats, wagons, bikes and trailers, and computer buddies.
- Put small tables that fit only two children in various centers around the room, such as in table toys or the snack area.

Partner Work: While some children seem to effortlessly morph from solo players to dyad players, other children benefit from a more deliberate and structured approach. Teachers can set up buddy activities with specific guidelines to help some children make the transition. The best way to teach buddies how to work together is to model the kind of behavior you want to see. You can do this by first being the child's partner and later inviting another child to take your place in the dyad relationship. Make sure you stay with the two children long enough to help them work smoothly with each other. Here are some partner activities teachers have found useful in their classrooms.

- Create buddy back rubbers. Teach children how to rub or pat the backs of their peers at rest time. Make sure to model appropriate social skills, such as where it is appropriate to touch another person; to ask first if she would like her back rubbed; to stop when the child requests; and to ask how much pressure is appropriate to use. Some teachers assign the job of back rubber to children who don't nap or need less rest time than the others. You can also assign back rubbing as a rotating job so everyone has a turn.
- Pair children to push each other on the swings or pull each other in wagons.
- Assign two children to do a heavy job, such as moving a table or carrying a large container of balls or blocks.

Peer Mentors: Most young children appreciate the value of adults. After all, adults are the ones who feed them, bathe them, take them out to eat, and read them books. Dyad play requires that children begin to see their own peers as valuable resources as well. Encourage children in your group to share their talents and strengths with each other.

- Each one teach one. Buddy up children to help each other learn new skills such as pumping on the swing or finding their name card.
- Seek out child mentors on an ongoing basis. When a child says, "I don't know what to do with my painting," try saying, "Go ask around and find a kid who can help you." If this seems overwhelming to the child, try directing her to a specific child who has the information she needs and the friendship skills to share it. Say something like, "You know, I bet Peng knows what to do with paintings. Ask her."
- When a child is struggling at a particular time of the day, such as snack or cleanup, help him find a child mentor to partner with. Kids can often learn from peers more easily than they can learn from adults.

Support Small-Group Play

Many preschool children are at the stage of small-group play, and most early childhood classrooms are already set up to encourage groups of three to five children to work together. Some young children struggle to enter small-group play because they are unfamiliar with what and how the children are playing. These children need adult support and intervention to learn how to play games such as House or Building an Airport.

Small-Group Play Areas: Here are some ideas for setting up space in your classroom so small groups can practice working and playing together.

- Many classrooms use the dramatic play and block areas for small-group activities. Some teachers choose to limit the number of children who can use the area at any one time. You can put up a graphic showing how many children can use the area, a pocket chart with limited slots for children to put their name cards, hooks on which children can hang their symbol, or Velcro tabs on which children can hang their photos.

- Art tables can be set up to accommodate four children who must share common supplies. Use chairs to define how many children can participate at an activity table. Teach the group to use the number of chairs to figure out if there is space for them at the table. Say something like, "Uh-oh, Choua. All the chairs are filled up at playdough. Let's find something to do until a chair is empty," or "I don't know, Patrick. Let's see if there is an empty chair at the cutting table. Yep, there are two chairs empty. That means there is room for you to work there now."

- Mealtime is another opportunity for four children to interact as a small group. Seat adults at tables with children who need help working together as a small group.

- Some teachers also pull out small groups of children for teacher-directed work during center time.

"You Can't Say You Can't Play" Areas: Design one or two spaces in the room as "You Can't Say You Can't Play" (Paley 1992) areas where children can practice inclusion skills. These areas have no limit on the number of children who can play there and are not private play spaces. They are open to the entire classroom community in the same way a public park or shopping mall might be. The job of the children already in the center is to find a way to integrate new children into the group activity. You might find the chant "Find a way for (child's name) to play" helpful when reminding children of the guideline.

It's important that the "You Can't Say You Can't Play" areas be interesting and attractive to most of the children in the group, so there is an incentive for children to stay in that area and include others instead of just leaving the area for another.

For example, if Oscar complains to you that the children in home living won't let him play, you can remind the group of the cultural norm for that activity:

1. Go with Oscar back to home living, and have him ask again to be included in the play.

2. If the children say something like "We don't want Oscar here," you can remind them of the norm by saying, "Remember, this is a 'You Can't

Say You Can't Play' area. That means you need to find a way for Oscar to play."

3. If children include Oscar in the play, say something such as, "You figured out a way for Oscar to play. That was friendly."

4. If the children refuse to allow Oscar into the play, remind them that their choice is either to let him play or they can leave the area and find another place to play. "This is a 'You Can't Say You Can't Play' area. Your choice is to find a way for Oscar to play or find another area to work in. Which will you choose?"

What if you find when given a choice between including a specific child or leaving the area, the children choose to leave the area? Wouldn't that be humiliating to the child who tried to join the activity?

As with all strategies in this book and recommendations from others, sometimes they work the way you want them to and sometimes they don't. Sometimes you can tweak a strategy or "go in the back door" to get around resistance. For example, if you find a particular child is always abandoned in the "You Can't Say You Can't Play" area, try these ideas:

1. If the children leave, say, "Okay. Oscar and I will finish building the fire station together," and join in the play. Most likely, the appeal of playing with a teacher will override the appeal of leaving the area. If children change their minds and choose to stay, have them ask Oscar how they can play. Prompting Oscar to make an inclusive response will increase his chances of being included next time.

2. Another strategy for a child who is usually excluded would be to invite that child to be your first partner for a special project. For example, if you are adding potting soil and seeds to the sensory table, invite Becker to be the first child at the activity. Let other children know that if they would like to join Becker, they can ask him how they can play. If needed, coach Becker to make an inclusive response.

3. A variation on this strategy is to become involved in a desirable activity with an excluded child, such as shooting baskets during outdoor time. When other children want to join the play, have them ask the first child how they can play. Remain with the group long enough after the other children join in to make sure the play is working smoothly.

4. When children begin to include the previously excluded child, make sure to give them positive reflective feedback such as, "Masha, I saw you found a way for Hope to play wagons with you and Tessa. That was very friendly."

Family-Style Dining: Family-style dining helps build strong bonds in the classroom community and provides opportunities for adults to model how to eat in a group. In family-style dining, food is placed on the table in community bowls and is passed around the table. Each child and adult serves himself or herself a portion.

You can model appropriate mealtime manners by asking for a dish to be passed and by being attentive to the needs of others. When somebody drops or spills something, model how you would handle this with a table of adult friends.

Comments like "Oops! Let me help you," or "Oh dear, would you like a new plate?" help children learn the social scripting they will need for success in school and in life.

Adults can also lead mealtime conversations. These conversations should be similar to those you would have with your own friends. Talk about upcoming plans, common memories, likes and dislikes, movies, books, and music.

Support Large-Group Participation

Trying to include children who are at the parallel play and dyad play stages in large-group activities is often frustrating for the teacher, the child, and the other children in the group. Without special accommodations or support, these children will quickly become fussy, noisy, distracted, and disruptive. Repeated reminders and threats to attend to the large-group activity only serve to frustrate and discourage everyone. At the same time, some children in the group are ready for large-group activities. How, then, can large-group activities be conducted while meeting the developmental needs of all children in the group?

Model and Coach: If you are in a two-teacher classroom, while one teacher is conducting large group, the other teacher can sit near one or more children who are still learning large-group skills. That teacher can model group skills and help coach the children to keep them on track. For example, "Hunter, I can't hear the story when you talk to your friends. Please be quiet for a few more minutes," or "Mason, look at the bear in the story. What do you think will happen next?"

Identify Peer Mentors: Help a child who is struggling with large-group skills identify someone who knows how to do the activity. Encourage the struggling child to match the other child when the struggling child is off-task. For example, Shastina has identified Viranda as a child who knows how to do story time. Before group time starts, say, "Shastina, remember to check what Viranda is doing if you are not sure what to do when we read our book." You might even seat Shastina next to her model and ask Viranda to help Shastina.

Use Front-Row Seating: Seat children who are not ready for large group directly in front of the teacher with their backs to most of the other children. Many children in this situation will have the illusion they are in a smaller group and will have an easier time.

Assign Special Tasks: Give a special job to a child who is still learning large-group skills. He can turn the pages in a book, pass out materials, or hold the props.

Dismiss Children Early: Start large-group time with all the children together. After the first short activity, tell children who are still learning large-group skills that they are free to work in quiet centers. Over time, those children will be able to stay longer and longer.

Divide the Group: Break large-group time into two smaller groups. In classes with two teachers, each one can lead one of the groups. In classes with one teacher, one group can be at large group while the other is at a center-time activity, and then the groups can switch. Some teachers like to divide groups randomly. Others like to have one group for children proficient at group skills and the other group for children who are still mastering group skills.

Teach Group Skills Explicitly: During center time, pull over a small group of children who are learning group skills. Help them figure out how to stay in their own body space, how to ignore distractions, and so on. You can find many ideas on activities in the chapter about self-regulation (see page 99).

Make Large Group Optional: Make large-group time an optional activity instead of a mandatory activity. Allow children to come and go as they wish.

Activities to Support Friendships

Children's development of connection comes from your personal interactions with the children and the group culture you have established for the classroom. From time to time, however, you might want to supplement the curriculum with some special activities to promote friendship skills.

Same and Different Book

Guide children to recognize and celebrate diversity with a "Same and Different" book.

1. Help children find partners.
2. Work together with the pair to help them find a way they are the same and a way they are different. Avoid using clothing as same/different characteristics.

3. Take dictation from the children to complete sentences such as "We are the same because we both_____. We are different because (name of one child) (how child is different) and (name of other child) (how child is different)." For example, "We are the same because we both like to play computer games. We are different because Jeremiah has a dog at his house and Monte has a goat at his house."

4. Take a photo of the two children together that they can mount on the page with the dictation, or have the children work together to illustrate their page.

5. Bind pages together into a book with a front and back cover. Put the title on the front and label the back as a family-response page.

6. Read the book to the class and have children take the book home to share with families. Encourage families to comment on the back cover.

Picture Graphing

As children learn about each other, they tend to form best friends and small friendship cliques. This is a normal stage of development for young children. At the same time, we want to make sure children don't form exclusive cliques. Some clues this might be happening are comments such as, "She can't play with us because she wears pants like a boy," or "He can't play with us because he can't run fast."

Help children learn that while they have some things in common with one group of children, they have something else in common with a different group of children. Picture graphing is a visual way to represent this to children. One way to use picture graphing is to change the theme of the graph on a weekly basis. Help children notice they are with a different group of children each time the topic changes.

1. Mount photos of children on individual pieces of poster board and cover them with clear contact paper. Photos that are two-by-two inches seem to work well for this. Attach Velcro fastener tabs to the back of each photo.

2. To make a reusable graph, divide a plain piece of poster board with a bold horizontal line. Either laminate the board or cover it with clear contact paper. Attach Velcro fastener bits or strips on both halves of the paper. Make sure there is enough Velcro fastener on each half to hold all of the children's photos.

3. Decide on a theme and label each half of the graph with a "choice." Use both words and pictures to label choices. Some ideas include the following:

   • Which food I like better: hamburger (top half), pizza (bottom half)

   • Which I am: boy (top half), girl (bottom half)

   • Which I like to do more: water table (top half), sand table (bottom half)

4. Have each child affix her picture to indicate her choice.

5. Point out to children that children in each section are similar to each other and different from the children on the other half of the graph. Each time the theme of the graph is changed, children will be grouped with different kids. Help them notice that the groups change, depending on the topic.

Buddy Jobs

Smooth dyad play requires a delicate dance in which the partners shift from being the leader to being the follower. Help children learn this skill with the structure of buddy jobs. Instead of assigning classroom jobs to individual children, assign them to buddy pairs. Children can be paired up to do classroom jobs in a way that each child has a chance to be an "expert" as well as a "trainee." Learning how to be both a leader and a follower are useful skills for school and for work, families, and adult life as well.

1. You will need to create one job for each buddy pair, so divide the total number of children in the room by two.

2. On a big piece of poster board, print the classroom jobs down the left side of the page. Use photos or clip art to illustrate each job. Draw horizontal lines between each job to help the children read the chart. Put two tabs of the loop side of Velcro next to each job, leaving enough room to put one child's photo on each spot. You can use a pocket chart instead of Velcro if you have one the right size.

3. Make two-by-two prints of each child's photo and label them with his name. Cover each one with contact paper to make it durable. Put a tab of Velcro (hook side) on the back of each photo.

4. Pair up children so two children are assigned to each job. Put the children's photos next to the job on the job chart.

5. For the first week only, you will need to teach one child in each pair how to do that job. You might begin the year by adding only one or two jobs every day so you have time to train the children.

6. The child who knows how to do the job is now the "expert." Their partner is the "trainee." As children do their job for the week, the expert coaches and trains her partner.

7. At the end of the week, move all the experts to new jobs. They become the trainees, and the children who were trainees now become the experts.

8. Each week, continue by moving the current expert to a new job.

Here's a sample of what this kind of job chart might look like:

Job	Expert	Trainee
Water plants	Chester	Tyrone
Feed hamster	Melinda	Joseph
Push in chairs	Ephraim	Daphne
Straighten book corner	Tyler	Kelsey

Buddy Art

Some children need a bit of extra support to move from parallel to dyad play. Think of including partner activities with clearly defined roles that need very little negotiation. The art area is one good place to start.

1. Have each child draw a picture with a black marker. Have children exchange drawings and color in their buddy's picture with colored markers or watercolors.

2. Have children do body tracings for each other.

3. Put two children at one easel with one piece of paper and two brushes. Guide one child to paint one side of the page and the other child to paint the other side of the page. For some children, you may need to actually draw a vertical line down the middle of the page to reduce the amount of negotiation they need to do.

Author and Illustrator

Language and literacy is another area that lends itself to clearly defined roles in dyad play. The beauty of the art activities above and the literacy activities that follow is they leave children with concrete, visual products created by both children. Help children recognize the teamwork needed to create their work by saying something such as, "Look at the picture you painted together!" or "You guys are working hard together to do your story."

1. Have one child dictate a story and have the buddy illustrate it.

2. Have one child draw a picture and the other child tell a story based on the picture.

Friend Books

Children who are learning dyad play find it helpful to see photos of themselves playing with others. Most children are visual learners, and they like to look at books and pictures as they are learning new skills or integrating new information.

1. Take pictures of children playing with each other.

2. Allow children to mount the pictures in blank books.

3. Take their dictation of who they were playing with and what they were doing.

4. Put the finished books in the class library. Read the books at group time or when children request them, and lend the books to families to read at home.

Buddy Play Pictures

~~Children form a vision of themselves from the messages that they get from the outside world.~~ Post photos of children playing with others in various areas of the room so they can see evidence of themselves having a friend and being a friend.

1. Take pictures of children playing together during the day.

2. Enlarge and mount the pictures on poster board or construction paper.

3. Have the children give dictation about what they were doing in the picture.

4. Hang the pictures on the wall at children's eye level in a "We Are Friends" display area or in centers.

Tea Party

Tea party is a predictable, sequenced activity to teach pairs of children how to take turns and share. Both boys and girls alike are drawn to the ceremonial feeling of taking tea. Use a small, inexpensive, breakable (not plastic; china or glass) tea set, a tablecloth, real food, and tongs to add to the special feeling of the activity and help children focus on the play sequences. Many teachers keep a waiting list for children who want to play. As soon as one child finishes, the next child on the list is called. Because children are so interested in this play, a child will usually participate even if it is without a "best friend." This encourages children to interact with new friends and helps children who have previously been rejected to be able to play successfully with others. Some teachers model the activity by being the "tea partner" for the first few days the activity is put out. After children have learned how to "do tea," they begin to work as child-child partners.

1. Gather a child-sized ceramic tea set, a basket with very small snack items (such as broken graham crackers), a pair of tongs, a container of watered-down juice, a container of disinfectant bleach solution, an absorptive tablecloth, and a small table with two chairs. Keep the snack food small and low-key and the "tea" (a juice/water combination) very

dilute. This activity is not a snack. It is a chance for children to learn to control their behavior and interact with a partner. The tablecloth not only adds ambiance but also absorbs spills to keep the area neater.

2.   Invite two children to sit together at "tea."

3.   Instruct children on how the game is played using the following guidelines:

- Children take turns using the tongs to serve themselves one piece of snack food, which they place on their cake plate, and pouring themselves "tea" from the ceramic pitcher into their teacup.

- Children can serve themselves more food or drink when they have finished the portion on their plates.

- Children must use the tongs and may serve themselves only one piece at a time.

- Children can be quiet or talk to each other, but may not carry on conversations with others outside the game.

- When one of the children is done playing, he should give his dishes to the teacher for her to dip into the disinfectant solution. The teacher will reset the table for the next child.

- Rinse the cloth in the disinfectant solution at the end of the session, and hang it to dry for the next session.

Discussion/Reflection Questions

1.   Compare time spent dealing with children's behaviors with time invested in teaching children how to have a friend and be a friend. Keep track during a typical week at your program. How much time did you spend on each? As you invest more time in teaching children friendship skills, how does that affect the time you spend managing their behavior?

_____

_____

_____

2.   Do you think lacking friendship skills might affect children's academic learning? If so, how? If not, why not?

_____

_____

_____

3. How might you design an outdoor play area to accommodate children at each of the play stages—solo, parallel, dyad, small group, and large group?

_____

_____

_____

Exercises

1. How are you currently acknowledging children's families in your program? Do your environment and materials reflect the diversity of family structures and traditions? Look back at the suggestions in this chapter to support children's sense of family belonging. Select two strategies to weave into your program.

_____

_____

_____

2. Observe a challenging child in your group. Pay attention to how well she functions alone, next to another child, interacting with another child, in small-group situations, and in whole-class activities. What is the highest level at which the child does well without adult support? Do you have new ideas about the underlying causes for the challenging behavior?

_____

_____

_____

3. Conduct a physical survey of your classroom and review your daily schedule. Does your program and your room support children at each of the stages of play development? How might you modify your environment and your daily program to better serve individual developmental levels?

_____

_____

_____

Reflection/Journal Assignment

Think about the first week or so that you worked in your current job. Reflect for a few minutes on how comfortable or uncomfortable you were in this new job, and what made it so. Was there an orientation before you began? Were you partnered with a buddy to help you get your bearings? How did you find out details such as the location of the adult restroom, how and when and if you needed to create lesson plans, and who was responsible to clean the room at the end of the day? How important do you think these first two weeks are for integrating new members into an existing community?

_____

_____

_____

_____

_____

_____

_____

_____

_____

_____

_____

_____

_____

_____

_____

_____

_____

Belonging Is Key

Children want to belong and understand how bad it feels not to belong. How many times have you heard one child say to another, "You're my friend, right?" And how many times when they are angry have you heard them say things like "You're not my friend" or "You can't come to my birthday"? Belonging, whether to a family, a church, a club, or a classroom, helps children feel secure and guides them to learn social rules and expectations for behavior.

Think About It

Reflect back on your own connections with others at work or in your community. Perhaps you've served in the military or are active in a religious community or regularly gather with extended family. What do these connections mean to you? How have these connections guided you in your life? Help the children in your life begin to understand their own connections to others, beginning with their own family.

Some Ideas

- Help children build their identity as a member of your family. Put together a photo album that includes pictures of them as they are growing up as well as pictures of your immediate and extended family at all different ages. Share stories with your children about your own positive childhood memories.

- Be clear with children about your family's values. When explaining rules and limits, think of saying, "In our family, we (say please, don't eat meat, braid our hair)." When your child does something against family rules, say something like "Robinson children don't take things that don't belong to them."

- Start family rituals such as eating spaghetti every Friday night or planting seeds on the first day of spring or reading books at the Laundromat.

- Help your child make friends by inviting another child along to join you at the park or join your family for supper.

Chapter 3 Resources

Delpit, Lisa. 1995. *Other People's Children: Cultural Conflict in the Classroom.* New York: New Press.

Doherty, William J. 1997. *Intentional Family: How to Build Family Ties in Our Modern World.* Reading, MA: Addison-Wesley.

Espinosa, Linda M. 2010. *Getting It RIGHT for Young Children from Diverse Backgrounds: Applying Research to Improve Practice.* Boston: Pearson.

Fitzgerald, H. E. 2006. "Cross Cultural Research during Infancy: Methodological Considerations." *Infant Mental Health Journal* 27 (6): 612–17.

Gestwicki, Carol. 2011. *Developmentally Appropriate Practice: Curriculum and Development in Early Education.* Belmont, CA: Wadsworth Cengage Learning.

Gonzalez-Mena, Janet. 2008. *Diversity in Early Care and Education: Honoring Differences.* 5th ed. Boston: McGraw-Hill.

Heidemann, Sandra, and Deborah Hewitt. 2010. *Play: The Pathway from Theory to Practice.* St. Paul, MN: Redleaf Press.

Paley, Vivian Gussin. 1992. *You Can't Say You Can't Play.* Cambridge, MA: Harvard University Press.

Sobel, Jeffrey. 1984. *Everybody Wins: 393 Noncompetitive Games for Young Children.* New York: Walker.

Trumbull, Elise, Carrie Rothstein-Fisch, Patricia M. Greenfield, and Blanca Quiroz. 2001. *Bridging Cultures between Home and School: A Guide for Teachers.* Mahwah, NJ: Lawrence Erlbaum Associates.

York, Stacey. 2003. *Roots and Wings: Affirming Culture in Early Childhood Programs.* Rev. ed. St. Paul, MN: Redleaf Press.

Zepeda, Marlene, Carrie Rothstein-Fisch, Janet Gonzalez-Mena, and Elise Trumbull. 2006. *Bridging Cultures in Early Care and Education: A Training Module.* Mahwah, NJ: Lawrence Erlbaum Associates.

FOUR

Self-Regulation

*I can manage my emotions
and empathize with others.*

We all know from experience that kids who can't control their emotions can cause chaos at preschool. But did you also know that researchers, such as Clancy Blair and Rachel Razza from Pennsylvania State University, are finding that the ability to self-regulate is also one of the most important predictors of later academic success? The standards below from Utah, Washington State, Maryland, and South Carolina are probably similar to those you will find in your own state. In this chapter, you will find ways to help support children's development of self-regulation.

- "Identifies own emotions (e.g., happy, sad, angry, frustrated, bored, lonely, afraid)." *Utah Pre-Kindergarten Guidelines*

- "Children regulate their feelings and impulses." *Washington State Early Learning and Development Benchmarks*

- "Understand basic feelings such as happiness and sadness, as expressed by others verbally or nonverbally." *Maryland Model for School Readiness: Framework and Standards for Prekindergarten*

- "Demonstrate empathy by responding to feelings and needs of others." *Good Start Grow Smart: South Carolina Early Learning Standards for 3-, 4-, and 5-Year-Old Children*

"Bye, Tata Mary. You come get me after naptime?" asked Mario.
"Sí, mijo. After nap," she agreed.
"I'm sad. I don't want you to go, Tata," he said with tears in his eyes.

"Come give me a hug, mijo. You'll have fun today. You'll see."

Mario still felt a little sad when his Tata left, but soon ran off to join his friends at the climber. One of his friends accidentally bumped into him. Instead of pushing back, Mario called out, "Hey, stop crashing me." When the chime rang, Mario met up with his teacher at the door and sat at circle for morning meeting. His friend Angelo became anxious when he couldn't find an empty spot. Mario noticed and scooted over, making some room, and called out, "Here's room, Angelo!"

What Does Self-Regulation Look Like?

Mario is well on his way to establishing self-regulation. He was able to express that he felt sad and found a way to help the sadness pass. He didn't strike back when he was bumped. And he showed his caring for others when he invited Angelo to sit by him.

Children who can self-regulate can identify feelings in themselves and others, understand that feelings change over time and are not permanent, and are able to separate their feelings from their actions. As children gain a deeper understanding of their feelings, they can begin to learn how to manage their feelings by self-soothing and other strategies. Finally, they are ready to learn how to express their feelings to others and use assertive language instead of impulsively striking out when they are upset. Isn't this exactly what we hope to see from all the children in our care?

When Things Go Wrong

With these skills, Mario has a relatively easy time moving through his school day. Not all the children in his classroom are at the same level. Some children in his group still have trouble managing their emotions and are quickly overwhelmed and out of control. Other children are oblivious to the feelings and needs of others. You might see them push a child away from a desired toy or be confused why a child cries when he is hit. When children have tantrums, hit out of frustration, can't calm down from excitement, or ignore the feelings of others, it is useful to take a closer look to see if they are missing one or more key skills of self-regulation.

Hannah swung a toy telephone and hit Rachel on the side of her head. Moments later, when the teacher got there, Rachel was screaming, with tears pouring down her face. Hannah was looking on, bewildered.

"Hannah hit me," Rachel sobbed as a bright red bruise began to appear on her cheek.

The teacher gathered Rachel into her lap and pulled Hannah over. "Look at Rachel's face," she said. "Look what you did. How do you think she feels?"

"Sor-ry," Hannah replied in a mechanical singsong voice.

"Sorry's not enough, Hannah. You hurt your friend. Look at her face. Look what you did. That was so mean what you did. You could have poked her eye out. You made that bruise on her face."

"I didn't do it," Hannah said. "We were playing and the telephone hurt her."

"Yes, you did hurt her. You were very bad to do that," the teacher said.

Hannah said again, "The telephone hurt her. Can I go now?"

"You can go sit down and think about what you did, young lady. You are being very naughty," the teacher replied.

Later the teacher told her director that this was typical behavior for Hannah. She would hurt somebody and immediately say sorry in that distant, insincere voice. When pushed, she would deny any responsibility for what she did. The more the teacher tried to make her feel bad for hurting others, the more distant and blank Hannah's face would become.

The story of Hannah clearly shows that making children feel bad does not help them act good. Instead of helping Hannah understand how her actions affect others, blame, shame, and guilt only served to put Hannah on the defensive. What the teacher found out later by observing Hannah as she moved through her day was that Hannah didn't yet understand cause and effect in general. She wasn't aware that her actions were what caused hurt and damage to other kids. She also didn't seem to understand the feelings of other children.

Hannah's teacher began to give Hannah reflective feedback many times a day in nonthreatening situations to help her become aware of how her behavior had consequences—"You wiped up the water and now the table is all dry," "You put on your shoes and now you are ready to go outside," and "You let Jalessa sit by you, and now she feels happy."

When Hannah hurt others, her teacher took the role of guide and partner in helping her develop empathy and consideration for others: "You hit Ivan and now he's hurt. He needs some help." After Ivan's needs were met, the teacher went back to Hannah. "You wanted the stickers so you hit Ivan. That hurt him. We need to keep kids safe here at school. Come on, let's practice a safe way to get stickers so nobody gets hurt." The teacher took Hannah back to the activity table and the two of them role-played asking each other to share the pile of stickers. In a few weeks the teacher noticed that Hannah hit less often, and when she did she was much more concerned and remorseful.

Help Children Understand Emotions

You may sometimes hear or read about these skills as "emotional literacy" or as Daniel Goleman called this skill "emotional intelligence." According to Goleman, we are not born with emotional skills but we are born with the ability to learn these skills. The first of these teachable skills is for children to begin to identify the feelings in themselves and others. It is helpful for children to recognize that feelings are responses to real or imagined events and that feelings come and go over time. Help children learn to recognize their emotions by having them notice how they feel physically. Clarify for children what may have triggered their emotions, and help them understand that feelings change.

Supportive Interactions to Help Children Understand Emotions

The ways we respond to children's emotions and the conversations we have with children about emotions helps them form the foundation for emotional intelligence. By using a rich emotional vocabulary, we help children to discriminate between and label the wide range of emotions they experience. By pointing out to them what triggered their joy or noticing aloud that they no longer seem sad, we help children learn that emotions come and go. Through our calm and controlled interactions with children who experience strong emotions, we send the message that emotions are nothing to be feared. Try to weave some of the interaction strategies that follow into your daily interactions in the classroom.

Respond to Children's Emotions

The greatest gift we can give to others is to truly listen. When we listen with compassion and understanding to a child's emotions, it supports the adult-child relationship. It also increases emotional literacy and boosts the child's sensitivity to the feelings of others. As teachers, though, we are multitasking at such a frantic pace that we slip much faster into the "problem-solver mode" than the "listening mode." Listen carefully to children's words to hear whether they are asking for information or for emotional support.

Is the child expressing an emotion such as frustration, disappointment, fear, hurt, or joy? When you hear a sentence that expresses a feeling, reflect the feeling back. Name the feeling in your answer to help children begin to build an emotional vocabulary. Let the child know you are really listening, you care, and you will help her express her strong feelings. As you empathize with children and model respect for the feelings of others, you are also planting the seed for the child's development of his own empathy for others.

You might want to . . .	Sounds like . . .
Ask how the child is feeling.	"Are you upset about that?"
Guess how the child is feeling.	"Your face and voice tell me you are very happy about your grandpa visiting you."
Mirror what you hear.	"I hear that you're angry that your shoe keeps falling off."
Validate feelings.	"I can see why you feel frustrated."
Empathize.	"You must feel so disappointed."
Let the child know that her feelings are a reaction to a trigger.	"You got scared when the fire alarm went off, huh?"
Reassure the child that his reaction is normal.	"A lot of kids are scared of loud noises."

Beware of these less effective ways of responding to children's emotions.

When you . . .	It . . .
Gush with sympathy—"Oh, you poor little thing. How mean of Allegra to say that to you."	Promotes victim mentality.
Give advice—"Here, let me show you how to put the bead on the string."	Sends the message that the solution is more important than the feeling.
Use humor—"You look like a volcano ready to explode. Ha, ha, ha! Is a bunch of hot lava going to come out of you?"	Makes light of the child's strong emotions.
Reassure—"Oh, don't feel like that. He didn't really mean it. He was just angry with you."	Sends the message that the child shouldn't feel the way she does.

Listen carefully to the words children use so you can tell if they are expressing an emotion or simply asking for information. When a child uses the words *who, what, where, when, why,* and *how,* he is usually looking for information, not empathetic responses. When children don't use those words, they are probably not looking for information and it might be best to try an empathetic response first.

When a child says . . .	Feeling or information	Try saying . . .
"Nobody will play with me."	Feeling	"You sound lonely to me."
"Where does this block go?"	Information	"Look on the shelf and find the shapes that match."
"I can't draw a horse."	Feeling	"You aren't happy with how your horse looks?"
"How many crackers can we take?"	Information	"The sign shows that you can take two crackers."

Name and Validate Feelings

We might fall into this trap with children: we not only want to control their behavior, but we also want them to stop feeling angry or sad. Is feeling happy superior to feeling sad? Many of us were raised to believe some of our feelings were okay and some were not. Happy might feel a whole lot better than sad, but the feeling itself is not superior. Making value judgments on children's feelings blocks their ability to monitor their behavior effectively. It may also prompt them to lack empathy for the distress of others. For example, you might hear one child call another child a crybaby. It takes the full range of feelings for children to develop their moral compass. Children learn as much from the feeling of disappointment as they do from the feeling of joy. When something they do triggers feelings of disappointment, it serves as a message to them to reexamine their behavior.

Strive to name and validate all the feelings—"good" and "bad"—that children express in your classroom. A good way to validate feelings is to reflect back to children your best guess about what they are feeling while withholding any judgment.

Instead of saying . . .	Try . . .
"What's that face supposed to be all about?"	"I wonder if you are feeling frustrated (hurt, scared, disappointed)."
"Pouting isn't going to get you anywhere."	"It looks like you want to use the soccer ball first."
"There's no reason to be angry."	"You're angry, and that's okay."
"There's nothing to be upset about."	"I can see you're upset, and I understand."
"Don't feel that way."	"I'm sorry you feel that way."
"Go sit on the beanbag chair until you can come back with a smile on your face."	"What do you need? What do you want?"

Discover What's Underneath "Angry"

Anger is sometimes called a "secondary emotion," which means that it is used to cover up a more vulnerable emotion such as frustration, disappointment, hurt, or fear. Whenever possible, guide children to name or identify their primary emotions instead of using the more aggressive word *angry*.

- Frustrated: You want something and are having trouble getting it.
- Disappointed: You thought something was going to happen and it didn't.
- Hurt: You feel physical, emotional, or social pain.
- Fear: You have anxiety about what might happen.

Instead of saying . . .	Try . . .
"You seem angry that you have to wait for a turn."	"You seem frustrated that you have to wait for a turn."
"I bet you're angry that it isn't your show-and-tell day."	"I bet you're disappointed that it isn't your show-and-tell day."
"When Emmaline said your shoes are ugly, you felt angry."	"When Emmaline said your shoes are ugly, you felt hurt."
"You're angry that we have a new teacher-helper today."	"You're scared about the new teacher-helper today.

Emotional Vocabulary

Helping children build a broad emotional vocabulary helps them become increasingly aware of their own emotions and the emotions of others. It also helps children to accurately communicate with others just what it is that they are feeling. Use the following list as a starting point, and add to it as more ideas come to you. You might want to ask parents of your dual-language learners to translate these emotion words into their home languages, and you might also want to learn some key emotions in American Sign Language. During times of intense emotion, using the child's own language to describe the emotion can be a valuable soother.

annoyed	bored	calm
confused	embarrassed	excited
generous	ignored	impatient
joyful	safe	unafraid
worried		

Help Children Understand That Feelings Are Responses

Many young children have no idea where their feelings come from. Think of the infant who cries to be fed or because she feels cold. Babies feel the emotion, and they react without knowing that the hurt in their belly is because they haven't eaten in three hours or the cold that they feel comes from wet bedding. Before they can manage feelings, children need to have an understanding of what triggers their feelings. As children become aware of cause and effect, you can begin to help them understand that their emotions stem from an outside cause. Not only do events and other people affect them, but they themselves have an influence on the feelings of others as well. Understanding that our behavior can have an effect on the feelings of others is one of the essential building blocks for the development of empathy. Weave sentence templates such as those that follow into your daily language with children to guide them to make these connections.

When . . .	Template . . .	Example . . .
Outside events have an impact on their feelings	You feel (emotion) because (event).	"You feel excited because Josie is coming for supper" or "You feel tired because you worked so hard on the climber."
Other people's actions have an impact on their feelings	When (person) (action), you felt (emotion).	"When Margaret said you couldn't go to her birthday, you felt sad" or "David shared his blocks, and you felt happy."
Their actions have an impact on other people's feelings	When you (action), (other person) felt (emotion).	"When you pushed Denise, she felt hurt" or "Jose liked it when you asked him to sit by you at circle."

Help Children Notice That Feelings Change

"When something bad happens to Ciara, it's as if her whole world is over. I'm not talking about just big things here. I mean if somebody won't play with her right then, or if she has trouble printing her name, or if she was hoping to be the one to turn off the lights but it's somebody else's job that day. She totally falls apart and starts that 'I never get to . . .' or 'Nobody ever plays with me' kind of stuff."

"I try to explain to her that I will help her or her turn will come or that her friend will play with her later, but she just can't move on. Her whiny ways begin to really get on my nerves. I just want to scream, 'Get over it, will you?'" The teacher laughed self-consciously at this point. "Of course I don't," she continued. "But I'm so tired of hearing her complain all day. Now I just hope that ignoring her will make it stop."

Some kids like Ciara have trouble visualizing that time passes, feelings change, and events move on. This can lead them to feel hopeless, stuck, and powerless over their fates. Before children can learn effective problem solving and decision making, they need to understand that time passes and that they have a hand in designing their futures. Ignoring Ciara might just make things worse by confirming to her that, indeed, nobody cares and life is hopeless. Instead, the teacher might try some activities and language that will help Ciara begin to understand that later is another opportunity and tomorrow is another day.

Young children don't realize feelings ebb and flow over time. When children are upset, they expect to feel that way for the rest of time. To move away from letting emotions control their behaviors, it is important for children to learn that they can manage their emotions and that feelings change over time. Help children notice that *happy* isn't permanent, but neither is *sad*. Make it a habit to recognize and reflect to children when their personal feelings have changed. Use a sentence pattern such as: "You felt (feeling) and now you feel (feeling). Feelings change."

"This morning you were frustrated with John, and now you two are having fun with the police cars. Feelings change."

"You used to not like to eat salad and now you do! Feelings change."

"You were so sad this morning when your nana left. Then you played with your friends and you felt better! Feelings change."

Change Children's Destructive Self-Talk

Some children talk in negative terms about themselves when they're upset. The words a child says to himself are part of what builds his view of reality. When you hear a child using destructive self-talk, encourage the child to recognize and name the underlying feelings. The following are some examples of how you might approach this.

Instead of . . .	Suggest . . .
Nobody likes me.	I want somebody to play with.
This is too hard for me.	I need somebody to help.
I can't do this. I'm dumb.	I'm frustrated.

Help Children Regulate Emotions

Many of the challenges preschool children pose can be traced back to a lack of emotional regulation. For example, after an exciting game of chase on the play yard, children need to be able to calm down enough to go back inside for lunch without bringing their high excitement into the classroom. Children who haven't yet developed the ability to regulate their emotions can become so overwhelmed that they lose their ability to think before they act. Think for a moment of how easily a group of young children can get out of control during transitions, around holiday time, or on the first day of water play outside when the weather gets warm. Their excitement or anxiety seems to totally overtake them, and regaining control can be quite a struggle. One of the reasons for the chaos is that at those moments children are having trouble regulating their emotions. They are anxious or excited at a high level and don't have the skills or support they need to calm themselves down.

Children often begin emotional regulation with comfort items or the support of a trusted adult. A child who is scared might regulate his emotions by moving closer to a teacher, or a child who is unhappy may get a comfort item from her cubby. Integrate emotional regulation supports throughout the daily life of the classroom to help children begin to find their own life strategies to self-regulate when their emotions get the best of them.

When you infuse your daily schedule, rituals, and routines with opportunities for children to develop and practice emotional-regulation skills, you will find your days magically smoothing out and becoming more peaceful.

Support Emotional Regulation through the Classroom Culture

Chaotic environments often result in chaotic emotions, such as anxiety. Anxiety can be especially troublesome during transitions when there is less structure in the classroom. Transition time seems to trigger aimless activity and conflicts. Use the classroom culture to support emotional regulation with strategies to minimize anxiety and by including ways for children to soothe themselves when they do become agitated.

Picture Schedules

For many children, the uncertainty of what is happening next can lead to anxious and escalating behaviors. Unfortunately, young children can't look at a clock to figure out what happens next. You can help children by giving them predictable rituals and routines. Once children become familiar with the routine, they know that if they are outside playing, lunch must be next. If lunch is over, it must be rest time. And if afternoon snack is done, it must be time to go home. This knowledge can help children feel confident and relaxed, and free them up to peacefully participate in activities and socialize with their friends.

Reinforce your daily schedule with a picture schedule posted at the children's eye level to help them visualize their day.

1. Take pictures of all major program portions of the day. For example, morning meeting, center time, outside time, lunch, afternoon meeting, rest, quiet play, outside time, go home.

2. Label each picture with its title, such as "Morning Meeting." For young children, it is not necessary to add the actual clock time, although you can if you wish.

3. As you move from activity to activity, refer to the posted schedule to help children learn how to use the tool. For example, point to morning meeting on the schedule and say, "We're done with this activity. Let's look now and see what comes next. Who knows what this is a picture of? You are right, next is center time."

4. When an individual child asks you if it's "outside time" or "go-home time" yet, bring him over to the picture schedule and help him find the information he needs.

Some teachers put their picture schedule in a pocket chart and have children move the pictures from the left column to the right column as the activity is completed. Others bind the pictures in book form with a plastic spiral binder and have the children flip the pages as each activity is finished to see what comes next. It wouldn't be overkill to use all of these methods in one classroom if you had a number of children who needed help getting oriented.

One, Two, Three, It's Me!

There is a lot to worry about at preschool. "Who will I sit next to?" "Will I be line leader?" "Will there be a space for me?" Provide additional support to children by giving them a predictable place to be at transition time. Transitions can be difficult for children who need predictability in their environments. Transition most often means that the child will be moving physically from one space to another. If this transition will require a negotiation of space, such as when children are told as a group to line up to go outside, some children will become so anxious that they strike out at others for no apparent reason.

If you have one or two children who fall apart when lining up, think of assigning each of them a special numbered place to be in line to minimize their anxiety and acting out. Whether the child gets there first, last, or sometime in between, that child knows she is always in the same spot. Number three is a useful position since many children can count to three. The singsong "one, two, three, it's me" is catchy and fun to say. Third in line is also a "neutral" place, unlike "line leader" or "last kid." If you have two children needing support, think of number five for the second child.

Make sure all the children know that Freddy's place in line is number three so they move to make space for him when he gets there. Most children will be very helpful and supportive with a one-two-three child in their group. Children typically will support strategies that lead to more peace and safety.

Red Dot

This strategy is similar to one-two-three, except it is used for group time when children do not have assigned seats or sit-upons.

Put a red sticky dot on the floor to indicate the child's predetermined place at group time. Make sure everyone knows that the red dot is Freddy's space. Having a clear vision of where to go helps some children calm down and reduces inappropriate behavior.

Sit-Upons

If many children get anxious when gathering for group time, consider using a system to assign predetermined places for each child. One method to do this without assigning permanent seats is to use individual sit-upons.

1. Have each child make his or her own sit-upon with colored paper and art materials.

2. Cover the sit-upons with contact paper to make them durable.

3. Assign a rotating job to arrange the sit-upons in the group area before children gather.

4. When children transition to large-group time, each child finds his or her sit-upon and sits in the designated spot.

5. Make sure there is a firm rule that children must sit where they find their sit-upon. If children are permitted to move their sit-upons, the predictability is lost.

Cleanup Job Board

Cleaning up after center time can be one of the most challenging transitions of the day. "I didn't take that out." "I already put some blocks away; Anthony needs to do the other blocks." "I never played there." Time and attention that you need to spend helping anxious children transition gets siphoned off by the constant distraction of monitoring the cleanup activity. Make life easier for the children and for yourself with a "Cleanup Job Board."

1. Put photos of each center in the left-hand pockets of a pocket chart.

2. Assign pairs of children to be in charge of each center and put their names in the right-hand pockets next to each job.

3. If there are too many children, add additional transition jobs such as pushing in all the chairs, using the carpet sweeper in the carpet area, or washing the tables.

4. Have the assigned children clean up their assigned area regardless of whether they used the materials that day.

5. Scan the room to see if the area is clean. Send the assigned children back to finish an area if it isn't done.

6. Try not to rotate jobs more often than once a week. Predictability and routine are key for children to feel calm and in control.

When you use a cleanup board like this, make sure to also require children to pick up after themselves as they move from one area to another during the work period.

Self-Soothing

Self-soothing is an important tool for managing emotions, yet we often make the mistake of trying to break children's self-soothing habits! Respect and honor children's self-soothing techniques unless they present a danger to self, others, or property. Some children already have coping techniques such as rocking, thumb sucking, hair stroking, or cuddling a baby blanket. Expose children to a wide range of soothing strategies to help broaden their available repertoire.

-   Some kids do well with a familiar comfort item to help themselves calm down when they are agitated. Some ideas for items that a child might use are family photos, a Koosh ball, a small cloth, a teething toy, or a small stuffed animal.

-   If a child ends up tossing these things around, see if you can attach the item to her belt loop with a short string. Some things, such as picture frames or Koosh balls, are available as key chains that can then be easily attached to clothing.

-   While many kids do well storing their comfort items in backpacks or cubbies, some children need their items closer at hand. Have these children use a fanny pack and encourage them to take out the items when they need help regulating their emotions. If they can keep items close without holding them in their hands the whole time, they will be freer to participate in activities.

Exploratory Materials

Children find it easier to express themselves with actions rather than with words. Provide kids with daily opportunities to work with open-ended materials such as water, wood, clay, and sand. Many children discover that working with sensory materials helps them to calm down and relax. Other children find they are able to express a full range of emotions through manipulating these materials.

Use Water as a Soother

Many people describe anger as red or hot. These people can find relief by using water as a soother. If you have children in your group who have frequent angry outbursts, you might want to explore this idea with them.

1. Very soon after the child has calmed down, ask, "Is your anger a color? What color do you think it might be?"

2. If a child describes the feeling of anger as the colors red or orange or describes it as a hot feeling in his head or hands, suggest that next time you will show him a way to chase the red or the hot away.

3. Another time you might ask, "How does your head feel when you are angry? How do your hands feel?"

4. The next time you see him beginning to escalate, invite him to get a drink of water, wash his hands or face, use a spray bottle of water to clean a table, or play at the water table. If this strategy works, make sure the child has access to water as a soother whenever he feels the need. Let the child know that many people use water as a way to calm themselves down.

One-Person Areas

Learning how to regroup when we are losing control is an important life skill. Many people find that leaving the situation for a short period of time helps them regain control and perspective. Help children explore this strategy by including places within the classroom where they can go to center themselves when they begin to spin out of control.

Some people like solitude while they calm down. Have one or more one-person areas in the room where children can retreat without being bothered by others. You can make an "office" area with a small desk, drawing tools, and maybe a lava lamp. You can make a "cave" on the bottom shelf of a built-in wall unit; add pillows and use carpeting for the floor. A table fountain or aquarium helps soothe some children.

Explore Relaxation Techniques

Different people have different temperaments and use different types of strategies to cool off. At home, I clean the refrigerator. Some people like to run, some people like to listen to music, some people like to chat with a friend, some people just want to be in a quiet corner and read a book. Give children the space and opportunity to explore different avenues and different strategies for soothing and relaxing when they are feeling anxious or stressed or are beginning to feel out of control.

- Some children find they can calm themselves by taking deep breaths.

- Becky Bailey, author of *Conscious Discipline*, describes a variation on this method that she calls "STAR Strategy": Stop, Take a deep breath, And Relax. Cut a star out of cardboard or buy a stuffed star to give children a physical and visual cue to remember the strategy.

- Children can sit alone in a beanbag chair or a rocking chair.

- Some children find that working with art materials helps them manage emotions.

- Music helps some children relax. Keep a tape, CD, or MP3 player and headset available for those children who need it. In his book *Living Like a Child*, Enrique Feldman recommends using slow classical music with a tempo of sixty beats a minute.

- Many boys and some girls find that large-motor activities help them calm down. Either take the child outside for a few minutes to burn off the energy or provide a large-motor area in the classroom for the child to use when he needs it. This might be a two-foot-square area with a hop ball or a small trampoline.

Some teachers conduct large-group breathing and stretching exercises for relaxation during morning meeting. Other teachers find that vigorous dancing or calisthenics helps their group to relax and get ready for more quiet work. Many teachers play soothing music at rest time to help children unwind from their active morning.

Symbolic Organizers

When children do break down and have a tantrum or lose control, envision that as a temporary disruption in their internal organization. Our task is to help them move from that disorganized state back to internal organization.

Just because a child has stopped the tantrum (or the swearing and shouting) does not necessarily mean the child is back into an organized state. Be careful about sending these children back into the mainstream while they are still a bit internally disorganized. In this state, they are more vulnerable to having another breakdown. How can we make sure they are truly ready to rejoin the group?

Most children find that working a very simple puzzle helps them regain their internal organization and control. Children use this symbolic activity of moving the puzzle from disorganization to order as a way of moving themselves from disorganization to order at the same time.

1. Sit the child at a small table on the floor with a small, four- to six-piece puzzle.

2. Remove the pieces and ask the child to put the puzzle back together.

3. Sit with the child while she does this small task. While she puts the puzzle back together, say, "You are putting everything back where it belongs," or "The pieces are all getting put together again," or similar type statements. Emphasize that she is making order and putting things right.

You can use other materials in the same way.

- Give the child a handful of Unifix cubes and have him attach them all together. Some older children do well if you make a pattern with about six cubes and ask them to continue the pattern with more cubes. Use a very simple A-B pattern such as red-blue, red-blue.

- Give the child a handful of math sorters and have him sort the objects into meaningful piles. Some examples are a handful of mixed coins, buttons, seashells, or jewels.

Physical Activity for Strong Emotions

Some adults choose to go for a run or shoot baskets to cool off when they are angry. Provide something similar for the children in your classroom who need physical activity to pull themselves back together. Early on in my work with children who are angry, it was recommended to encourage them to vent their feelings by hitting a pillow. Now, however, we have learned to discourage destructive or violent outlets for anger such as tearing up an old phone book or using a punching bag because they produce chemical changes in our bodies. These chemicals might relieve difficult feelings and lead to feelings of excitement and euphoria. Children might find these feelings very pleasurable and make a dangerous connection between violence and destruction and feeling good. This misconception can escalate later to vandalism and violence toward others.

For some children physical activity works as a good venting strategy. Instead of hitting or destruction, provide those children an opportunity to run around outside, climb a climber, or ride a bike for a few minutes. One teacher I met makes a "Squiggly Square" in a corner of her classroom. She marks off a three-foot square on the floor with masking tape. When children want to jump up and down or let their bodies go loose and silly, they are invited to use that small, safe area. This is a great technique to give children the physical release they need without having to wait for outside time.

Activities to Support Emotional Regulation

These additional activities and games can occasionally be worked into the weekly lesson plan to reinforce emotional-regulation skills that children have learned through interactions and the classroom culture.

Class-Made Books

Help reinforce the concepts that children can manage their feelings and that feelings can change. When you make a class-made book with the children's ideas and artwork about these concepts, they will be drawn to it over and over again, giving them the practice and review they need to learn the difficult concepts.

1. Make a Big Book with the class on managing feelings called "Feelings Change." Have children fill in sentence templates such as "I get afraid when _____. I help my feelings change by _____."

2. Print the words on the bottom of the page and have the children illustrate their ideas. You might begin by modeling your own page. For example, you might say, "I get annoyed when I lose my glasses. I help my feelings change by getting a drink of water."

3. Bind the book together with a cover and back page. Label the front with the title, and the back page as a family-response page.

4. Read the book to the children and allow them to take turns bringing it home to share with their families. Invite families to make comments on the back cover.

Plan-Ahead Charts

Children start out with very few strategies to manage their emotions. Some children, in fact, think they are the only ones who ever feel anger or sadness! Help the children in your class understand these two truths: everyone feels strong emotions and different kids use different ways to manage their emotions.

1. At large- or small-group meetings, introduce the subject by talking about your own experience. Say something like, "Last night I was so scared. I was sleeping and then the storm came and the thunder woke me up! I was really scared. Does anybody else here ever get scared?" This introduces the idea that everyone—children and grown-ups alike—gets scared sometimes. Let children share their own experiences of times when they were scared. Many will copy you and talk about being scared of the storm. That's fine. Others will want to share how brave they are and how the storm didn't bother them at all. That's fine too. Validate each child's experience with reflective feedback. For example, say, "So, Brandon, you aren't scared of thunder," and "Emilia, big dogs can be scary, can't they?"

2. Next, begin sharing techniques to manage fear. Again, start with your own experience. "You know what I did when I got scared last night? I turned on the light. When I was a kid, I used to go to my mom's bed. Then I felt better. I wonder what you guys do to help yourselves feel better when you get scared." Invite each child to share techniques he uses to successfully manage fear.

3. You might want to record children's ideas on a chart. You can later have children illustrate their emotion and technique for a page in a class Big Book.

4. Repeat this activity at another time with another emotion, such as excitement or frustration.

5. Review the compiled lists of ideas or Big Books often, and add to them over time. Refer to the lists when a child is struggling to manage a difficult emotion.

Don't forget to look for examples of people managing their emotions in stories you read to children. Help children identify how the character managed that emotion.

Sand Tray

Children can work through many emotional issues in their play when they are given the right props and opportunities. Many children find sand trays ideal for this purpose. Although sand trays are traditionally used for play therapy, you can adapt them for the classroom too.

1. Fill a bus tub or similar-size container with a few inches of clean sand.

2. Provide some containers with a variety of small props. Include the following items, and add other tiny toy and representational figures:

    - People figures of all ages, abilities, and colors

    - Animal figures, including some wild animals, dinosaurs, snakes, and bugs

    - Plastic trees and fences

    - Fantasy figures, including queens and kings, fairies, witches, wizards, jewels, and crystals

    - Helper props such as police and firefighters, doctors, and ambulances

    - A variety of small vehicles

3. Set the sand tray in a one-person area out of the traffic paths of the room. Invite children to use the sand tray to make a world. If you wish, when a child appears to be almost done, invite her to tell you about her world.

Recently, a teacher reminded me of a boy we had in our class a few years ago named Bentley. His mother was recently remarried, and they had just moved to a new house. Bentley had been more disruptive than usual, and nothing seemed to help very much. One afternoon we pulled out the sand tray and all the props and invited Bentley to play. He immediately took the three boxes of props and dumped them into the tub. We thought the activity was a failure until we asked him, "Tell us about your sand world." His answer? "My world is a total mess." How revealing! No wonder this child was having such a hard time at school. We used this information in the classroom to make sure that Bentley's school day was simple, orderly, and predictable, and very soon his school behavior improved.

Keep in mind that teachers are not therapists. If children reveal disturbing information while using the sand tray, refer the child to the appropriate support personnel or agencies. Remember that as a preschool teacher, you are a mandated reporter.

If You're Happy and You Know It

By modifying this song, you can help children not only label emotions but also come up with strategies to manage those emotions.

1. Make up new verses for the song, using emotions that the children are learning. Some common ones for children are happy, scared, angry, and hurt.

2. The second line of each verse should be a strategy that children can use in the classroom. Some ideas:

   - If you're happy and you know it, give a smile.
   - If you're scared and you know it, find a friend.
   - If you're angry and you know it, count to five.
   - If you're hurt and you know it, get a hug.

Here's an example of how one teacher sang this song with her group. Notice how she handled the child who came up with an inappropriate strategy for handling anger.

The children gathered around Holly for a song before lunch. Holly started clapping and had a big smile on her face. "Happy, happy, happy," chanted Teddy, jumping up and down.

"If you're happy and you know it," she started singing. Most of the kids joined in with big smiles. "Clap your hands!" they finished. "If you're happy and you know it, clap your hands," they all continued together. "If you're happy and you know it, then your face will surely show it" (they all smiled and squirmed around). "If you're happy and you know it, clap your hands."

"What should we do next?" asked Holly.

"Scared. Do scared," called John.

"Okay. Let's do scared. What does scared look like? Show me how you look when you get scared," she said to the group, as she modeled herself what her own scared face looked like. "What can you do if you get scared in school? Who has an idea?" continued Holly.

"I want a hug. I get scared," said Brandy.

"Okay. Let's sing that we get a hug. Ready? If you're scared and you know it, get a hug. If you're scared and you know it, get a hug. If you're scared and you know it, then your self will surely show it—let me see your scared self! If you're scared and you know it, get a hug. Okay, go find somebody to get a hug with."

The children sang and acted out the scared verse and then gave hugs to each other.

"Let's do one more feeling. We did happy and we did scared. I wonder what we can do now. Who has an idea?"

"I wanna do mad," said Francisco. "I punch his face when I get mad."

"Okay. Let's do mad. How can we do mad at school so we can all be safe, Franny?"

"I punch his face," Francisco answered.

"You get mad, and you feel like you want to punch. At school, we keep everyone safe. Do you have an idea how to do mad with no hurting at school?" Holly gave Francisco time to think of an answer.

"I don't know," said Francisco.

"Hmm," Holly said to him. "I wonder who you can ask in our class who might know. Who would you like to ask?"

"I ask Mitchell. How you be mad, Mitchell?" he asked.

"Count to five," answered Mitchell. Holly had taught the children to count to five if they felt they were getting out of control.

"Okay, count to five is safe. Let's use that," said Holly. She led the children in the last verse of the song.

Help Children Learn Impulse Control

When children act on their feelings without thinking first, we sometimes call that impulsive behavior. For example, a child who feels crowded at group time might push or hit the child next to her. When children learn to take a moment to think before they act, we call that impulse control.

Grace ran out to the yard and looked for the red bike with the blue seat. Campbell got outside before her and was already riding around the yard on what the kids called "the good bike." Grace ran over and grabbed at the handlebars.

"Get off, you stupid. That's mine," she said.

As Campbell tried to pull away from her, Grace pushed hard. Campbell and the bike both fell to the concrete. Their teacher, Isela, shook her head in frustration as she went to attend to the problem.

"Grace, that's it for you. That was your last chance. No bikes for you the rest of the week."

Grace immediately ran to another unused bike and tried to get on. "I said no," Isela told her, carrying Grace off, kicking and screaming. "That child is so quick to grab things from others. She can tell me that grabbing is not all right and that we use words at school, but as soon as she gets out there in the action, she loses it."

Some children and adults act on their emotions without taking a moment to reflect first. Grace was one of these impulsive children. She would feel something, like the urgency to have the "good bike," and then act on her feelings without thinking first. Children who meet their wants and needs of the moment without thinking a moment ahead can pose a challenge in the preschool room. At cleanup time, they may continue playing because they don't want to stop and don't feel like cleaning up. When it's time to go outside, they may refuse to stop for a moment to put on their jacket because putting on a jacket isn't as much fun as playing outside.

Punishing impulsive behavior does nothing to teach impulse control. Instead, Isela might have tried to validate Grace's feelings and then guide her behavior. She could have said, "You really wanted that bike, huh?" When Grace agreed, the teacher might have said, "You want the bike really bad, and Campbell is already using it. Let's see what we can do now to keep everybody safe." Maybe the teacher could have started a waiting list for the bike. Or the teacher could have helped Grace find the words to ask Campbell for a turn. The teacher might decide to add various strategies to the daily program to help Grace learn to think before acting. By working on the missing strength instead of on the behavior, the teacher could have helped Grace learn what she needed to know to manage her own impulsive behavior.

Supportive Interactions to Promote Impulse Control

Help children take ownership for the consequences of their actions on themselves, others, and their environment.

"Marcus hit me," Hernando cried to Mr. M.
"I saw," said Mr. M, giving Hernando a hug. "You tried to push him off the bike, so he hit you, huh?"
Hernando had a confused look on his face. "Marcus hit me," he said again.
Hernando made no connection between his pushing Marcus and Marcus hitting him. To him, they were totally random and separate acts.

Once children make the connection between action and consequence, they can start to control their impulses and make more deliberate choices based on their predictions of the results.

What's Your Plan?

Impulsive children act before they think. They chatter during story time, they run instead of walk to the door, or they serve themselves seven scoops of pudding at lunch. These children move through the world reacting to what's around them without stopping a moment to think first. The objective of "What's Your Plan?" is to help these children put a moment of thoughtful behavior into their impulsive activity.

Use this technique when you see a child who appears to bounce around the room without getting involved anywhere. Over time, this practice in impulse control will pay off in less random and more thoughtful behavior overall.

1. Approach the child, get down on his level, gently hold his hands in yours, look into his eyes, and ask, "What's your plan?"

2. A child's plan can be as simple as pointing to the water table or as complex as "I'm gonna give the dinosaurs a bath in the water table."

3. Say, "Okay, go," and release the child.

One More Thing

When you are working with a child who flits quickly from one activity to another, try to keep him engaged for one more moment by saying, "One more thing." Often, this strategy will even extend a child's focus past that "one more thing."

When you are playing with a child . . .	Try saying . . .
in blocks	"One more thing. Can we add three more blocks to the tower?"
in home living	"One more thing. Would you get me some pretend supper before you go?"
at the water table	"One more thing. Would you hold this funnel a minute so I can pour this big pitcher?"
at the writing table	"One more thing. Would you find me Orson's name card?"
in the book center	"One more thing. Before you go, would you find me a fun book from our bookshelf that I can read?"

I Hear You

> Ms. Garcia asks the children in morning meeting, "Who knows which animal gives us the eggs we're using in the cooking project today?"
>
> As hands wave wildly in the air, Topanga yells out, "Chickens, chickens!"
>
> Ms. Garcia says, "Topanga, I'm calling on kids who are raising their hands right now. Hunter, do you know which animal gives us eggs?"
>
> Topanga crosses her arms over her chest and juts out her chin, and her eyes fill with tears. She wonders what she did wrong. Ms. Garcia wanted to know which animal gives eggs, she was able to help, and instead Ms. Garcia asked Hunter, who doesn't know anything about farm animals. If Ms. Garcia wanted to know something and Topanga knew it, why couldn't she tell the teacher? "This is a dumb school!" she cries out.

If there are some children in the group who need to be the ones to answer, it can be helpful to develop a signal to use with them. Teach them that if you look at them and touch your nose with your index finger it means, "I hear you," which lets them know that you know they know the answer. It also gives other children the space they need to think and respond as well.

Cause and Effect

Sometimes we mistakenly assume children understand there is a connection between their behavior and what results from that behavior. However, most preschool children are just beginning to connect their actions with the consequences.

Use reflective language that focuses children's attention on cause and effect, especially on their actions and what the result was. One simple way is to use the sentence template "You (action) and (result)."

"You turned the crank and the clown popped up."

"You mixed red and yellow and look what you got."

"You wiped up that spill and now the table is all clean again."

Tell and Retell the Story

Help children analyze their personal stories with a three-step story process. Help them find the trigger feeling, their response, and what resulted.

To use the stories when a child has made an unsuccessful action choice, use the "tell and retell" method. This process helps children revisit a situation and discover alternative responses that they might have made. By using this process regularly, you will help children learn to think through their own personal situations before they choose a response—something that few children are able to do by themselves when they are sitting in a time-out.

First, tell the story in three steps, the way it happened. Use the third-person point of view to tell the story. Focus on the three major points:

1. What emotion was the child experiencing? (trigger feeling)
2. What did the child decide to do? (action)
3. How did it turn out for everyone? (result)

"Once there was a girl who wanted to ride a bike. She looked and looked for the bike, and then she saw that somebody else was riding it. She was very disappointed. (trigger feeling) The girl went over and pushed the bike over. (action) The bike fell and both kids cried. (result) That's how that story went."

Continue by working with the child to come up with another response that might lead to a happier ending.

"Let's do the story again and figure out what that girl could do to have a happy ending." Start by retelling the story as closely as you can to the original, but pause before the character decides on an action.

"Once there was a girl who wanted to ride a bike. She looked and looked for the bike, and then she saw that somebody else was riding it. She was very disappointed. (trigger feeling) Last time she pushed the bike over. That didn't work. I wonder what else she could try?"

Allow the children to come up with another solution and continue the story from that point.

"Okay. So she decided to get the teacher. The teacher came and helped the children decide how to take turns. The girl and the other child took turns on the bike, and they had fun. That's how that story would have ended."

Or . . .

"Okay. So she decided to call the kid Stinky Butt. The kid got mad and told the teacher. The teacher came over and told her, 'We don't name-call at this school. Go away from the bikes now.' The girl had to walk away. She was still sad because she wanted the bike. Uh-oh, that didn't work. Let's think of another ending."

When telling and retelling, it is usually more effective to tell the story in the third person. Instead of saying, "You wanted the shovel," try saying, "The boy wanted the shovel." Many children have an easier time talking about a theoretical child than they do talking about themselves. When the story is told specifically about the child, children will focus on the details and will do a lot of correcting and sidetracking such as, "I didn't say that" or "He said I could have it."

Support Impulse Control through the Classroom Culture

Some children are more sensitive than others to all of the distractions that typically are going on in an early childhood classroom. This distraction is only made worse when the room itself is cluttered and unorganized. The following suggestions can help minimize distractions for these children and help them stay in control.

Help Children Concentrate

Sitting still and focusing on a task can be more challenging for some children than for others. These kids may be interested and excited about the work, but they find the physical environment so distracting (or uncomfortable) that they can't focus or complete the task. Try a variety of different strategies to help children concentrate on a task.

- Help distractible children focus by giving them a toy to hold quietly during work.
- Some children concentrate best when they can sit on a large ball or stand when working at a table.
- Make sure that chairs allow children to sit with their feet flat on the floor.
- Kids who get distracted by noises sometimes do well with earmuffs or headphones that are disconnected.

Going to the Office

Set up a small area of the room as an "office" where a child can go to work without being disturbed by others. This is not a punishment area or a time-out area. It's a quiet place in a room full of activity where a child or adult can withdraw to concentrate on work.

Some teachers set up a small desk in an attractive corner of the room. Face the desk toward the wall and decorate it with a lamp, calendar, pencil cup, discarded telephone, and other items to help make it look like an attractive office space.

Invite children who get distracted easily to take their "work" to the office. Make sure children understand that when someone is using the office, he is not to be interrupted or disturbed.

When you first set up an area like this, expect that all the children will want to explore it and have a turn to work in it. You might want to post a sign-up sheet on a clipboard and hang it on the wall next to the desk. Once the novelty wears off, you will probably find that those who don't need the area quickly lose interest, while those who do keep returning for more.

Pay Attention to Transitions

> As the children finished cleaning up and got in line to go outside, Cooper jumped on top of Emilio and tackled him to the floor.
>
> "He just attacked Emilio for no reason," Mr. Karo reported to the director as he brought Cooper to the office. "This is the third time this week that Cooper has hurt a child. I have no idea what to do."
>
> "Why did you jump on Emilio, Cooper?" the director asked him. Cooper shrugged.
>
> The director decided to spend the next morning observing the classroom. Sure enough, Cooper pushed and hit others several times—while gathering for morning meeting, during cleanup, and when getting in line to go outside. All three times were transitions. Was this merely a coincidence?

Young children thrive with organized time, space, routines, and rituals. Transition times often lack this organization. For children like Cooper, transitions can feel unpredictable, frightening, and chaotic. Cooper became very anxious at transition time, and he expressed that anxiety by impulsively striking out at other children. Punishing Cooper for his impulsive behavior did nothing to stop the problems. For Cooper, the solution turned out to be a simple matter of giving him structure at transition times to replace his impulsive reaction to anxiety with a safer response. When he was given the task of pushing in chairs at every transition and then reporting directly to one of the teachers, he immediately calmed down and stopped hurting others.

Create Organization

Organization is important for children all day long, not only for transition time. The importance of organization and the impact it has on behavior cannot be emphasized enough. When children feel organized inside, they are more purposeful and directed and express less impulsive behavior. An internally organized child has a stable idea about her place in the world and what to expect. Without a sense of organization, young children struggle to make sense of how the world works. Their behavior may be impulsive, chaotic, random, and unfocused.

For children to become internally organized, they must experience external organization in their daily lives. External organization refers to the efforts we make to organize the child's environment with routines and rituals, organized space, and clear expectations—all of which lead children to internal organization.

"Louis never seems to relax and have a good time here," Ms. Ortega said. "He doesn't get involved in play. His eyes are always darting around the room. At snacktime, he hoards food instead of just taking one portion at a time. During group activities, if a child even bumps against him lightly, he makes a big deal of it and complains that he was hurt on purpose."

Louis's actions might tell us that he looks at the world as a scary and unpredictable place. As he goes through his day, he stays constantly on guard for potential changes and surprises. He has no idea about what might happen next, who's in charge, or the rules of the game. Most of Louis's day is spent feeling anxious, apprehensive, confused, and fearful. To Louis, the world is a random and unstructured place where one never knows what might happen next. Louis's confused feelings lead to many impulsive and destructive behaviors. Here are three keys to providing external organization for children like Louis.

1. Make the physical environment orderly and predictable.

2. Structure time so children can begin to predict what will happen next.

3. Set clear and consistent expectations.

As children experience this external organization, they are able to relax into work and play. Children begin to predict what will happen next in their day and where to find the materials and supplies they need. They find it easy to comply with expectations and guidelines because those limits are consistent from moment to moment and day to day. They experience less anxiety and tend to move more toward thoughtful, rather than impulsive, responses.

Activities to Support the Development of Impulse Control

The famous Russian psychologist, Lev Vygotsky, made an amazing discovery about dramatic play. He found that a child who ordinarily was unable to stay still and quiet was much more able to do so if being still and quiet were a part of play. For example, a child who struggles to stay quiet during story time might be more able to stay quiet during a game of hide-and-seek, or if he were pretending to be asleep in the dramatic play area.

Scaffold children's abilities to control themselves by adding pretend games to your weekly lesson plans. During these games, children can test their impulse control. Ask them to be very, very quiet in order not to scare a pretend mouse. Another time, have children stay very still so the pretend butterfly can land on their hands. Join in the dramatic play area and help the children all go to sleep until you give a signal to get up, or pretend you are in a rowboat and encourage the children to sit very still so the boat doesn't tip over into the crocodile-infested river. Activities such as these give children enjoyable and valuable practice in extending their abilities to control their emotions and their impulses.

Body Bubbles

Tucker was one of those children who seemed to run blindly through the classroom, crashing into others and leaving a path of destruction and chaos behind him. Children like Tucker need support to replace impulsive and random movements with more conscious awareness of the space of other people and things. One effective strategy for body awareness that children enjoy is to use Body Bubbles, which helps them visualize an imaginary bubble that surrounds their bodies.

1. Use your arms to make a circle around your own body to demonstrate, and have the children do the same.

2. Have children try to dance or walk around the room without "popping" one another's bubbles.

3. When gathering for a meeting or beginning a movement activity, review the "body bubble" concept to help children be thoughtful about where they sit or stand.

Homemade Picture Books or To-Do Lists

Classroom schedules highlighting major activities of the day—such as meals, outdoor times, and rest times—are enough support to help most children navigate their days. Some children do well with even more personal support.

1. Work together with children to make little photo-illustrated picture books or to-do lists to help them visualize their days.

2. These pictures should feature the children doing the activity. Include activities as well as transitions, and make sure to include their arrival to and departure from school. Be especially careful to include pictures of the more difficult transitions of the day.

3. Read the book often to the children, send it home for families to share, and use it to "preview" the next event. For example, as lunch ends, bring the book or list to the children. Help them find the lunch picture and then guide them to identify the next event.

Simon Says

Simon Says is a wonderful game to help children practice impulse control. The trick to Simon Says is to stop and think before you act. The problem with the game in its traditional version is that the children who have the most problems with impulse control are eliminated early in the game. In other words, the children who most need to practice impulse control are the children who end up getting the least practice! In this version of Simon Says, nobody is out and everyone gets the practice they need.

1. Gather the children into either a small or large group. Have them stand a couple of feet away from each other.

2. Tell the children you are going to play Simon Says. Tell them that you are going to do things with your body, and sometimes they should copy you. If you tell them "Simon says," then they should copy you. If you don't say "Simon says," then they should not copy you. Remind them that it is a very tricky game and they need to listen carefully before they copy you.

3. Modify the original game so when children make a mistake, they are not eliminated from the game. They are merely prompted to listen carefully and try again. The goal is to keep all the children in the activity for the entire game so everyone gets to practice impulse control.

Here's an example of Randi playing a round of Simon Says with her kids.

"Remember, stop and think," Randi reminded the children as they began the game. "Before you move, what do you need to think about?" she asked the group.

"Do the same thing," suggested Marisella.

"Uh-huh," agreed Randi. "You are exactly right. You do the same thing if I say the words 'Simon says.' Remember? And Mari, if I don't say 'Simon says,' you stay . . ." Randi paused here for Marisella to finish the sentence.

"Stay still," said Marisella.

"Okay, ready? Here we go. Listen hard. Simon says put your hands on the floor," she modeled the motion as she talked. Randi waited until all the children had their hands on the floor. "You waited to hear me say 'Simon says.' Yes."

"Okay. Here's a tricky one. Listen hard. Put your hands way high in the air." Randi kept her hands on the floor. Two children put their hands up. A few children called out "Simon didn't say," and Randi waited for the two to put their hands down again. "That was so tricky. Let me trick you again. Listen hard. Simon says put your hands up in the air." She said "Simon says" louder than the rest of the words, then put her hands up. Again, she waited until all the children had their hands up before moving on.

Randi included one "stop and think" song or game in her lesson plan three times a week. After a few weeks, she was able to play Simon Says a little faster and with fewer prompts. The children were beginning to learn how to "stop and think" before they acted.

Obstacle Course

Many children are challenged by shifting gears from active play to more quiet play. These children need more practice with modulation activities. These activities are specifically designed to help children move from loud to quiet, from using large muscles to using small muscles, from moving quickly to moving slowly. When children practice modulation in play activities, they can begin to transfer that learning to other times when you need the children to settle down, such as during rest time. Obstacle Course is one of these modulation activities you might want to organize from time to time.

1. Set up an obstacle course with large-motor activities, such as climbing through a tunnel and jumping over a log.

2. In the middle of the course, set up a small table with a small-motor activity on it. This can be something like stringing a few beads or putting together a three-piece puzzle.

When children go through this course, they need to be able to shift themselves from one mode to another. This shifting helps develop internal controls needed to "stop and think."

Call-and-Response Songs

Call-and-response songs are another way to help children process information before they act. These are game-type songs in which a leader sings a line first while the children are quiet, and then it's the children's turn to sing a response. When children become familiar with a song, it's challenging for a kid to hold back and not sing until it is time for a response. Two popular children's call-and-response songs are "Did You Feed My Cow?" by Ella Jenkins and "Candy Man" by Greg and Steve.

As a bonus, "Candy Man" helps teach the concept of whispering and thinking the words—both useful life skills. After children have learned the skill of thinking the words, teach them to use the strategy when they have the urge to say something hurtful or to call out of turn. "This is a time to just think the words." Some teachers like to use the singsong "Should it be said or kept in your head?" as a prompt to just think the words.

High-Low ABCs

Another song for modulation practice requires children to sing with energy, immediately shift to a whisper, and then go back to singing forcefully again. Songs like these help children learn to quiet down from energetic play.

1. Sing the "Alphabet Song" while sitting and patting your legs with your hands.

2. Sing and pat one line loud, soft on the next, loudly on the next line, and so on. For example: "A, B, C, D," (loud) "E, F, G," (soft) "H, I, J, K," (loud) "L, M, N, O, P," (soft) "Q, R, S," (loud) "T, U, V," (soft) "W, X," (loud) "Y, Z" (soft).

Like the obstacle course, this game requires children to be conscious of their energy and activity levels and gives them a fun way to practice modulation control.

Freeze Dancing

Like High-Low ABCs and Obstacle Course, Freeze Dancing provides children an enjoyable and nonthreatening way to practice controlling their impulsive urges.

1. Play music while the children dance freestyle.

2. Turn the sound off. Tell the children when the music stops they have to freeze in position.

3. If you call out, "Stop and freeze," when you turn off the music, the same words can be taught for emergency situations such as can occur on field trips or in the play yard.

You can also use the Ella Jenkins song "Stop and Go" (this song is on two of her recordings, *Play Your Instruments and Make a Pretty Sound* and *Songs Children Love to Sing*) to practice a similar dancing game. Another variation is to play Freeze Tag outdoors. The rule for Freeze Tag is that one person is "it." The rest of the children run about and must freeze in position when touched by the child who is "it." There are no winners or losers in this game. The fun is in the freezing. Some people use the rule that children who are free can tag children who are frozen to "unfreeze" them, which can make the game last longer!

Let's Talk about Time-Out

Traditionally, time-out has been used in classrooms as a punishment for poor impulse control. Should a child be separated from the group when she is angry and out of control? How does time-out fit with our goal that children become intrinsically motivated and learn to manage their emotions and behavior? Is time-out being used as an extrinsic control to make a child feel bad in the hopes that she will then act good? Or is time-out a self-regulation skill that children can take with them through life?

A match is a tool that can be used to light the stove or burn down the house. Similarly, time-out is a tool that can be used to build up or tear down. It's not the tool itself that is good or bad, it's how the tool is used and the intent behind its use that determines whether it is helpful or hurtful.

For a moment, think about time-out as a possible life skill. When adults are out of control, when adults are angry and acting impulsively, what would we hope that they do? We would hope that they can begin to identify feelings in themselves when they're going to be dangerous to themselves or others or property and pull themselves away to a place where they can cool off. Waiting until the police officer comes to send you to time-out in jail is not the answer. We want children and adults to be able to identify in themselves when it's time to pull out of a situation to avoid acting impulsively, foolishly, carelessly, or dangerously. We want them to find a way to bring the heat of the emotion down to a safe and manageable level.

You teach what you model. One way to teach the skill of pulling out before things get dangerous is to model it for kids. You might say to children early on in the year, "Sometimes I start to feel anxious. When I feel like that, I'm afraid I might make some poor choices. So this is what I do: I go to the window, look outside at the trees, and take a few deep breaths. And then I come back and join the class. So if you ever see me say 'excuse me' and walk to the window, it's probably because I need to calm down."

Take a moment to model this behavior for the children. Say, "Excuse me," walk to the window, take some deep breaths, and return, so children can see what it looks like. Have a group discussion to share with each other that everyone feels the need to pull out sometimes. Brainstorm different places in the room where people might go to calm down.

Should we be sending children to their calm-down area? Certainly—if you model it as caring behavior for our community of learners. Tell the children that sometimes you get anxious and irritated and you don't even notice what's happening to yourself. Tell them that if they see this happening they can say, "Do you need to go to your calm-down place?" Model and role-play how saying that looks and what tone of voice would be appropriate as a gentle and loving reminder that they might need to go to their calm-down place. Make it a group practice that when you see someone—adult or child—losing control, anyone can suggest to the person that perhaps he might want to go to his calm-down area.

But what if you suggest a child uses her calm-down place and she doesn't want to go? Do you drag her there, kicking and screaming? If you force a child to go to her calm-down place, does it become a punishment?

When strategies don't work the way you envisioned, it's important to step back and regroup before acting. Somehow, dragging someone to a place that you are trying to define as a comforting area doesn't make much sense to me. At the same time, adults often sense when a child is overstimulated and needs to take a break from the action. What then might be some options to respect the peace and calm of a child's chosen place while at the same time helping an overstimulated child to calm down?

- You might take the child with you to your own calm-down spot and attempt to help the child calm down there.

- You might make it a point to spend some warm and comforting one-on-one time with a child in her chosen spot during center time when she is calm. During that time you might comment on how nice and comfortable the spot feels.

- You might find if the child is too overwrought he is hard to redirect. You might try to spend a few days observing him more closely so you can catch him as soon as he starts to get anxious. Inviting him to join you in his calm-down spot to spend some one-on-one time together for a few moments may be inviting enough to get him to try it out.

- Remember that not every strategy works for every child. Going to a calm-down area is just one of many centering strategies you will accumulate. If this particular strategy doesn't work for a particular child, introduce other strategies until you find a good fit.

What about children who, in the middle of group time or story time, stop and go to their calm-down area? Isn't that disruptive to the rest of the group? Shouldn't they have to wait until the activity is over? In fact, getting up and leaving immediately is exactly what you want children to do. You want them to become aware of when it's time to remove themselves from a situation and regroup. If you insist the child stay in the activity even when she knows she needs to remove herself, her anxiety and her behavior will probably only escalate further. Quickly, you'll reach a point where you will have to intervene and send her to time-out, the hallway, the office, or home for the day. It's far better for everyone in the room if children are permitted and encouraged to leave and calm down when they need to.

Help children learn to appreciate taking some time to calm themselves down. Instead of using it as a tool to punish children who have disappointed, hurt, or frustrated you, present time-out as an essential life strategy, a gift for children and adults who need to "take a moment."

Remember that regaining control of emotions is an important step, but it is often only the first step when dealing with problems and conflicts. Problems and conflicts cannot be addressed until all the people involved have managed their emotions and reestablished internal organization. Once everyone has moved from their emotional selves back to their thinking selves, the hard work of problem solving and conflict resolution can begin.

As you work with out-of-control children, don't lose sight of the real goals. You don't want to be tethered to that child all day, trying to control and manage his behavior. The goal is that children learn to manage their own feelings and take responsibility for their own behavior. When children have made thoughtful choices, you want them to feel satisfaction and pride in themselves. When children have chosen behavior that has damaging consequences, you want them to attempt to fix things the best they can. Think twice about interventions and strategies that shift responsibility away from the child and put it on you, the adult. Be the child's ally in celebrating his success and profiting from his mistakes as he learns how to manage himself.

Calm-down areas are only one of many strategies that children find useful to help them regain control when they become anxious or agitated. Introduce children to a variety of calming strategies they can begin to make a part of their own self-soothing techniques.

Promote Empathy

Zack pushed Trisha off the bike he wanted and rode off. Seeing what had happened, one of the teachers snagged Zack while another went to get the first aid kit to clean up Trisha's scraped elbow.

"Look at Trisha's face, Zack. How do you think she feels?" asked the teacher as she hugged a crying Trisha against her.

"I dunno," answered Zack.

"Look at her, Zack. Look at her elbow. That's where you hurt her."

"I wanna go play," Zack said after looking at the bloody arm.

Zack hasn't yet become aware of the feelings of others. He still needs help to read faces and body language. In this scene, the teacher might have helped him by saying something like, "Do you see that Trisha is bleeding? Look at her face. Do you see the tears coming out of her eyes? That means Trisha is hurt and sad."

After children have developed skills to identify their own emotions, they can begin to notice and label emotions in others. Use some of the suggestions that follow to help the children in your group become aware of the emotions of others.

Supportive Interactions to Promote Empathy

By introducing your own supportive interactions as you help children identify and manage their own emotions, you are actually modeling for them how to identify and respond to the emotions of others. Children who feel supported in their own emotions are likely to be more sensitive to the emotions of others. When children are tuned into the feelings and needs of others, it is sometimes referred to as empathy. Teach children how to recognize feelings in others based on what they see and hear.

Help Children Identify with Others

It is easier for children to empathize with others when they feel connected to them in some way. You can help children feel these connections by pointing out similarities. Weave comments about commonalities among children throughout your program day.

Morning meeting	"Who heard that big thunderstorm last night? Oh my goodness, I see a lot of you heard it. Look around at how many children heard that storm."
Story time	"Marcin, you ride the bus to school with your mommy just like the boy in our book. Angel, you ride the bus with your mama too, just like Marcin."
Mealtime	"Robert, look at MaryLynn's plate. I think she might like applesauce as much as you do. MaryLynn, are you an applesauce lover too?"
Outdoor time	Say to the children on the climber, "I see three kids who like to play on the climber—Akin, Steven, and Sunny. All three of you like to climb."

Model Perspective Taking

One essential skill for empathy is the ability to take the perspective of another person. In our role as teachers, we are constantly observing children to figure out what they feel and want. When we talk about this process aloud, we help children begin to see the world through the eyes of others and become aware of how they can be helpful. There are four steps to this process:

1. Describe what you see.

2. Guess the emotion.

3. Imagine why the child feels like that.

4. Model how to take helpful action if it is needed.

Describe what you see	Guess the emotion	Imagine the reason	Take action
"Mila has a big smile on her face."	"I think she might be happy . . ."	". . . because we have glitter and glue today."	"Mila, do you want to work at the art table this morning?"
"Jacob has tears in his eyes."	"He looks like he might be sad . . ."	". . . because he lost his lion keychain."	"Let's go help Jacob."
"Hannah's face is getting red and she's starting to talk very loud."	"She might be upset . . ."	". . . because Wagner crashed into her."	"Hannah, do you need help with something?"

Recognize Helpfulness

When children become aware of how their words and behaviors affect others, they can begin to distinguish between what kinds of behavior are helpful and what behaviors are hurtful. When they grab a toy away, they can look at their friend's face and discover that grabbing is hurtful to others. When they help a friend find his missing keychain, they can see the smile on their friend's face and discover what behaviors might be helpful. Help children develop this awareness with a simple sentence template such as "You (action) so (impact). That was helpful." Here are some examples:

> "You moved over so Emilia could sit down. That was helpful."

> "You worked with Stephan to get all the balls back in the crate. That was helpful."

> "You found Dexter's car in the yard and gave it back to him. Look how happy he is now. That was helpful."

Eventually, you will notice that children are familiar with various ways they can be helpful to others. At that point, you can begin to prompt them to come up with their own helpful and friendly behaviors.

Instead of . . .	Try . . .
"Give Amit some of the blocks."	"See if you can help Amit find a way to play blocks."
"Stacy needs a doll too. Paul, give her one of yours."	"Let's help Stacy be able to play babies with you."

(continued on next page)

Instead of . . .	Try . . .
"Stanley, move over so Albert can sit at circle."	"We need to help Albert find a place to sit." (Then just wait.)
"LeBron, Abby is crying because her mama just left. Can you paint with her at the easel, please?"	"Abby feels sad because her mama just left. How can we help her feel better?"

Activities to Support the Development of Empathy

Help children develop empathy with pictures and stories of children experiencing a wide range of emotions. Continue to use activities that help children be aware of cause and effect. Focus children's awareness of how their own behaviors affect others, both with helpful and hurtful results.

Emotion Photo Cards

There are many commercial posters and other materials available that illustrate faces with various emotions. Some of these show drawings of children's faces while others are actual photos. Instead of using these commercial materials, think about making your own emotion cards using photos of children in your group. Children are often far more interested in visiting, revisiting, and talking about pictures of children they know than they are in commercial photo cards.

1. Invite children to pose for pictures illustrating various emotions such as happy, sad, surprised, angry, and scared.

2. Take close-up digital photos of just their faces.

3. Print out the photos and glue them onto card stock or old, unused playing cards.

4. Keep the photo cards in a basket for children to explore during free-choice time.

5. Think of using the cards for teacher-directed math activities such as sorting by emotion or copying A-B-A-B patterns with two different emotions.

Emotion Necklace

Prepare children to be able to read the emotions of others by using emotion necklaces. Children find it much simpler to identify an emotion by looking at a simple happy-face card or sad-face card than they do by attempting to read individual faces.

1. Prepare ten small cards about two inches square with simple happy or sad faces.

2. Punch a hole at the top of each card and lace a long piece of yarn through the card. Tie the ends together to make a "necklace."

3. Keep these emotion necklaces in a small basket that is easily available to the children.

4. Teach the children how to select and put on an emotion necklace that expresses how they are feeling. Make sure you wear these cards yourself.

5. Model for the children how you can tell how somebody else is feeling by looking at their face card. Say something such as, "I see Maddy has a sad-face necklace on. I wonder why she's sad today? I think I'll go ask her." Or, "Luci, you have a happy-face necklace on today. I wonder why you're feeling so good? Did something special happen?"

Cause-and-Effect Toys

Children need to have an understanding that actions have consequences. For children to learn that their actions have an impact on things and people, they need to experiment and explore every day. Through this exploration, children form an understanding of how actions and behavior affect the outside world. Be patient as children test their understandings by repeating the same thing many times. Provide children with materials and activities that reinforce cause-and-effect understanding.

- Include materials in the classroom such as a jack-in-the-box, surprise boxes, marble mazes, balls and ramps, and magnets.

- Place cups, funnels, and bottles in the water table for children to explore. Set out red, yellow, and blue water and eyedroppers so children can experiment with mixing colors.

- Provide cooking projects and open-ended exploration with a variety of art materials.

- Point out cause and effect as you read storybooks to children. Ask the children questions such as: "Why do you think the Little Red Hen kept all the bread to herself?" "Why do you think the wolf couldn't blow down the brick house?" "Why do you think the hungry caterpillar's belly is getting bigger and bigger?" Children find these questions interesting because they are just beginning to realize that events are related in cause-and-effect chains. Dirty Harry rolled in the mud and got dirty, so his family didn't recognize him, so he got the scrub brush, so they washed him, so he turned white with black spots again, so they recognized him. These are not random events. They logically follow one another in a cause-and-effect manner.

Beginning-Middle-End Stories

Guide children's understanding of the flow from feelings to actions to consequences by helping them break down stories into three steps: the feelings that started it all, how somebody noticed that feeling, and how that person was helpful or friendly. You can do this with many of the picture books you already read to the children. You can also use stories you make up about incidents in the classroom.

For example, in *The Kissing Hand*, the little raccoon feels scared to go to school and be away from his mother. His mother sees that he is scared and gives him a kiss on his palm to take with him to school. The kiss helped the little raccoon feel better. Guide children to see this by asking the questions:

- How did the little raccoon feel at the beginning of the story? (focus on the feeling)

- What did his mom see? (focus on the identification of feeling)

- What did the mom do to be helpful? (focus on how the other characters were helpful or friendly—showed empathy)

When there have been problems in the classroom, make up a story with pretend names. One approach is to tell the whole story with a solution already in place. For example: "Once upon a time, in a school far, far away, a bunch of children came to circle to listen to a story. They all sat down, and then Logan came from the cubbies, and he couldn't find a place to sit. He looked and looked and there was no place. Logan felt very sad and lonely. Peter saw that Logan looked sad. 'Do you want to sit by me?' he asked. 'Sure,' said Logan. Peter moved over and Logan sat down. He had a big smile. 'You're my friend, Peter,' said Logan."

Guide the children by asking questions like:

- How did Logan feel at the beginning of the story? (sad, lonely)

- What did Peter do when he saw that Logan was sad? (made room for Logan to sit down)

- How did Logan and Peter feel at the end of the story? (happy)

As the children learn problem solving, let them help you finish the story. For example: "Once upon a time, in a school far, far away, a bunch of children came to circle to listen to a story. They all sat down, and then Logan came from the cubbies, and he couldn't find a place to sit. He looked and looked and there was no place."

At this point in the story ask questions such as: "How do you think Logan felt?" "What might you do if you saw that Logan felt sad?" "How would everyone feel if you did that?"

Behavior Affects Others

Sometimes we give children a false sense of their power over the feelings of others. While children's behavior may have an impact on somebody's feelings, it is important not to encourage children to think they can control the feelings or behavior of others. Some hurting and troubled children will try to use this mistaken view of their power over others to be hurtful in an attempt to help themselves feel better. Be crystal clear that while feelings are a reaction to events, nobody can make others feel or do anything.

Instead of using the word *make* . . .	Try "When you _____, I feel _____."
"Tell Raymond how he made you feel."	"Tell Raymond that you don't like it when he calls you names."
"Don't make me call your mother."	"When I call and you don't come in, I feel very frustrated."
"Look at his face. How did you make him feel?"	"When you told Benjamin he couldn't play, he felt bad."

The Magic of Babies and Doggies

Two very exciting projects are showing how babies and dogs can help young children develop empathy. In Canada, Mary Gordon began a program called Roots of Empathy. Mary brought babies and their mothers into early childhood classrooms once a month for a year. The children cooed and laughed and helped the mothers care for their babies. Even the most troubled children, who never seemed to get along with other kids their own age, melted when they got near the little ones.

Pam Gaber, of Gabriel's Angels, found similar results when she began bringing her first therapy dog, Gabriel, to children at a crisis nursery. Just as Gordon found with her babies, Pam found that her dog brought out the nurturer in young children, even those who had suffered abuse and neglect in the past. Children watched Pam give loving attention to Gabriel just as Mary's mothers modeled loving care to their babies. In both cases, children followed the models and demonstrated their own loving care and empathy.

While not every program can implement a yearlong baby visit project or can find the services of therapy dogs, you can try to house a small pet such as a hamster or invite a baby sibling in for a visit. You might want to start small and adopt a teddy bear for the classroom. Have the children name the bear and include the teddy in your classroom routines, modeling loving care and empathy. You might want to create one of your classroom jobs around taking care of Teddy during the program day. For some children, babies, pets, and even stuffed toys are a less threatening way to begin to practice empathy and caring.

Make sure, of course, that you stay close to children who might need extra help to stay gentle with vulnerable babies and creatures.

Discussion/Reflection Questions

1. Keep track of problem behaviors that you encounter in your group for one day. What problems might have been the result of children not being able to regulate their emotions? What are some problems you observed that are a result of children being unable to control their impulses? If children were able to better control their impulses and regulate their emotions, what impact might it have on your group?

   _____

   _____

   _____

2. Describe how an adult might behave who has trouble managing impulses and emotions.

   _____

   _____

   _____

3. How might you model empathy for each of these situations:

   • Mikel has climbed to the top of the climber and looks scared as he is trying to get back down.

   _____

   _____

   _____

   • Dee-Dee is weeping because Ebony is washing tables when it was supposed to be her turn.

   _____

   _____

   _____

- Giuliana's birthday is tomorrow and she's bouncing around today, which is interfering with other children's play.

_____

_____

_____

Exercises

1. Think of a child in your class who has demonstrated a low level of impulse control or emotional regulation. What one or two strategies will you implement to help the child build those strengths?

   _____

   _____

   _____

   _____

   _____

2. Look at your schedule, the physical environment, and your class-room routines with an eye toward organization. What are some of the strengths of your current program? What changes might you make to improve external organization?

   _____

   _____

   _____

   _____

3. Think about your current practices. How do you already model empathy in the classroom? What new strategy will you try?

   _____

   _____

   _____

   _____

Reflection/Journal Assignment

Thinking about your own emotional life, how do you manage your own strong emotions? Do you have a soother for when you are feeling angry? Anxious? Sad? Do your own soothers give you any ideas of strategies that might be useful for children to manage their own emotions?

_____

_____

_____

_____

_____

_____

_____

_____

_____

_____

_____

_____

_____

_____

_____

_____

_____

_____

_____

Children and Self-Control

In school, teachers expect children to learn about and control their emotions and to understand and be thoughtful of the emotions of others. Teachers expect children to learn how to be angry or disappointed without hurting themselves, other people, or property. Teachers expect children to learn how to do things that they don't want to do, such as cleaning up or coming inside when outdoor time is over. And they expect children to be aware of when another feels left out and needs to be included or feels sad and needs comforting.

Think About It

What messages did you get as a child about your feelings? How did the elders in your world model how to handle anger? What did you learn about responding to the feelings of other people? How did these lessons serve you or hinder you later on in school, in the workplace, and in your adult relationships? Reflecting on your own experiences, what kinds of lessons would you like to teach your own children about understanding and managing their own emotions?

Some Ideas

- Children learn a lot about behavior by observing their elders. Let children watch you safely manage your own strong emotions. For example, you might say, "I am so angry right now that I am going outside by myself for a few minutes until I'm not so angry anymore. You need to leave me alone for a few minutes."

- Children are able to practice skills such as staying still or remaining quiet for longer periods of time when these skills are part of a game. Playing games such as hide-and-seek or pretending to be Sleeping Beauty are good practice for children to develop controlling themselves.

- Helping to care for pets and plants are good ways for children to begin to develop empathy for others. Ask your child to notice how the pet looks hungry or looks like she wants to play. Ask children to water the plant because it looks like it needs a drink.

Chapter 4 Resources

Bailey, Becky. 1997. *There's Gotta Be a Better Way: Discipline That Works.* Oviedo, FL: Loving Guidance.

———. 2000. *Conscious Discipline: Seven Basic Skills for Brain Smart Classroom Management.* Oviedo, FL: Loving Guidance.

Barnett, Mark A. 1987. "Empathy and Related Responses in Children." In *Empathy and Its Development*, edited by Nancy Eisenberg and Janet Strayer, 146–62. New York: Cambridge University Press.

Blair, Clancy, and Rachel Peters Razza. 2007. "Relating Effortful Control, Executive Function, and False Belief Understanding to Emerging Math and Literacy Ability in Kindergarten." *Child Development* 78 (2): 647–63.

Brooks, Robert, and Sam Goldstein. 2001. *Raising Resilient Children: Fostering Strength, Hope, and Optimism in Your Child.* Lincolnwood, IL: Contemporary Books.

Center on the Social and Emotional Foundations for Early Learning. http://csefel.vanderbilt.edu.

Committee for Children. 2002. *Second Step: A Violence Prevention Curriculum.* Seattle: Committee for Children.

Committee on Integrating the Science of Early Childhood Development. 2000. *From Neurons to Neighborhoods: The Science of Early Childhood Development*, edited by Jack P. Shankoff and Deborah A. Phillips. Washington, DC: National Academy Press.

Covey, Stephen R. 1997. *The 7 Habits of Highly Effective Families: Building a Beautiful Family Culture in a Turbulent World.* New York: Golden Books.

Dinkmeyer, Don, and Gary D. McKay. 1973. *Raising a Responsible Child: Practical Steps to Successful Family Relationships.* New York: Simon and Schuster.

Feldman, Enrique C. 2011. *Living Like a Child: Learn, Live, and Teach Creatively.* St. Paul, MN: Redleaf Press.

Gabriel's Angels: Pets Helping Kids. http://www.gabrielsangels.org.

Gestwicki, Carol. 2011. *Developmentally Appropriate Practice: Curriculum and Development in Early Education.* 4th ed. Belmont, CA: Wadsworth Cengage Learning.

Goleman, Daniel. 1995. *Emotional Intelligence.* New York: Bantam Books.

Gordon, Mary. 2009. *Roots of Empathy: Changing the World Child by Child.* New York: The Experiment.

Gordon, Thomas. 1970. *Parent Effectiveness Training: The Tested New Way to Raise Responsible Children.* New York: P. Wyden.

Gould, Patti, and Joyce Sullivan. 1999. *The Inclusive Early Childhood Classroom: Easy Ways to Adapt Learning Centers for All Children.* Beltsville, MD: Gryphon House.

Koralek, Derry. 1999. *Classroom Strategies to Promote Children's Social and Emotional Development.* Lewisville, NC: Kaplan Press.

Leong, Deborah, and Elena Bodrova. 2006. "Developing Self-Regulation: The Vygotskian View." *Academic Exchange Quarterly* 10 (4): 33–38.

Taylor, John F. 1997. *Helping Your Hyperactive/ADD Child.* 2nd ed. Rocklin, CA: Prima Publishing.

Wheat, Rebecca. 1995. "Helping Children Work through Emotional Difficulties—Sand Trays Are Great!" *Young Children* 51 (1): 82–83.

Whelan, Mary Steiner. 2000. *But They Spit, Scratch, and Swear! The Do's and Don'ts of Behavior Guidance with School-Age Children.* Minneapolis: A-ha! Communications.

Ziegler, Robert G. 1992. *Homemade Books to Help Kids Cope: An Easy-to-Learn Technique for Parents and Professionals.* New York: Magination Press.

FIVE

Collaboration

I am learning how to work and play with others.

Working and playing well with others requires more than just "being nice." To be able to collaborate, children need to learn how to take turns, solve social problems, and share community space and stuff. Some children even need help to learn how to play cooperatively. The following examples from Hawaii, Maryland, California, and Wisconsin outline many of the same collaboration skills you will find in your own state standards. This chapter will help you meet those standards.

- "Understand what people need to do to work and live together in groups." *Hawai'i Preschool Content Standards: Curriculum Guidelines for Programs for Four-Year-Olds*

- "Identify and demonstrate appropriate social skills such as listening to others, settling disagreements, and taking turns that help people live, work, and play together at home and at school." *Maryland Model for School Readiness: Framework and Standards for Prekindergarten*

- "Child learns how to understand the needs of other children and to negotiate constructively within the constraints of social rules and values." *California Desired Results Developmental Profile—Preschool*

- "[Child] engages in social problem-solving behavior and learns to resolve conflict." *Wisconsin Model Early Learning Standards,* second edition

LaVita looked around the room and decided to go to the craft table where children were making pattern necklaces. Sitting at one of the empty chairs, she spied the dish of red beads and pulled them over to her workspace. "I love, love, love red!" she said. "See, I have red ribbons, and my mama painted my nails red too. See?"

"Wait," cried Daniel. "I was using the red ones to make my fireman necklace with the red like the fire and the white like the smoke."

"I need them too," said LaVita. "Miss Bernadette says we need to be fair."

"Okay," answered Daniel. "Let's do My Turn, Your Turn. I'll take a red one, then you take a red one, then I take a red one, then you take a red one. Okay?"

"Okay," replied LaVita. "My Turn, Your Turn."

What Does Collaboration Look Like?

LaVita and Daniel are both on a path to developing the skills they need to work and play together. When they found themselves in conflict over using the red beads, they took turns expressing their needs and listening to each other with courtesy. They are beginning to internalize the teacher's promotion of fairness and were able to come up with a solution that they could both agree with. Working and playing together is complex indeed.

Each society and culture develops its own norms for social skills. Miss Manners and Amy Vanderbilt are popular resources for some adults who have questions about the right thing to do. We call it etiquette: "How should a wedding invitation be worded?" "What should I say to a friend who has just lost her father?" "What is the appropriate graduation gift to give to the son of a colleague?" The answers to these questions are not universal. They are different for different cultures. They change over time. And you may even have found that many of these "rules" are different depending on where you work or live.

Children don't need to turn to Miss Manners or Amy Vanderbilt to learn what is expected of them. Families are constantly sending children messages about what kinds of behaviors they expect of them. Some cultural traditions dictate, for example, that all toys in the household belong to all the children—even those toys that have been given to one child as a birthday gift. In other households, children may have their own bedrooms with their own belongings, over which they can dictate who can join in and who cannot. Some children are given strong messages to "stand up for their rights," using force if needed. Other children come from families that guide them to "just walk away" from the aggressive behaviors of other children.

The "Miss Manners" guidelines of your classroom may be more familiar to some children than to others. Make yourself a resource for information about the customs and traditions at school for interacting, both for the children and their families. Working and playing alongside others at school usually requires knowledge of social norms such as sharing, taking turns, and resolving disputes peacefully.

There are three critical things children need to learn to navigate the school culture:

1. waiting, taking turns, and sharing

2. conflict resolution

3. play skills

When Things Go Wrong

While children might want to work and play with their peers, many of them lack the basic skills that LaVita and Daniel possess. Collaboration is not inborn. The desire to have a friend and be a friend may be inborn, but the skills needed to execute this desire are learned. When children don't know how to wait, take turns, and share space and things; resolve conflicts; or enter and exit play, the result is often chaos. Do the following scenarios sound familiar to you?

> Nicholas had been looking forward all morning to getting into the dress-up collection and putting on the new firefighter hat and gigantic boots. As soon as morning meeting was over, he headed straight to the dramatic play area and saw Lily had gotten there first. She was already decked out in the new props.
>
> Saying, "Ha, ha!" Nicholas snatched the hat off Lily's head, put it on his own head, and ran off to find the big fire truck from the block area.
>
> Lily ran to the teacher to ask for help. The teacher was busy getting snack ready and told Lily to tell Nicholas to give the hat back. Lily told Nicholas that the teacher said to give back the hat. When Nicholas ignored her, she tried to grab the hat back. In a moment they were on the floor hitting each other and yelling for help.
>
> Seeing the chaos, the teacher came over and took the hat. "If you two can't figure out how to play nicely together, nobody gets to use the hat," she said, putting the hat in the closet. "Go find something else to do," she told the kids.

Unfortunately, the teacher missed a couple of teachable moments when she could have helped Nicholas learn how to wait a turn and helped both children learn how to resolve conflicts peacefully.

Madeline finished snack and decided to go to the block area to build a dog hospital. Plopping herself down in the middle of the action, she began to work.

"Hey, Madeline. Quit taking those. Me and Ryan and Jacob are building a car wash. Move over," Terell complained.

"I can play if I want," said Madeline as she took another few blocks from Ryan's pile.

"You need to move over. You're breaking it with your feet," he answered, as he pushed her feet away.

Angry, Madeline kicked out and purposefully knocked down their whole structure. Jacob picked up a block and threw it at Madeline while the other boys ran off to get a teacher.

Although Madeline was right that the class materials were community property, she had no idea how to enter play peacefully. Instead of negotiating her way into the block scenario, she disrupted the ongoing activity, resulting in chaos.

Children who learn how to share and take turns and who begin to internalize that others have feelings and needs move more smoothly through their daily lives at school than children who haven't yet learned these skills. Observe challenging children to see if they demonstrate these skills as they move throughout their classroom day. Identify missing friendship skills and mistaken behavior. Help relieve your problems and theirs by integrating a host of strategies into the daily program that model, coach, and teach the friendship skills, norms, and customs children need to collaborate and move successfully through the school day.

Help Children Learn to Wait, Take Turns, and Share

People live and work together most peacefully and productively when they know how to share resources fairly. Often this involves waiting (standing in line at a movie theater), taking turns (negotiating a four-way stop intersection), and distributing resources equitably (splitting a pizza among friends). When children don't yet have these skills, we often see escalating behavior such as yelling, grabbing, hitting, pushing, and tantrums. Use some of the following ideas to teach children to wait for a short time, take turns, and share resources.

Supportive Interactions to Help Children Wait, Take Turns, and Share

As children begin to play with others at school, they need to learn the skills of taking turns and sharing. Some children in your group probably come from homes where sharing is a natural part of home life. Others, however, may struggle a bit with sharing space or materials with others. It is even harder for these children to share if they are already using the materials in question. However it is that you want children to behave, make sure you model that behavior in your interactions with them.

Model Waiting, Taking Turns, and Sharing

As you play with children, remember that they see and hear everything you do. If Daija grabs markers with both hands and plops them on her paper, and we react by grabbing them back and saying sharply, "You can't take all the markers. Put those back!" we have just modeled that grabbing and harsh words are appropriate strategies in the classroom. Instead, if we say, "Daija, I want to share the markers too. Please put them in the middle so I can share them with you," we have demonstrated an alternative way that our class should handle conflict. Which method would you like to see the kids use? Look for opportunities to teach the language of sharing and taking turns as you play with children. Make comments like these:

"Jeremiah, can I use the glue bottle when you are done?"

"My turn?"

"Let's play My Turn, Your Turn."

"Can I have it when you're done?"

"Let's play blocks together."

"Let's play two-people water table."

Support Waiting, Taking Turns, and Sharing through the Classroom Culture

For some of the children in your group, sharing is an integral part of their family and community culture. In these families, there isn't an emphasis on ownership and personal property. A toy given to one child in the family becomes community property in the household. For these children, the transition to a classroom full of community property might be a relatively easy concept. However, because all toys are communal, they may be less familiar with the idea of having to wait or take turns. Other children may come from families in which children can make decisions about who can use their personal belongings and when. They may be taught that if they are using something first, such as a video game that belongs to everyone in the house, they don't have to share with other children in the group. In effect, the child who is using it has temporary ownership. These children may be used to the idea of waiting or taking turns, but may be less familiar with the concept of community property.

When there are conflicts between your expectations at school and the expectations at home, remind children that there are often different rules for different places, just as one might wear a bathing suit for water play but not wear a bathing suit to go to sleep, for example. Help all children in the group learn school expectations of waiting for a turn, taking turns, and sharing school materials and supplies.

Use Timers

Timers can empower children and help them organize their understanding of how the world flows. Young children have little concept of how long "five more minutes" or "in a minute" are. Timers are an interesting, visual, and concrete way to introduce children to the concept of how time is measured. Try using timers along with your five-minute warning for cleaning up or to structure a child's turn at show-and-tell. There are many inexpensive timers available at local stores and discount outlets. Try the kitchen department for egg timers and kitchen timers. Timers have many advantages over the teacher keeping time:

- First, you don't have to add "timekeeper" to your already full job description.

- Children can learn how to use common timers and build an understanding of how timekeeping and taking turns works.

- Children are much less likely to argue with a timer than they are to argue with a person keeping track of time.

Use timers sparingly, however, to limit children's access to an activity. Allowing children to use a center or piece of equipment for as long as they want encourages them to get deep into their play. It's a better strategy to have the flashlights out for a week without limiting turns than to have them out for a day or two, giving each child only a three-minute turn. For sharing and taking turns with materials or areas, consider using waiting lists instead. Each child then can use the activity for as long as he likes during that session. When he is done, or when the next session begins, the next person on the list has the opportunity to use the activity.

Waiting Lists

When teachers take on the role of Timer Police, moving children in and out of activities in an attempt to let everyone have a turn, they cheat children of the opportunity to learn how to manage scarce resources on their own. Use waiting lists for popular areas, such as computers or the art easel, or for new and interesting toys added to the classroom. Waiting lists have a number of valuable advantages over teachers keeping track of turns.

- Waiting lists are concrete, visual representations of taking turns. Many children find it easier to learn visually in addition to listening to the teacher.

- Children can consult each other to figure out whose turn is next.

- Waiting lists are objective and children are less likely to dispute something in writing than they are to debate endlessly with the teacher.

- Children can eventually learn to manage waiting lists with minimal adult help. This gives them a life skill and gives the teacher extra time for more essential roles.

- Waiting lists help children develop an internal organizational vision of how taking turns works.

Here are different ways to use waiting lists, based on your teaching objectives and the children's skill levels:

- Put up a clipboard and marker. Teach children to "write" their names, one under the other, when they want a turn. It doesn't matter that some children can't make any letters. Teachers might want to keep an eye on the sheet and lightly print the child's initials next to her "signature" until they can recognize each child's typical mark. When it is the next child's turn, the teacher can cue the next child by saying, "Is this your name here? That means it's your turn."

- You can use charts with pockets or Velcro boards as waiting lists. Children put their name cards in the slot. When the child completes his turn, he puts his name card back where it belongs.

- Make photo cards for each child using a digital camera and printer. These cards are used in the same way as the name cards above.

- Put names on or attach small photos to spring-clip clothespins. Have children attach their clothespin to a piece of poster board to show that they want a turn next.

- As the children become accustomed to waiting lists, you can establish that when each child is done she looks at the list, crosses off her name (or removes her name card), and lets the next child know it's his turn. Completely teacher-free turn taking!

Talking and Listening Stick

When children are not anxious about having a turn to speak, they are more able to relax and listen to the child whose turn it is to talk. Use a talking stick or a small stuffed toy to help children learn to predict when it will be their turn to talk at group time. The predictability of when the stick will arrive helps some children with the waiting process.

1. Make a talking stick by having children decorate a small branch with paint, glitter, beads, and other decorations.

2. Explain that the stick will be passed around the circle and everyone will get a chance to talk.

3. The child who is holding the stick or the toy is the speaker. The children without the prop are the listeners.

Turn-Taking Scripts

Social scripts help everyone in the classroom communicate easily. As adults, we use social scripts in our daily interactions. For example, if you bump into somebody at the grocery store you might say, "Excuse me" or "I'm sorry." These two quick little social scripts communicate that our bump was not intentional. Children already enter your classroom with unique scripts they have learned at home. Having uniform scripts is like a common language to help children communicate meaning and intent. These scripts are also very helpful for dual language learners and some children with special needs such as autism and speech delays. Think of the turn-taking scripts below as starting points to creating your own social scripts for your classroom.

• Sometimes a child doesn't want to play with others or take turns. If it is acceptable in your program, teach children to say, "I want to play alone right now," and make sure others understand what that means.

• Children might worry that if they give somebody a turn with a toy, they might lose it for good. Teach children to say, "You can look at it if you give it right back."

• For children who grab from others to get a turn, teach language instead, such as, "Thomas is using that. Ask him for a turn. Say, 'Can I have a turn when you are done?'"

Sharing Group Supplies

Introduce the concept of sharing by having children pass out community supplies to peers. It is easier for some children to "share" things they are not currently using. Introducing sharing this way helps children get ready for cooperative play with others later. Here are some ways to apply this idea.

- Have children pass out paper or markers for a large-group activity of some sort.

- Let them help you set the table for snack or lunch by passing out plates or cups.

- Have them pass out scarves for a dancing activity.

My Space, Your Space

In most schools, teachers want children to respect the personal space and personal property of others. They encourage children to say things such as, "Don't take that, I'm using it right now" or "Move over, you're sitting too close to me." Props and visual cues help children begin to define their personal space at school and the space of others. With practice, they'll be able to define space without these cues.

Children will often come to your program with different skill sets. For children from homes that practice community rights to all space and possessions, hearing words such as "I'm playing here" and seeing teachers defending another child's play space is a new concept. Use concrete props and visual cues with those children who need prompting, and phase out those props and cues as children become more conscious of the concept of personal space.

- Use carpet squares, masking tape, or hoops on floors to define a child's personal workspace.

- Have children decorate colored construction paper. Cover the paper with contact paper to make durable sit-upons.

- Set a large appliance box on its side in the block area to make personal space for one child.

- Help children define personal space at the water table by using individual dishpans.

- At an art table, use cookie sheets to define a workspace for individual children.

- Make sure children have individual, labeled cubbies to keep a few personal belongings.

Activities to Teach Waiting, Taking Turns, and Sharing

Help children learn how to take turns by creating activities where turn taking is an essential part of the play theme. Join into the play yourself and model taking turns through your language and actions.

My Turn, Your Turn

This activity helps teach taking turns to young children.

1. Take a stack of unit blocks and sit at a small table.

2. Invite one child at a time to play with you.

3. Build a tower of blocks by taking turns adding a block to the structure.

4. As you take turns, chant "My turn, your turn," and encourage the child to join the chant. Let other children observe the play. They will learn by watching, and you will save time by not having to teach the skill to others individually.

As children become skilled at taking turns in the game, allow two children to do the activity together while you observe and continue to coach the My Turn, Your Turn chant. Eventually, children will be able to take turns without direct adult guidance. If problems develop, remind children that it is a My Turn, Your Turn activity.

Dramatic Play Themes

You already know that children learn best through play. Use your dramatic play centers to help children practice waiting and taking turns in real-life settings. Some ideas are: setting up a doctor's office with a waiting room and sign-in sheet, a bakery with number tickets, or a post office with a line where you wait for a turn at the counter. Because many children come to these activities with little experience, be sure to join in the play at first to model how the system works.

1. Sign in, take a number, or get in line.

2. Say something like, "I see there are some people ahead of me. I'm gonna have to wait till it's my turn."

3. Each time somebody's turn is done, say something like, "It's getting closer to my turn, but not yet. I still have to wait."

4. When your turn comes, show the children how you know. Say something like, "My turn. My name is next on the list" or "My turn, I'm next in line."

Teach Children How to Resolve Conflicts

Even after children have learned how to wait, take turns, and share, conflicts will come up. Conflicts between the wants and needs of two people are a normal and expected part of social interactions. Resolving conflicts with others is a very complex process. Most young children need a lot of support and guidance from adults to solve conflicts peacefully, just as many adults need the help from small-claims court to resolve their own neighborly conflicts. Your goal isn't to prevent all conflicts from happening. Instead, your goal is to teach children how to resolve their conflicts fairly and safely. The process we teach is called conflict resolution. In chapter 6, you will see a very similar process we call problem solving. In this book, the term *conflict resolution* is used to refer to disputes between two or more children. The term *problem solving* used in chapter 6 refers to problems such as losing a personal item, being overwhelmed with all the dress-up clothes that need to be put away, or not being tired at rest time. While the processes are very similar, you will also notice some differences in the way the teacher walks children through each process.

"You hurt me, so I'll hurt you" is common playground logic. Retaliation works on the belief that if a child can make the offender feel bad enough, he himself will feel better and the offender might shape up. Do you recognize any of these examples?

- Na'Quan bit Manuel on the arm, hard enough to leave marks. "He got paint on my paper on purpose," he said through his sobs as he tried to explain his biting to the teacher.

- "You can't come to my birthday," Arial spat out at Shastina after she refused to share the stickers. "And you're not my friend anymore. Lilly's my best friend now, and you can't play with us."

- "Tae'Hun knocked down my blocks so I knocked down his blocks back," Celine said to the teacher. "He did it first."

- "My daddy tell me if somebody hit me or call me names, I supposed to punch them back," said James to Mrs. Lewis.

Most young children work on the theory that in order to get others to behave and cooperate, they need to use force, threat, exclusion, and other methods of coercion.

Moving children from blame and retaliation to peaceful conflict resolution is one of the most challenging tasks facing caregivers of young children. "Go back and use your words," may work from time to time, but the skills required for resolving conflicts are very complex for young children. During the preschool years, children depend on adults to teach and facilitate the process.

Teachers set the stage for the development of conflict-resolution skills by the way they themselves approach everyday problems.

Interactions to Support Conflict Resolution

Conflict resolution is a step-by-step interaction between the two people having a difference of opinion. It is based on the premise that neither person is right or wrong and there are two sides to the story. Through the process, each person has a chance to communicate his or her point of view and be heard by the other person. Once there is an understanding of everyone's needs and wants, it is easier to come up with solutions that work for everyone—truly a skill for life. Conflict resolution for children consists of five steps.

1. Calming down
2. Talking about what they need and listening to what their playmate needs
3. Understanding the conflict
4. Thinking about and trying ways to solve the conflict
5. Going back to resolve the conflict again if the first solution doesn't work

Help Children Calm Down

Kids might be so emotionally charged that they can't even begin to engage in the conflict-resolution process. Before they can start, they need to move from their emotional state to a thinking state.

When faced with a conflict, children may feel fear, anxiety, frustration, disappointment, or hurt. They may immediately become defensive or argumentative, certain that their perspective is the "right" perspective. Conflict resolution is a thinking process involving the cerebral cortex portion of the brain. When children are in this highly charged emotional state, the thinking part of the brain goes on vacation while the "emotional brain" takes charge. The first step in conflict resolution, then, is to use emotional-regulation skills to move from an emotionally charged state of mind to a thinking state of mind. Until children are proficient at these skills, they need a lot of support from adults to calm themselves down enough to begin to think about what caused the conflicts and how things can be resolved.

Help children regain control by acknowledging that there is a conflict and suggesting a strategy to calm emotions. Keep your comments neutral. Assigning blame at this point in the process is only sure to escalate emotions.

Neutral statement	Biased statement
"Wow, it sounds like two children are very upset about something. Let's stop for a minute so we can all hear what the conflict is all about."	"It sounds like you're upset that Benjamin took the stethoscope you were using."
"Whoa. It sounds like we have a conflict here. We'll fix this so it works for everyone. First, let's do some STAR breathing. Stop, Take a Deep Breath, and Relax."	"I see that Angel isn't letting you have any space to work."

(continued on next page)

Neutral statement	Biased statement
"Uh-oh. It looks like we have a conflict about feeding Fishy. Let's all get a drink of water and then we can figure things out."	"Whoa. It sounds like it was Amie's turn to feed Fishy but Ricardo pulled the food away from her. Let's all get a drink of water and then we can figure things out."

When children feel heard, they often calm down enough to move on to the next step.

Refer back to the chapter on self-regulation (page 99) for more language and approaches to help children settle their emotions and move into an internally organized state of mind.

Help Children Say What They Need and Want

The next step is to give each child a chance to figure out and express what it is that he or she wants. This is not a very easy task for children, or for adults. Children will want to give you the whole story about what happened—who was there, how it all started, what happened next, who said what to whom. This venting is part of the process. Let children talk until they wind down. And then ask the critical question: "What is it that you want?" When the child has told you the need or want, reword it if necessary to keep it focused on what the child wants, not on what happened earlier.

What the child says . . .	How you reframe it . . .
"I want Pia to give me my book back."	"So you want the book, is that right?"
"I want Frederick to give me a turn at the computer."	"You want to use the computer, is that right?"
"I want to set the table all by myself. I don't want to do it with Leah."	"You want to set the table by yourself. Is that what you said?"

Don't engage the child in conversation during the venting process. It will only extend the process and may escalate emotions again. Simply listen, nod your head, and say an occasional "I see" or "Uh-huh." The goal at the end of this step is to have a simple need/want statement from each child.

Help Define the Conflict

Even when children can state what they want and need, young kids often have trouble defining conflicts. Defining a conflict requires seeing two sides to the story, and when young children are in the midst of a conflict, it can be challenging for them to see the world through the eyes of another person. They can only see a conflict from their point of view. It's often up to adults to look at the clues and make their best guess as to what the conflict is really about. Once you have gotten a clear "want statement" from each child, it should be relatively simple to turn it into a neutral problem statement. Most of the time it will work to start your sentence with the words "Two kids both want . . ."

The clues	The conflict is . . .
Gabriel is arguing with Kyrha over who will use the wagon. Each one says that they want to use the wagon.	Two kids want to use the same wagon.
Tyreck and Caden jostle with each other so they can better see the new rat. Each one says they want to see the rat.	Two kids both want to see the rat.
Daniel is using the red beads and LaVita moves the beads to her side of the table. Each one says they want to use the beads.	Two kids want to use the same beads.

Notice that in each case the conflict is defined in neutral language that doesn't make assumptions about who is at fault or invalidate children's strong feelings. Good problem statements avoid implying fault or blame. For example, "two kids want the same beads" is a neutral problem statement whereas "LaVita took the beads that Daniel was using" implies that LaVita is to blame for the conflict. Check with the children to get agreement that the neutral problem statement reflects their feelings. For example, say, "So, the problem is that two kids both want to use the same beads. Is that right?"

Help Children Find Resolutions

A good way to prompt the children to begin to think of solutions is to say something like, "What can we do when two kids both want . . . (to use the same beads, to water the garden, to wash the paintbrushes)?" Until the children become accustomed to solving problems, you may need to continue prompting them.

- What are you going to do?
- Tell me some ideas.
- How could you solve this conflict?
- What could you do now that is helpful?
- What could you do to resolve your conflict?

Help children begin to brainstorm possible solutions. First graders and older children usually like to generate a long list of possible solutions before moving on to the next step of choosing the solution. However, younger kids do much better when we combine the two steps. With preschoolers and kindergartners, evaluate each solution together and decide whether to try it. If the solution is discarded for some reason, think up another solution.

Sometimes children might not come up with possible solutions. For some children, it's because they are new at the skill. Others are used to having adults solve things, and they are just waiting for the answer to be given to them. And still others have learned to avoid taking responsibility by letting adults take on the entire burden. As tempting as it is to jump in, save time, and solve the conflict yourself, control your impulses. Children will only learn the process by stretching and practicing.

If . . .	Try . . .	Sounds like . . .
The child is very new at brainstorming solutions.	Suggest one or more solutions, such as sharing, taking turns, or finding duplicate items.	Instead of saying, "You can find more markers or put your name on a waiting list," think of saying, "Some children decide to find more markers on the shelf and some children like to put their name on a waiting list." Using this format helps children think of solutions without the teacher taking control of the process.
The child has had ample experience brainstorming solutions.	Encourage the child to find a peer to help.	"Would you like to find another friend to help you think?" "Who might know?" "Who can you ask?"
	Help the child break through his or her block.	"Pretend you're a kid who has an idea. What would you say?"

Some common solutions to young children's conflicts include sharing, trading, waiting, getting a duplicate item, leaving, finding something else to do, getting adult help, making amends, and fixing what went wrong. As children become more familiar with the process, you'll probably find they are amazingly inventive and often think of solutions far out of the ordinary that work out just fine. For example, two children might decide they will both wash the baby doll at the same time, one washing the head end while the other washes the feet end. If both children agree, be willing to try it out.

Evaluate the Solution

Some solutions work and some don't. When they do, give children descriptive feedback to focus their attention on how the process worked. For example, say, "Ricardo shook the food into Amie's hand, and Amie dropped it into the water. You came up with a good solution."

When a solution doesn't work, simply guide the children through the process again. "You decided that LaVita would wait for Daniel to be done with the red beads. But LaVita has been waiting, and Daniel isn't done yet. Hmm. Two kids want to use the beads. What else could you try?"

Is It Fair?

Only the kids know the answer to this question. Be wary of deciding that a proposed solution isn't fair until you hear what the children think of it. For example, suppose that Ella took the red truck from Ivan, who was playing with it. In the conflict-resolution session, Ella might propose that she gets to play with the truck as a solution. This might not seem fair to an adult, since Ella took the truck from Ivan to start with. But we don't know what Ivan's truth is. He might have been done with the truck or not care very much about playing with it. He might be willing to let Ella have it once he feels that justice has been served through the conflict-resolution process. If Ivan says he doesn't want to let go of the truck, then the adult can support him and Ella in finding another solution. But if Ivan is happy with Ella's solution, it's not up to the adult to decide it isn't fair.

What if you are concerned Ivan is afraid of speaking out to Ella, that he really wants the truck but will concede just to keep the peace? Of course you can coach Ivan to use assertive language with Ella (see previous sections). But in the end, Ivan is the only one who can decide when something is worth asserting himself. If adults decide for him, he might never come to the point of saying no or of asking for what he wants. If the class models assertion and conflict resolution over and over, eventually children like Ivan find their own voices.

Conflict Resolution in Action

1. **Calm down.** Allow each child to briefly talk and be heard about the issues so they can move from their emotional state to their thinking state. Listen but don't get involved in the backstory. End this exchange by saying, "What is it that you want?" Here is a sample script:

Mr. R:	Okay, you guys. It looks like we have a conflict here. Shanae, you talk first and then Tre'vone, it will be your turn.
Shanae:	I was doing the computer game and I was winning, and Tre'vone came over and he pulled me and made me lose.

2. **Help children express their needs and wants.** During this part of the conflict-resolution process, don't focus on what happened. Instead, focus on what will happen next.

Mr. R:	Uh-huh. So what do you want?
Shanae:	Tre'vone needs to go away and leave me alone.
Mr. R:	Okay. Tre'vone, tell me what's going on.

Tre'vone: Yesterday you told me I could do computer after circle and I was supposed to do it, and she sat down fast and started to play and it's my turn so I made her stop.

Mr. R: Okay. So what is that that you want now?

Tre'vone: I want to do my turn.

3. **Define the conflict.** Form a neutral problem statement based on what both kids want or need.

Mr. R: So, it looks like two kids both want to have a turn at the computer now. Is that right?

Tre'vone: It's my turn.

Shanae: I was using it first.

Mr. R: So two kids both think it's their turn. Is that right?

(The children agree.)

Mr. R: So let's work together to resolve this so everyone is okay. Remember, at school we take care of each other and we take care of ourselves [two of their classroom-guiding principles of behavior], so we need to make sure that this works out for both of you.

4. **Brainstorm resolutions and predict the consequences.** As each child comes up with potential solutions, have each ask the other child if that solution would work. You can guide this conversation by saying something like, "Ask (other child) if that will work for (him/her)." Resist the urge to involve yourself in the exchange. The goal is to facilitate the conversation *between* the two children involved. If one of the children has a language delay or speaks a different language than the other, you may need to do a bit of translation. Think of saying something like, "Brandy is saying, 'Let's use the timer.' Tell him if that's okay with you."

Mr. R: I wonder what you guys can think of that we can do now.

Shanae: He needs to let me finish first.

Mr. R: Ask Tre'vone if that would be all right.

Shanae: Let me finish, okay?

Tre'vone: No. You'll use all the time and I won't get a turn, and Mr. R said I could do it today.

Mr. R: Nope, that idea won't work for Tre'vone. Let's think of another idea.

Tre'vone: (*To Shanae*) Let me go first, then you can have it back tomorrow.

Shanae: No. I was going first. You use it too long, and I never get a turn.

Mr. R: Nope, that's not okay with Shanae. Let's keep thinking.

Shanae: (*Folding her arms*) Tre'vone won't let me do my turn. He never lets anybody do computer except him.

Mr. R: We'll keep thinking until we find something that works for everybody. You know, a few years ago some kids had a conflict like this. And they decided to use the timer from the cooking center so both of them had time that day.

Shanae: We could use the timer.

Mr. R: Ask Tre'vone if that would be okay.

Shanae: Tre'vone, we could use the timer and then we both could have a turn.

Tre'vone: Okay. But I need to go first.

(*Shanae does not respond.*)

Mr. R: Shanae, Tre'vone said the timer would work for him if he can go first. He's waiting to see if that is okay with you.

Shanae: Okay, but I need to get a turn too.

Mr. R: So, you guys will get the timer and each take a turn this morning. Do you need my help to figure out how much time to set?

Shanae: Yeah. You make sure I get time too.

Mr. R: Okay with you, Tre'vone?

Tre'vone: Yeah. I wanna go now. She can do the timer.

Mr. R: You guys figured out how to solve the conflict. You took care of yourselves and you took care of each other.

(*Mr. R and Shanae go off to take care of the timer while Tre'vone goes to the computer to start his turn.*)

5. **Follow up.** Check back to see if the resolution worked. If it did, congratulate the children. If not, repeat the resolution process.

Mr. R: I see you each got a turn on the computer. Your idea of using a timer worked for you!

or

Mr. R: Uh-oh. I see the timer didn't help you both get what you wanted. Let's figure something else out.

Not every classroom conflict calls for conflict resolution. Perhaps you saw one child push another out of the way at the swings. There's nothing wrong with moving in and resolving the issue then and there.

The biggest reason for using conflict resolution is to help children learn how to do the process. Use conflict resolution during teachable moments of the day when you have the time and space to do so. The easiest and best conflicts to practice on are conflicts over space and stuff. For example, two children both want to use the yellow bucket or two children both want to be the line leader at the door.

Use conflict resolution when . . .	Don't use conflict resolution when . . .
You don't care how it gets solved.	You want the situation resolved your way.
You have space and time to work through the process.	You are rushed or too busy with other things.
Children are using the "thinking part" of their brains.	Children are in an emotionally charged state.

Demonstrate Conflict-Resolution Attitudes

Convey your belief that conflicts can be resolved. Help children stay mindful of expectations and limits of acceptable behavior. As you interact with children, make sure to model and use all the skills needed for conflict resolution often. Help children develop a conflict-resolution attitude by modeling that

- conflicts can be resolved;

- nobody is all wrong or all right;

- the goal is to figure out what's going to happen next, instead of assigning responsibility for what already happened; and

- a conflict is only solved when the solution works for everyone.

Here's an example of how a teacher might model a positive conflict-resolution approach. Imagine that there have been ongoing conflicts in the block area since the new first-responder figures have been added to the area. In their attempts to use this newly revitalized area, children are accidentally knocking down each other's creations and are complaining that they have no room.

In this case, some teachers might be tempted to say something like, "Okay. We're closing down the block area for the rest of the day. There is just too much fighting in here today." Look now at how a teacher might instead model essential conflict-resolution attitudes.

Conflict-resolution attitude	How to model
Conflicts can be resolved.	"Uh-oh. The block area is so crowded it looks like you are having trouble working. Let's find a way to solve this conflict."
Nobody is all wrong or all right.	"Nobody is doing anything wrong. We just have a conflict we need to resolve."
Figure out what's going to happen next; don't assign responsibility for what already happened.	"Let's look at what we can do so everybody has room to work."
The solution needs to work for everyone.	"How about we move this shelf over so we can find room for everyone. Does that work for all of you?"

Supporting Conflict Resolution in the Classroom Culture

Make the use of conflict resolution one of the foundations of your classroom culture. Invite children to come to you for help in resolving their conflicts with other children if they aren't able to do it themselves. Establish a classroom atmosphere in which both children and adults are encouraged to express their needs and set limits. Provide visual and kinesthetic cues that emphasize the classroom value of conflict resolution by setting up a small area clearly dedicated to that purpose.

Invite Children to Come to You for Help with Conflicts

As teachers, we seem much more accepting of children coming to us for help with their own conflicts than when they report conflicts happening with other children. When they tell us about things in which they aren't personally involved, we often call it "tattling"—a word with a negative connotation. Sometimes teachers object to children reporting what they see because they worry that the "tattler" is just trying to get somebody in trouble. They might respond with, "Just take care of your own self" or "If it has nothing to do with you, then please don't tell me."

Preschool-aged children are very curious about rules and what they mean. They often remind themselves and others about the rules. "Hey! You're not allowed to put your hand in the fish tank. The teacher said." For young children, rules are black and white. Asking a young child to make judgments on when it is or is not appropriate to report infractions is asking quite a bit. I'd much rather encourage children to look out for the welfare of themselves, others, and our environment than have them look the other way.

At the same time, we don't want to encourage children to turn in others for the sport of it. One way to encourage children to report and yet not make reporting a game of sorts is to listen respectfully and thank the child for letting you know something is amiss with no further fanfare.

If a child reports . . .	Try saying . . .
An incident in which the child is personally involved—for example, "He won't let me get on the slide."	"Do you need help solving this?" If the child says yes, you can move into conflict resolution.
An incident involving other children—for example, "Kim won't let Dallas get on the slide."	"Thank you." If the child pushes for a greater response, you might say, "I'm taking it under consideration."

If you decide to intervene, as with Kim and Dallas in the table above, avoid referring to the child who reported the incident.

Instead of saying . . .	Try saying . . .
"Kim, Dow said you won't let Dallas use the slide."	"Dallas, it looks like you're trying to use the slide. Are you having a conflict?"

Help Children Express Their Needs and Set Limits

In most preschools, teachers encourage children to speak honestly and respectfully about their thoughts, needs, and feelings. Most state early learning standards have items addressing children's ability to express their needs clearly and respectfully and to listen to others when they are talking about their own needs. We might call this assertive language.

Assertion is somewhere in the middle of a continuum that runs from passivity on one end to aggression on the other. Where children are on this spectrum may depend in large part on the kind of communication that is valued, modeled, and taught in the home. Many classroom problems can be traced to children being at different places along the assertion continuum. Although this is a continuum, for our purposes it's useful to think about three main tendencies or places along the continuum—passivity, assertion, and aggression.

Passivity

Children who use a passive approach can be exploited or bullied by children who are on the more aggressive end of the continuum. More passive children may allow more aggressive children to get their own way and might be reluctant to express opinions or preferences. For example, look back at the scenario between Daniel and LaVita over the red beads at the beginning of the chapter. Had Daniel been more passive, he might have said nothing when LaVita took the red beads, even though he wanted to continue using them.

Aggression

On the other end of the spectrum, children who use an aggressive approach frequently get into physical confrontations with others. Some teachers might describe them as all-about-me or selfish and self-centered people. Looking again at the opening scenario, had Daniel been aggressive, he might have said something like, "Quit it, you stupid. Give those back," or he might have reached over, grabbed the dish of beads from LaVita, and pinched her arm as a warning not to invade his space again.

Assertion

Assertion balances needs of self with needs of others. Daniel's response in the scenario was assertive. "Wait," he said. "I was using the red ones to make my fireman necklace with the red like the fire and the white like the smoke." When children use assertion, they state their own preferences and limits without verbal name-calling or physical aggression. Assertive children are neither aggressive toward others nor do they allow others to overrun their own rights. Help children at both ends of the spectrum develop the assertion skills they need to do well in the school environment.

Approach	Looks like/Sounds like
Passive	Just gives up and retreats. "That's okay. You can have it."
Assertive	Expresses wants and needs. Open to hearing what the other party to the conflict feels and wants. "But I want to use it too."
Aggressive	Might threaten, bribe, or use physical means to get what they want. "If you don't give it to me, I won't be your friend." Or "Gimme it."

It's as important to teach limit-setting language to children who use a passive approach as it is to help children who are more physically or psychologically aggressive. It can be difficult to avoid the trap of "rescuing" passive children. Because they don't stand up for themselves, adults often jump in to enforce passive children's rights and set boundaries for them. If Kianna grabs a doll from Geoff and Geoff allows it, a teacher who witnesses the scuffle might step in and tell Kianna to return the doll. Without support to develop assertion, children who allow others to run over them in the classroom are likely to become children who allow that in many different settings. Help passive children learn assertion to set boundaries now—teach all children how to use assertive language to state their needs, assert their rights, and set boundaries for others.

Whether a child uses aggressive or passive behavior, you can use these teachable moments to help children learn assertive responses.

When . . .	Children can say . . .
A child is allowing another child to interfere	"I don't want you to help. I'll do it myself."
A child is the object of name-calling or profanity	"I don't like those words. Stop it."
A child is being bullied	"I don't like that. I'm going to play with somebody else."
Someone is grabbing a toy from a child	"Stop it. Ask for a turn."

When you give children assertive language, you might have to tailor your response depending on how passive the child is or how fluent the child is in English. For example:

- You might say, "Did you like it when Kianna took the doll?" If John says no, say, "Go tell Kianna, 'Stop. I don't like it when you grab.'"

- You might say, "John, it's okay to tell Kianna you were still using the doll" or "John, do you need help to get the doll back?"

- If John tends to talk softly and avoid eye contact, have him rehearse his "strong voice" with you. Model and practice a firm yet respectful tone of voice and assertive body language.

- Provide your own physical support if the child needs it. Get down to John's level, put your arm around him, call Kianna, and say, "Kianna, John has something to tell you." Then say to John, "Tell her 'I was still using the doll. Give it back, please.'"

- For dual-language learners or for some children with speech delays, think of teaching very short responses such as "Stop" or "No."

Break down assertive language into baby steps. Some children need to start with very simple assertive language whereas others are ready for more complex language.

	Teach	Includes . . .	For example
First	"Stop" or "No."	A single word to set a boundary	"Stop."
Second	"I don't like that."	Expression of a feeling	"I don't like that."
Third	"I don't like it when you (behavior)."	Expression of feeling in response to the action of another	"I don't like it when you call me names."
Fourth	"I don't like it when you (behavior). I want you to (suggestion for change)," or "I don't like it when you (behavior). I'm going to (action)."	Expression of feelings, the action of another, and a suggestion for change or action	"I don't like when you call me names. I'm going to play with somebody else."

Walking away can be an assertive skill. Model it for children, and coach them how to leave a bad situation with a feeling of strength and control. Emphasize leaving as a sign of strength and wisdom, not a feeling of intimidation, defeat, weakness, or shame.

Model Assertive Language

Of course, one of the most powerful tools you have to teach assertive language and behavior is to model it yourself in your daily interactions with children.

When a child . . .	Instead of . . .	Try saying . . .
Calls you a name	Sending the child to time-out	"I don't like those words. I'm going to walk away right now."
Talks while you are trying to read a story	Saying, "That's so rude to talk while I'm reading"	"When you talk I have trouble reading. I wish you could be more quiet."
Calls another child a rude name	Saying, "Be nice"	"When you call Paloma names, I wonder what you are trying to say. Let's see what's wrong and find another way to say that."
Grabs a toy from another child	Grabbing the toy back and returning it to the child	"I don't like it when you grab toys. We take care of people in our classroom. I want you to give the squirter back to Dana."

Conflict-Resolution Center

A conflict-resolution center in the classroom is visual and concrete evidence that talking things out and respectfully listening to the views of others is valued.

The requirements for a conflict-resolution center are few. It might be a small table with two chairs or a corner with a beanbag chair. The wall might have photos or drawings of children talking out their differences. Most conflict-resolution centers also have pictures and words to help guide the process. One example is the chart below. Note how the conflict-resolution steps from earlier in this chapter have been reworded into more child-friendly language. The language is simpler, but the steps are the same.

Conflict-Resolution Steps
1. Take a deep breath.
2. What do I want? What do you want?
3. What can we do?
4. What did we decide?
5. How did it work?

Conflict-Resolution Activities

As the children in your group become fluent in the conflict-resolution process, you can add these strategies to decrease children's reliance on you to facilitate the entire process.

Peer Mediators

Once the group has learned the conflict-resolution method, children can learn to be peer mediators. Even children as young as four years old can guide their classroom peers through the process. It is helpful to have a conflict-resolution center or table set up when using peer mediators, because the environmental cues help keep the children on track.

1. If a child wants the job as a peer mediator, let her join you for a few conflict resolutions with other children and coach her through the mediator process.

2. When a simple conflict comes up between two children and you are too busy to facilitate, ask the children involved if they would like a peer mediator to help.

3. Have the three children go to the conflict-resolution center to work on the issue. Most four-year-old peer mediators use a rather free-flowing facilitation style, which is fine.

4. If the children still can't resolve the conflict, make an appointment with them to help out as soon as you have a moment. If they do resolve the conflict, congratulate the three children for their productive work.

Solution Wheel

A solution wheel is a quick reminder of some generic solutions to conflicts.

1. Draw a large circle on a piece of paper and divide it into eight pie sections.

2. In each section, write down one generic technique used to solve young children's conflicts. Here are some ideas you might use: share, trade, get another one, wait for a turn, play something else, fix what you broke, say "I'm sorry," or go to the conflict-resolution table to solve it.

3. You might remind kids of this resource when they come to you with a conflict, and have them choose a solution from it.

Some teachers make small copies of the circle and glue it on poster board cards with a spinner. The kids are then invited to spin the spinner to find a possible solution to their conflict. Some teachers let children spin the wheel over and over until it lands on a choice the child wants. Others just let the child choose from the available choices.

Support Developing Play Skills

Moving from working and playing with one friend to working with a small group of children is no small task. The friendship skills required to navigate multiple relationships at once can be challenging. Even when children have the skills to wait, share, take turns, and resolve conflicts, they still might have trouble negotiating the world of play with others.

In order to work and play well with others, children need to figure out how to join ongoing play without disrupting the action, how to leave play when they are finished, and how to be an active participant in large-group activities.

Start children on a happy path to negotiating their social worlds, working with them to learn the skills of negotiating play with others in small and large groups.

Entering Play

Think of that very high-achieving, bright, and accomplished adult you might know who just can't seem to go with the flow at a staff meeting. As wonderful as she might be, she just can't seem to join into a chat in the break room without barging in and disrupting the ongoing conversation. Think of yourself sitting and sharing an intimate lunch with a close friend. Suddenly, a mutual acquaintance comes to the table and asks if she can join you. Do you sometimes feel like Little Johnny who says, "Go away. We're busy"? Clearly, the dynamics of a group of three or four people is quite different than what goes on between two close friends. And so it is with children.

Learning how to smoothly enter an ongoing activity is a challenge for many preschool children just as it is for some adults. Mia sees some children building a tall structure in the block area. If she doesn't yet have the skills and language to join in the play, what might she do? How might she attempt to join in? Most likely, she will knock down the tower, push in, or grab blocks. It's not enough to tell her, "Go over there and use your words." Many children haven't yet learned the words to say. If she knew them, she probably would have used them.

As you play with children, model scripts and skills they need to join in ongoing play with others. Here are some of the most useful strategies:

- Ask "How can I play?"
- Model how to join the play theme.
- Decode play sequences.
- Invent play themes.
- Make three-step play sequence books.
- Help children reject play requests graciously.

Ask "How Can I Play?"

A useful beginning script to enter play is "How can I play?" The chance of a child being excluded is less likely when a child asks *how* rather than "Can I play?" "How can I play?" invites the other children to be creative and come up with a way to integrate the new child. This is especially likely to happen if you have modeled appropriate responses to "How can I play?" in your own play with children.

When you are teaching a child how to integrate himself into ongoing play, invite the child to come with you as you model the words and strategies.

1. Invite the child to join you as you enter the play. For example, invite Angel to come with you to help with the block structure that a few other kids are building.

2. Say to the children already there, "Hi. How can we play?"

Model How to Join the Play Theme

Successful players join into ongoing play themes. They watch the action for a moment, figure out a role for themselves, and often just blend into the action without asking or receiving invitations. Whenever you model how to join ongoing play, help the child figure out how to join in rather than changing the play theme. Don't go into a group that is playing doctor and suggest that they play bathing babies!

1. Invite the child to come with you as you attempt to join ongoing play.

2. Talk aloud to the child as you observe and figure out what is going on in the ongoing play. You might say something like, "Hmm. It looks like they are building something tall with the blocks. Let me listen to what they are saying. Ah, Yvette just said that it has to be tall enough to fly to the moon. I bet they're building a spaceship. What do you think?"

3. You might model how to ask the group if you can use your idea of how to play. For example, say, "I'm gonna get all the big blocks for you, okay?" or "I'm gonna build a road that goes to your spaceship."

4. Another approach is to just figure out an appropriate role and join in without asking. For example, say, "Ezekial, how about we help bring over more blocks for Yvette to stack up."

Decode Play Sequences

Groups of children who play together on a regular basis establish informal rules for how play works. We call these loose patterns "play sequences." These play sequences form a kind of social script.

Here's an example of a play sequence, and a child who hasn't picked up on it yet. Jake and Eric are playing car and garage in the block area again.

Earlier this year, a few of the children in the class invented a game, and it has been very popular for weeks. They made some ramps and are using one of the rectangle blocks as a garage door that they swing open and closed as they drive cars in and out.

Damiano is new to the class. He's been watching the play. He loves to play cars and moves over to where the other two are playing. Damiano picks up a truck and starts to crash it into the block structure.

"We're playing garage," says Jake. "Don't crash it down."

Damiano has never played garage before. His previous experiences playing with toy cars have been to crash them into things. He continues to smash his car into the structure.

"Get out of here, Damiano," Eric says. "Teacher, teacher, Damiano is wrecking our game."

The teacher comes over. "Damiano, you have to play nice in the blocks or you need to choose another area to play."

Damiano's face falls. He throws down the car and storms off, kicking the blocks as he leaves.

Damiano entered the situation feeling like a part of the classroom community. He had the desire to enter the play, but lacked the knowledge about how to "play garage." Doing the best he knew how with the play themes he had, he failed at his attempt to join in. What Damiano needed at that moment was a perceptive teacher to note the play theme he was missing. The teacher could have then sat for a moment to teach him how to "play garage" or could have guided one of the other children to model the play for Damiano. Armed with this knowledge, Damiano might have been able to join into the ongoing play, strengthening his feelings of belonging at the same time. Instead, the situation ended with Damiano doubting his connection to the group and still lacking the play theme he needed to enter the play next time.

When children avoid play with others or are unsuccessful at play with others, observe carefully to see if they need some instruction on common play themes or language. Always keep in mind that a major goal for a challenging child is to help him become a member of the class community more and more every day. Be wary of any strategy or intervention that allows that child to drift further from the others.

Invent Play Themes

Some children might come to your class with very limited play skills. To play successfully with each other, children need some basic, compatible play themes. A child who has come from a harsh or abusive home life might not understand the nurturing play of other "mommies" and "daddies" in the home-living area. Her idea of play might be to fling kitchen items against the wall while shouting, "Shut up or I'll punch you." She might treat the baby dolls roughly or punitively and use profanity with them. Teachers might find this play offensive, and peers might be frightened by what they are seeing and hearing. Other children may have various disabilities that hinder them from making sense of complex or rapid moving play.

Begin to teach these children more successful play themes with teacher-invented scenarios. Make sure these games include very scripted and clear guidelines for interaction. Include some sharing and taking turns. When children participate in teacher-invented games, they don't have to figure out what to do. Everything is predictable and nothing needs to be invented. Children who find success in these very prescribed "games" gain a sense of social competence that carries over into the rest of the program day. Create simple play themes, and teach them to all the children in the group. For example, you might invent a game called Car Wash.

1. Invite children to the block center to play Car Wash with you.

2. Work together with the children to build a car wash building out of blocks.

3. Model the play by taking a car and driving it through a "muddy" area, saying something such as, "Oh no. My car is full of mud. I need to go to the car wash!" Drive your car to the structure, pretend to spray water on the car (with all the sound effects, of course), and as you drive out of the wash say something like, "All clean."

4. Drive your car through the muddy area again and get your car dirty. Repeat the sequence.

5. Other children will pick up cars of their own to follow in your play. Some children more skilled at play might suggest that they take on the role of "washing lady." Others might modify the scripts. However, the basic theme of the play should stay consistent. Nonverbal children can follow the play sequence without talking, while children learning English can pick up basic language patterns such as "oh no" and "all clean."

Other ideas for teacher-invented play themes are post office, doctor's office, feeding the baby, shopping, shoe store, and cooking supper. Consider using the bike area outdoors for play themes like car wash. Use your climbing structure for themes such as Fire Rescue or Save the Cat in the Tree. Whatever the theme, keep it simple and make sure to include some basic scripts. Three steps are enough. When children lose interest in the play theme after a few days or a few weeks, invent another. Continue creating these simple themes for as long as you have some children in your group relying on them as a way to play with others.

Make Three-Step Play Sequence Books

Children learn some games like Duck-Duck-Goose from older children and adults. Other games just seem to evolve naturally and vary depending on the group. For instance, a group of children might invent a game of Daddy-Baby. The routine might include changing the diaper, feeding the baby, and then putting the baby in the shopping cart to go shopping. You might see these invented games anywhere in the program. On the swings, they might be "pumping to the sky." At the water table, children might be "making tornadoes."

Observe challenging children over a period of play sessions to determine if they understand the basic play routines that other children have established. Often when children have trouble figuring out the established play themes, trouble breaks out. Children playing "tornadoes" might physically or verbally push out a child who is not "playing right." They might say things like, "Logan can't play with us. He's stupid."

When you identify a child having trouble figuring out the play sequences, help children understand ongoing play themes with "Three-Step Play Sequence" books.

1. Make a blank book with a front cover and three blank pages.

2. Observe the children at play and figure out the three main steps. Look for the trigger, the action, and the closure. For example, in one class, ambulance play looked like this:

    -   Trigger—"Help, help!" calls one child.

    -   Action—Ambulance players run to the child and give aid.

    -   Closure—"All done. We fixed her," says one of the ambulance people.

3. Help your target child integrate into the existing play. Take photos of that child for each of the three steps. Mount the photos in the book. On each page, print the simple step. On the cover, put the name of the play, such as "Ambulance." This book, for example, might say, "Help, help!" under the picture on the first page. The second page might say, "Run and help the kid." The third page might say, "All done. We fixed her."

4. Teach the child how to play by reading and rereading the book as often as the child wants. Keep the book in the class library for all the children to read.

Help Children Reject Play Requests Graciously

As children move from playing alone to playing with others, there will be times when they still want to work or play alone. Often children will say things such as "You're not our friend," "Go away," or "We don't like her, do we?" when a new child attempts to join the play.

One thing you will have to clarify for yourself and your program is your policy about whether or not children can from time to time exclude others from their play. For example, if two children are "making lunch" at the sand table, is it okay for them to tell another child who tries to join the play that he can't right now? Or if three children are in the home-living area playing doctor, can they tell another child who tries to join in that there is no room for her?

If you do decide that there are times and places where a child might exclude others from play, give them the language they need to graciously reject the request. Here are two suggestions: "Not now, maybe later" or "No thanks." When you teach this script, make sure you also let children know that it is all right for children to want to work by themselves sometimes. It isn't meant to be a permanent rejection of friendship.

Exiting Play

Children who don't know the language to exit play might decide to throw toys or tear down the work of other children when they are done playing. As you play with them, model a simple two-step routine:

1. Put the toys down.
2. Say "Bye" or "I'm done" (optional) and walk away.

Young children need nothing more complex than this.

Working and Playing in Larger Groups

Adults have a unique role when they participate in large-group play with children. When children participate in parallel play, dyad play, or play in small groups, adults can most often allow the children to lead the play. They can sit back to model participation and gently coach children who need help with their play skills. Larger groups are different. Because most preschool children are very unskilled at managing large groups, it falls to the teacher to be the leader of the group as well as being a participant. As the leader of the group activity, you will decide the purpose of gathering the group together, you will guide assigning roles to the children, and you will keep gently directing children back to the activity at hand.

For example, think of joining a small group in the block area. If during ongoing play one of the children proposes tearing down the castle and building a farm instead and the others agree, the agenda can quickly change. Your role in that play would be to act as one of the child participants to model appropriate negotiation and compromise skills. On the other hand, think about one of the large-group activities you might be leading. Your role in that activity would lean more toward keeping the group on task to follow the existing agenda. Do you see the difference? In the first instance you are a participant, while in the second, you have the added responsibility of being the group leader. Even in those cases when you might have individual children lead parts of a large-group activity, they are acting in an apprentice role under your direct guidance and supervision. Here are some ways to be an effective role model and leader for large-group activities:

1. Make sure the agenda or plan is clearly communicated to the group.
2. Ensure that every group member is included in the activity, and accommodate any special needs individuals might have.
3. Gently redirect individuals back to the task at hand when the group strays too far off course.
4. Recognize each individual's contribution to the group effort.

Here's an example. Perhaps you are in a setting where all the children will move as a group from the classroom to the school library. As the leader of this large-group activity, you might want to take these steps:

1. Make sure the plan is clearly communicated: Say something such as, "We are all going to go to see Ms. Alexander in the library now so she can read us a new book about bugs. Remember, at school we need to walk down the hallway in a quiet line. Justin, you are line leader so you can go to the front of the line."

2. Ensure that every group member is included and accommodate any special needs: Integrate other children individually or in small groups. For example, "If your name starts with the letter B you can get in line. If you are wearing red pants you can get in line." If Priscilla and Austin have trouble walking down the hallway quietly in line, invite them to join you or another adult, or assign them a special job. "Priscilla and Austin, please come to the front of the line and help carry the book bin back to the library for us."

3. Gently redirect children as necessary: Remember what we learned from Vygotsky in the chapter on emotional skills about how we can scaffold children's abilities to control themselves using dramatic play. For example, if the children are getting too noisy, stop and whisper in an exaggerated manner something like, "Let's see if we can be so quiet that even the little mice can't hear us. Can you move your feet oh so quiet? Can you make your mouths oh so quiet? Let's see if we can get all the way to the library and not even wake up one little mouse. Let's go."

4. Recognize each child's contribution: As you enter the library, acknowledge individual children: "Justin, you led us all safely to the library. You are a good leader. Priscilla and Austin, you carried that whole box of books together down here. That was good partnership. Wanda and Freddy, you were so quiet walking down here. Mason, Luis, Jan, Tabby—you stayed right in line."

Discussion/Reflection Questions

1. Thinking about the topics we explored in this chapter—waiting, taking turns, sharing, resolving conflicts, and specific play skills—which of these skills is also important for adults in their neighborhoods and the workplace? Describe a situation when you had to work or interact with an adult who lacked these skills.

_____

_____

_____

2. Make a neutral problem statement for each of these situations. Start your statement with "It looks like two kids both . . ."

    • Johnisha and Neil are physically struggling over a book in the library center.

    _____

    _____

    _____

    • Ian comes to group time and sits next to the teacher. Wilbur approaches and tells Ian he was sitting there first but he had to wash his hands, and Pablo was saving his seat. Ian says that he's sitting there and he's not moving and that once you get up you lose your seat.

    _____

    _____

    _____

    • Maritza is absent today. Her job was to clean the guinea pig cage. Adrian decides to do Maritza's job at job time and begins to get the supplies. Meanwhile, Mychael has decided the same and tells Adrian he thought of it first. Mychael begins to open the cage to move the guinea pig to the carrier. Adrian yells for Mychael to go away because he was there first.

    _____

    _____

    _____

3. Create an original three-step play theme and introduce it to the children in your group. How did it work out? Did you find that children who normally don't play well joined into the play?

    _____

    _____

    _____

Exercises

1. Select a child who is having trouble taking turns. Every day for a week, play the My Turn, Your Turn game with him or her. When you see the child having trouble taking turns say, "Remember . . . this is a My Turn, Your Turn activity." Did you find any improvement in taking turns after using this activity?

   _____

   _____

   _____

   _____

2. Try to use the conflict-resolution process with children four or five times. Did you find it hard not to get involved in the backstory? What did you find challenging? What went well? How did the children respond?

   _____

   _____

   _____

   _____

3. Observe some of your more challenging children during free choice or outdoor time with a focus on their play skills. Did you identify any play skill challenges such as their ability to enter play or join in with existing play themes? Plan and implement a strategy to help a child build the play skills he or she needs to be successful in your classroom. What kind of effect did the new skills have on the child's ability to get along with others?

   _____

   _____

   _____

   _____

Reflection/Journal Assignment

Where are you on the passive-assertive-aggressive continuum? Do you have a consistent style, or does it vary depending on whom you are with? What impact has your style had on your professional life? Your personal life?

_____

_____

_____

_____

_____

_____

_____

_____

_____

_____

_____

_____

_____

_____

_____

_____

_____

_____

_____

_____

_____

Getting Along with Others

One of the biggest tasks for young children is learning how to work and play with the adults and other children at school. Some of the skills that children will need to do well in school are being able to share, wait for a turn, solve conflicts with each other without hitting or name-calling, use polite language, respect the rights and feelings of others, and take part in conversations.

Think About It

As a child, do you remember being reminded by your elders to share with your little sister, say thank you to the lady at the bakery who gave you a cookie, and to stop interrupting the grown-ups while they were talking? Merely by spending time with adults in society, children learn how we expect them to behave. In our busy, electronic lives, it can be a challenge to provide children with many opportunities to learn social skills from us, rather than from the media or outsiders who may not share our values.

Some Ideas

- **Family meals**—One of the best opportunities you have to help children learn many of the social skills they need to do well in school and in later life is to regularly share a family meal. A family meal can be anything from a home-cooked Sunday dinner to a take-out pizza or burger meal. What you are looking for is for everyone to sit together at the table, eating and talking together without the interruption of electronic devices such as cell phones or TVs. Even planning one family dinner a week gives you the opportunity to teach children how to take turns, chat politely, and be considerate about the needs of others. As a bonus, Dr. William Doherty from the University of Minnesota reports that children who share family meals do better in school and have less behavior problems than children who don't eat together with their families.

- **Invite a classmate**—If you think your child is having some trouble making friends at school, invite one of his or her classmates to spend an hour or two with your family when you go to the playground or an amusement park. When children share fun time together outside of school, they often become friends *at* school. As their friendship grows, think about inviting your child's friend for a sleepover!

Chapter 5 Resources

Bailey, Becky. 2000. *Conscious Discipline: Seven Basic Skills for Brain Smart Classroom Management.* Oviedo, FL: Loving Guidance.

Brooks, Robert, and Sam Goldstein. 2001. *Raising Resilient Children: Fostering Strength, Hope, and Optimism in Your Child.* Lincolnwood, IL: Contemporary Books.

Committee for Children. 2002. *Second Step: A Violence Prevention Curriculum.* Seattle: Committee for Children.

Covey, Stephen R. 1997. *The 7 Habits of Highly Effective Families: Building a Beautiful Family Culture in a Turbulent World.* New York: Golden Books.

Dinkmeyer, Don, and Gary D. McKay. 1973. *Raising a Responsible Child: Practical Steps to Successful Family Relationships.* New York: Simon and Schuster.

Fisher, Roger, and William Ury. 2011. *Getting to Yes: Negotiating an Agreement without Giving In.* 3rd ed. New York: Penguin Books.

Gestwicki, Carol. 2011. *Developmentally Appropriate Practice: Curriculum and Development in Early Education.* 4th ed. Belmont, CA: Wadsworth Cengage Learning.

Gordon, Thomas. 1970. *Parent Effectiveness Training: The Tested New Way to Raise Responsible Children.* New York: P. H. Wyden.

Hewitt, Deborah. 2012. *So This Is Normal Too?* 2nd ed. St. Paul, MN: Redleaf Press.

Koralek, Derry. 1999. *Classroom Strategies to Promote Children's Social and Emotional Development.* Lewisville, NC: Kaplan Press.

———. 1999. *For Now and Forever: A Guide for Families on Promoting Social and Emotional Development.* Lewisville, NC: Kaplan Press.

Levin, Diane E. 2003. *Teaching Young Children in Violent Times: Building a Peaceable Classroom.* 2nd ed. Cambridge, MA: Educators for Social Responsibility.

Mize, Jacquelyn, and Ellen Abell. 1996. "Encouraging Social Skills in Young Children: Tips Teachers Can Share with Parents." *Dimensions of Early Childhood* 24 (3): 15–23.

National Association for the Education of Young Children. 1988. "Ideas That Work with Young Children: Avoiding 'Me Against You' Discipline." *Young Children* 44 (1): 24–29.

Nelsen, Jane, Lynn Lott, and H. Stephen Glenn. 2000. *Positive Discipline in the Classroom: Developing Mutual Respect, Cooperation, and Responsibility in Your Classroom,* 3rd ed. Roseville, CA: Prima Publishing.

Saifer, Steffen. 2003. *Practical Solutions to Practically Every Problem: The Early Childhood Teacher's Manual,* revised ed. St. Paul, MN: Redleaf Press

Whelan, Mary Steiner. 2000. *But They Spit, Scratch, and Swear! The Do's and Don'ts of Behavior Guidance with School-Age Children.* Minneapolis: A-ha! Communications.

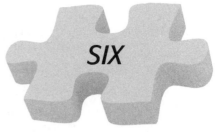

SIX

Contribution

I have a responsibility to myself and others.

Schools have always focused on helping children develop their talents and skills. However, we are now becoming increasingly aware of the need to guide children to use their talents and skills wisely and for the good of themselves, their families, their communities, and the larger world. The following examples from Head Start, Kentucky, Arizona, Oklahoma, North Dakota, and Louisiana highlight some of the components of the skill we call *contribution*. You will probably find similar skills in your own standards in Social-Emotional, Attitudes Toward Learning, Citizenship, or Social Studies domains. This chapter will help you meet those standards.

- "Shows confidence in a range of abilities and in the capacity to accomplish tasks and take on new tasks." *The Head Start Child Development and Early Learning Framework*

- "Shows a sense of purpose (future—hopefulness)." *Building a Strong Foundation for School Success: Kentucky's Early Childhood Standards*

- "The child demonstrates the ability to seek solutions to problems." *Arizona Early Learning Standards*

- "Recognize the importance of his/her role as a member of the family, the class, and the community." *Oklahoma Prekindergarten Curriculum Guideline*

- "Perform various tasks that contribute to the well-being of the group." *North Dakota Early Learning Guidelines*

- "Begin to demonstrate an understanding of social justice and social action issues." *Louisiana Standards for Programs Serving Four-Year-Old Children*

As soon as Mrs. Hernandez walked into the classroom, Isabella asked Ms. Hill if she could show her mother the new garden. "Mama, mira, come see. We're making food for the hungry kids."

Ms. Hill explained to Isabella's mother that the children had just started a vegetable garden and were planning on donating the harvest to a local food bank.

"Me and Natalie planted all the carrots. The seeds were so, so, so tiny little, and it took a hundred minutes," Isabella told her mother excitedly. "My dress was getting all dirty from the dirt, so I asked Ms. Hill if I could wear a painting smock. And see, no dirt!"

"You're a good girl, mija," said Mrs. Hernandez. "You make your family very proud."

What Does Contribution Look Like?

Isabella, like many typical four-year-olds, had the basic building blocks of contribution. One of the pleasures of working with very young children is their endless enthusiasm, excitement, and can-do attitude. Most children in this age range feel they can do anything and look forward to the future. Four-year-olds are beginning to grasp the concept of fairness and can often be heard reprimanding each other (and their elders) with "That's not fair!" when they feel they have been wronged. Given opportunities to show compassion, they can sometimes shock you with their honesty and love.

Years ago, one of our preschoolers was in a horrible car accident that killed his mother. During the next week, the children in the group kept asking when Jose would be coming back to school. To ease his return, his grandmother arranged for Jose to visit us for a short time in the morning at circle time so Jose could talk about the accident to his classmates. Parents of the other children were notified of the plan, and all agreed to allow their children to participate. We held our breath as Jose told of the car flipping over and the death of his mother. The children listened in total and respectful silence as Jose spoke. When he was done talking, they asked a few questions such as where he would live now and if he was sad. After he answered three or four questions, we ended the conversation and told Jose we looked forward to seeing him back after the weekend, breathing a sigh of relief that it seemed to go well enough. Then came the unplanned and unexpected. Every child in the group stood up and surrounded Jose with a group hug, saying "I love you." It was a morning of raw honesty and love that reminded all of us that children are capable of incredible compassion, given the right support and opportunities.

For children to become contributing members of society who leave positive footprints on the world, they need four main building blocks.

1. They need to recognize and nurture their talents and skills and develop a strong sense of hope and optimism about the future.

2. They need to learn how to approach challenges and roadblocks with a problem-solving attitude.

3. They have to identify the valuable role they play in their social relationships—family, school, and community—and begin to find ways to contribute to the well-being of those groups.

4. They need to recognize problems and injustice and begin to use their talents to address those issues with compassion and fairness.

As early childhood educators, we play an important role in supporting children on this lifelong path. In our daily interactions, we can help children learn to be persistent and see themselves as capable and talented individuals. We can send a consistent message to children that they need never lose hope and that they can always look forward to creating and living a better and stronger tomorrow. We can provide them with many opportunities to use their energies and skills to contribute to the group, as individuals and with others. We can work with children to recognize injustice, reject bullying, and consider the rights of the minority. We can search out opportunities for children to get involved in community activities, care for the environment, and help those in need.

When Things Go Wrong

"Christopher," called the teacher. "Come on back. You didn't finish washing the chair. It still has red paint on the back." It was a warm spring day, and the kids had taken all the chairs out of the classroom for a major scrub down.

"I can't," said Christopher. "The paint is too stuck."

"Come. I'll show you how to scrub it with the brush," said the teacher.

"I didn't make paint on it, so I don't have to," answered Christopher as he kicked over the chair.

"It doesn't matter who made the paint, Christopher. We're all washing all the chairs today to make our room nice and clean. So let's pick up the chair and finish up."

"Tell David to do it," said Christopher as he ran off to the other side of the play yard.

Christopher usually had trouble finishing a task and would often find excuses not to finish if pushed. When he hit a stumbling block, he would most often quit and move on to something else. He would get easily distracted or discouraged. The idea of working together for the good of the group was foreign to him. He would often complain if asked to help clean up an area of the room where he didn't play. He would typically serve himself the last three scoops of fruit at lunch, even when others clamored for him to leave some for them. He needed some support to push through challenges, solve problems, and balance his own wants and needs with the needs of others.

We would think that preschool-aged children would already come to us as excited and optimistic children. And many of them do. Think, for example, about children on the playground and the seemingly constant chant of "Look at me, Teacher" as children master and celebrate new skills. Or when you bring out some new magnifying glasses, how many of the children flock to be first to try them out. How often have you heard a child say, "I'm a good helper, aren't I?" after she has washed the paintbrushes? Or had a child report to you that Mia isn't being nice in the home-living area because she isn't sharing the babies. All of these behaviors are signs that children are beginning to develop the skills needed to be contributing members of our communities.

Some children, however, have already been written off as failures in life before they even turn six. These are the little guys who pose incredible challenges to parents and teachers with behavior that's rude, aggressive, weepy, manipulative, hurtful, or generally unlikable. Every day they are given feedback that they are somehow deficient, failures, or hopeless. Days full of sad-face cards, time-out chairs, notes home, and more subtle failure messages become so much of a way of life for the child that he begins to make that outside message his inside self-talk.

Christopher's life was full of snowballing problems. His low level of emotional regulation had led to many years of negative and discouraging messages. His mother referred to him as her "problem child," and he was well known among peers as the "bad one" and the "troublemaker." He had already been kicked out of two other preschools for being bad and was about to be asked to leave his current one as well. As the negative messages increased, Christopher's belief in himself failed. He felt increasingly more inadequate and incompetent, which made each day harder and harder to handle with his already low level of emotional regulation.

Christopher's problems weren't going to be solved in a day. However, Christopher's teachers made a commitment to consciously begin to change the way they reacted and interacted with him. They used more encouraging language and descriptive feedback for those times he was doing well. They worked on changing Christopher's vision of himself by helping him keep a journal of his successes. They eliminated the use of the color chart that only served as a visual cue for Christopher that he was a failure. And they began to help Christopher's mother appreciate her child's strengths by frequently sending home notes about the delightful things he had done during the day. Gradually, Christopher's behavior improved, both in the classroom and at home.

When we think of bullying, often we think of children much older than little four- and five-year-olds. However, the seeds of bullying behavior can be seen as early as the preschool years, according to the U.S. Department of Health and Human Services. Where do you see the seeds of bullying in these two stories?

Abigail and Sophia were happily playing together at the water table making "soup" in a big pot.

"I need to stir it now," said Abigail, trying to pull the big mixing spoon away from Sophia.

"Wait, I'm still doing it," said Sophia as she pulled the spoon back and continued stirring.

"You need to give it to me now," said Abigail, raising her voice and pulling harder.

"No. Stop it," said Sophia.

"You can't come to my birthday then," warned Abigail.

"Okay, you can have it," Sophia said as she handed over the spoon. "I can come to your birthday now, right?"

◆   ◆   ◆

Jose and Anthony were playing in the loft when Matthew climbed the ladder to join them.

"Get out of here, Matthew," said Anthony. "You can't play here." Turning to Jose, Anthony continued, "He's not our friend. Huh, Jose? We don't like him. He's stupid."

"Yeah, we don't like him," answered Jose in a quiet voice. "But you like me. Right, Anthony?"

In the early years, bullying behavior might start out as exclusion, name-calling, and threats of loss of friendship. It can be hard sometimes for teachers to catch these behaviors because children will often wait until an adult is not present before they engage in bullying. One thing we can do is to take children's complaints of exclusion or name-calling seriously. Follow up and make it clear that bullying behavior is not acceptable in your classroom. Include interactions and activities to model appropriate responses to bullying and give children positive reflective feedback for friendly and inclusive behaviors.

Most preschool children see themselves through rose-colored glasses. Because they grow, change, and learn so rapidly in the early years, they have confidence that if they are lacking a skill today, they are sure to have it tomorrow.

Help children keep this enthusiasm by making sure the daily program is accessible to all styles of learners. Establish a classroom that supports persistence, focus, and task completion. Provide a supportive environment where children can feel pleasure from using their talents to help others. Set up opportunities for children to work together to reach common goals. Instill a classroom norm of fairness and respect for the needs of the minority.

Help Children Develop Skills and Optimism

So often as we try to help children grow and learn new things, we focus on their areas of challenge and weakness. After all, those areas need work. For children with many areas of challenge, their reflected reality may seem to be that they are a big mess of problems with no areas of strength or talent.

Before children are three years old, everything they believe about themselves comes directly from what others tell them. Gradually over the next two years, however, the talk that children hear about themselves becomes their self-talk. Their minds become like tape recorders, playing and replaying those messages again and again. What children believe about themselves becomes their reality. Children who tell themselves they are failures, fail. Children who tell themselves they are stupid have trouble learning. Children who are told that nobody likes them behave in unlikable ways. One of the first steps in helping children change their unsuccessful behaviors is to change their self-defeating self-talk.

Help children develop self-talk that honors their abilities to grow and change in positive ways. Give them tools and language to visualize and celebrate their successes. Use language in your daily interactions with children to help them develop positive attitudes about themselves, their potential, and their futures.

Supportive Interactions to Build Skills and Optimism

Our daily feedback to children alerts them to what it is that we value. Help children work through challenges by recognizing their persistence in completing a task, cheering them on to let them know you believe in their potential, and appreciating their efforts. While it's often easiest for us to do some tasks ourselves, such as wiping up a spill, give many of the little tasks to kids so they can develop their own skills.

Recognize Persistence
Adults' talk to children becomes their self-talk. And children's self-talk becomes their reality. Use language that lets children know that you notice their efforts

and trust in their abilities. When you give praise by saying "good job" or handing out stickers, you are missing opportunities to highlight for children exactly what it is that you value. Use descriptive feedback when children exhibit persistence, focus, and task completion. Descriptive feedback allows children to become aware of their strengths and talents. Remember, too, that what gets recognized gets repeated. Children who are consistently recognized for persisting in a task are more likely to persist again in the future.

It can be helpful to align the kind of feedback you use with ways that families encourage their children. In some homes, children are encouraged to stand out and be proud of themselves. For these children, you might say something like, "Look how hard you've been working. I bet you're proud of yourself." In other families, standing out from the group is discouraged and seen as being arrogant and prideful. These families might encourage their children to succeed not for self-glorification but, rather, for how they can benefit their families. These children might be more comfortable when you recognize their accomplishments with words such as "I bet your daddy would be happy to see how hard you are working to write your name."

You can use the following descriptive phrases with most children to help them become more persistent and hopeful:

- You've been working a long time.

- You can do this.

- You're trying and trying.

Help Children Cope with Frustration

Help children develop self-talk that encourages persistence when they face frustration. You can sometimes hear children repeating your cheerleading sound bites to themselves as they dust themselves off and try again.

- I can help teach you if you like.

- You can do it.

- Don't worry. It takes practice.

- Don't give up. I have faith in you.

- It's okay to make a mistake.

- You tried really hard. Soon you'll get it.

- I'll bet you make it next time.

Use Encouraging Language

Praise and criticism are two sides of the same coin. Children who are often praised don't develop the skills they need to self-evaluate. Rather than trusting their own perceptions, they depend on others to do the evaluating for them. Work and learning lose their intrinsic value and instead become ways to get attention and verbal reward from others. Some children who get frequent praise become "praise junkies." They sound like this:

- Do you like this?
- Is this pretty?
- Did I do this right?
- Is mine better?
- Whose is best?
- Are you going to put a sticker on my paper?
- Mine is better than Juan's, right?
- Is this good?

Praise and criticism can cause other children to become discouraged. In fact, the more they are praised, the more discouraged they may become. Compliments such as "That is the most beautiful painting I ever saw" become words for worry. If that's the most beautiful picture (which I suspect it's not, thinks the child), then what do I do for an encore? If mine is the most beautiful, why did I hear her tell Juan the same thing about his? I feel like just experimenting with mixing the paint, but I'd better not cause it may turn out ugly and then the teacher will tell me it's ugly and she only likes beautiful pictures. Discouraged children sound like this:

- This is ugly.
- I can't do this.
- Mine is the stupidest one.
- I'm gonna tear mine up and throw it away.
- His is nicer than mine is.
- Do it for me.

Instead of praising children's work, try giving them descriptive feedback, focusing on the process instead of the product, or making a comment to encourage children to reflect on their own work. Encouraging, descriptive feedback is especially important when working with children who seek adult attention and praise and for children who appear discouraged.

Try these responses when a child asks, "Is this good?"

Descriptive feedback	Focus on process	Encourage self-reflection
"I see you made it all swirly up here on top."	"Tell me how you made this swirly part up here."	"What's your favorite part of this painting?"
"Look how many different colors you used."	"How did you decide what colors to use in this?"	"Do you like the colors you used for this painting?"
"That tower is almost as high as you are."	"That must have been tricky to build a tower so high."	"What do you think of that tower?"
"You got all the way across the monkey bars."	"You worked hard to learn how to get across those monkey bars."	"How do you feel about getting all the way across the monkey bars?"

Recognize Accomplishment

Some children naturally find pleasure in completing tasks, and some will even get uncomfortable if you don't allow them to finish their work. Other children, however, find it easy to abandon work that they find boring or too challenging. Prepare children for the demands of school and adulthood by helping them learn to find internal satisfaction in getting a job done. When you observe children completing a task, use reflective language to recognize their accomplishment.

"You're a kid who tries over and over again until you figure it out."

"Look at that! You got all the puzzle pieces put back."

"Let's see how great the block area looks. Every block is back in its spot. It was hard work to finish all that."

Are We Done?

Help children learn to finish tasks by coaching them to check their work one last time.

- Make it a practice to say to the children, "Are we done?" You can do this after you set the table for snack, after you put all the sand toys back in the baskets, or at the end of reading a picture book.

- For individual children, try saying such things as, "Let's check one more time. Are there any blocks (puzzle pieces, chairs, trash, and so on) out of place? If not, that means we're done."

Beware of "Doing For"

"Draw me a horse." "Zip my coat, please." "I can't pour without spilling." "Can you write my name?" We can do it better, faster, and easier than they can.

After all, adults have had many years of practice. When we jump in to help children do things they can do for themselves, they might be hearing the message that they are incapable. However tempting it is to "do for," children need opportunities to practice skills for themselves in order to perfect them. It is important to remember, however, that some children in your group may come from cultural traditions in which adults demonstrate their love and caring by helping children with what we sometimes call "self-help" skills such as eating, dressing, and hand washing. You may have to observe and listen very carefully to distinguish between a child asking you to write her name for her because she is afraid that she can't do it alone and a child bringing his shoes over to you for you to put on his feet because that's part of the nurturing routine at home. In the first case, you may want to encourage the child to write her name the best she can, whereas in the latter you might decide to put the child's shoes on and find other opportunities to practice skills. Teach, show how, coach, guide, support—but think twice before you "do for."

Promote Skills and Optimism through the Classroom Culture

What children see on a daily basis has an impact on their perceptions about the world. Red/green behavior charts and happy/sad face behavior posters can be constant reminders to struggling kids that they are deficient. On the other hand, displays and photos of children's work are a visual reminder of accomplishments and possibility. For those children who need reminders to stay on task, replace behavior charts with supportive tools such as visual schedules and checklists.

Post Children's Work

Remind children of their accomplishments by providing space for each child to display his or her own work. Some teachers post small pictures of each child around the classroom to indicate to children where they can post one sample of their work. When a child chooses to post another sample, she takes down the first one and replaces it with the new one. Children can take care of this task themselves without adult assistance. Just give them the tape and let them go.

Self-Correcting Tasks

Young children often have trouble figuring out what "done" means when they are doing a task. For example, a child who has wiped the paint off the floor for a minute or two might assume the job is finished, even though there is still paint on the floor. Help children learn how to reflect on their work and evaluate for themselves whether or not it is done by making available self-correcting materials and tasks.

Puzzles are one good example of a self-correcting tool for task completion. If all the pieces are in all the spaces, the task is complete. If there are extra pieces or extra spaces, there is more to do. At first, when children have put a puzzle together, help them determine if the task is finished. You might say, "I see all the pieces are where they belong! You finished the whole puzzle" or "Uh-oh. See these two pieces left over? That means there's more to do before the job is done." Once a child is familiar with how puzzles work, the puzzle itself will cue the child as to whether or not he finished the job.

Another self-correction strategy is to label shelves so everything has a place. For example, take a photo of each musical instrument and attach the photos to the shelf. Store each instrument on top of its corresponding photo. After music time, have a child check the shelf to make sure each instrument has been put back in its place.

Assign the rotating job of "Cleanup Inspector" to check all the areas at cleanup time to make sure everything has been put away. Have children check both for empty spots on the shelves and for materials left out on tables or on the floor.

Checklists

Checklists are a useful life skill for people who need external organizers in their daily lives. Children can begin to use picture checklists to help them focus and complete tasks. Checklists are particularly useful for children who have been diagnosed with ADD or ADHD. One way to integrate checklists into your daily program is by using one at your morning meeting.

1. Make a picture poster board of the morning meeting routine.

2. Take a photo of each of the activities and paste them on the board. Make sure they are posted in order, either from top to bottom or on a long strip from left to right, which also reinforces early concepts of reading.

3. Laminate the board so you can write on it and erase every day.

4. Check off each activity with a dry-erase marker as it is completed.

5. At the end of the meeting, have the children evaluate the list with you to make sure everything got done.

Activities to Support the Development of Skills and Optimism

Class-made books can be powerful tools to record and remind children of their growth over time and their hopes for the future. Think of adding some long-term projects to your lesson planning to help children learn the value of persisting with a task over a period of a few days or a few weeks.

The Important Book

This activity is based on *The Important Book* by Margaret Wise Brown. A class-made book helps children celebrate what they identify as their unique and special qualities.

1. Have each child make one page of this book.

2. Work with the children to help them complete this template. (Make a different template for girls and boys.) Prompt them if necessary, but make sure that the children identify their own qualities and that they are the ones to select which is the most important.

   The most important thing about (name) is _____.

   (S)he also _____ and _____ and _____.

   But the most important thing about (name) is (whatever was said on the first line).

   For example: The most important thing about Tyesha is that she loves her brother.

   She also has red hair ribbons and likes to play Hungry Hippos and eats ice cream.

   But the most important thing about Tyesha is that she loves her brother.

3. Have each child illustrate his or her page. Then put together the pages with a cover to make "The Important Book." Put a family-response page on the back.

4. Read the book to the class. After the first few times, children will enjoy guessing who wrote each page of the book. Circulate the book among the families and invite them to respond on the response page.

5. Keep the book in your classroom library.

"How I Am Growing" Journals

Young children are so focused on the here and now that they have trouble recognizing their growth and how much they change over time. When they are struggling to learn a new skill, such as tying shoes or managing hurt feelings, children need to be able to envision future success—to have hope. Help children remember how they overcame obstacles in the past to help them develop a sense that they will be able to continue to grow in the future.

1. Staple together a book of blank pages for each child.

2. Have children decorate their own book covers.

3. Establish a weekly ritual of helping each child record a stepping stone. Look for such stepping stones as: tasted a new food, played with a new playmate, worked with a new art medium, put on her own shoes, or put together a new puzzle. Major milestones are built from such tiny accomplishments.

4. Encourage children to illustrate their pages or give them photos of themselves engaged in their achievements to mount on their pages.

5. Have children bring their journal home to share with families. Leave room on the pages for families to comment. Add more pages as necessary to keep a running record for the entire year.

6. Some discouraged children benefit from having an adult regularly read through their journal with them to reinforce the self-talk that they are kids who have proven in the past they can learn new things and they will continue to do so in the future.

Hope Books

Help children anticipate a positive future by making "Hope Books," either individually or as a class Big Book project.

1. Select a theme for the book. Some possible themes include:

    - When I turn five I will know how to . . .

    - When I go to kindergarten I will learn . . .

    - When I grow up I will . . .

    - Someday . . .

2. Help children complete a sentence template for their page of the book. Take down their dictation and have each child illustrate a page. For example, ask the child to complete the sentence: "When I get big, I'm going to get a job as a . . ."

3. Put the pages together with a front cover and family-response page on the back. Read the finished book to the children either individually, in a small group, or during large-group time.

4. Allow children turns to take the book home to share with their families. Invite families to comment on the family-response page, and then keep the book in the classroom library.

My Life Books

Young children are just beginning to learn the concept of the passage of time—that there is a past, present, and future. Understanding the concept that time and events move along is a prerequisite to feeling hope and anticipation for the future. Making past, present, and future style books helps children visualize and internalize this understanding.

1. Give each child a blank page for the class Big Book called "My Life."

2. Take dictation from each child to complete three sentences: When I was a baby, I used to _____. Now I am (age), and I can _____. When I am a grown-up, I will be able to _____.

3. Have the children illustrate their pages with photos or drawings.

4. Bind pages together into a Big Book with a cover and a family-response page in the back. Read the book to the class and let children take it home to share with their families.

5. Encourage families to add their responses to the back cover of the book.

6. Keep the finished book in the class library.

Long-Term Projects

Part of developing the concept of hope is the ability to look forward to tomorrow. One way to help children grasp the concept of hope is to include some project work that takes two or more days to complete.

When you do long-term projects with children, make sure to help them review the progress that was made each day and to anticipate what will be done the next day. Some ideas include:

- Have children make items from materials that harden and dry over time, such as plaster of paris, papier-mâché, or playdough. When the items dry, allow the children to paint and decorate them.

- Build and decorate a gingerbread or graham-cracker village.

- Make simple puppets one day and put on a puppet show the next day.

- Bake muffins one day and serve them for snack the next day.

- Plan a celebration with the children. Brainstorm with them what they need and how to do it. Help them execute the plan.

- Conduct one or more long-term studies, which can take place over a number of days, weeks, or even months. Some classes have done studies on different kinds of shoes. Others have studied how a house gets built or that geese come from eggs. For more information on how to conduct long-term studies or projects, check the bibliography at the end of this section for books by Sylvia Chard, Margie Carter and Deb Curtis, and Lilian Katz.

Help Children Become Problem Solvers

"All day long I feel like I'm solving problems for the kids! This kid wants a red marker, that kid can't find his jacket, the other kid wants to know if there's room to play at the sticker project table," Alisha grumbled. "When are they going to learn to solve some of these little problems by themselves?"

"Little children, little problems. Big children, big problems." Today it's a problem about finding a red marker. In ten years, it will be a problem of what to do when someone offers her drugs. And in twenty years, it will be a question of how to deal with sexual harassment in the workplace. Just as a new skier starts learning on the bunny hill where there is a minimum of risk, a new problem solver must start on the problem-solving bunny hill. It's only by practicing on low-risk problems like red markers and missing jackets that children develop the problem-solving skills they will need to tackle the major problems just around the corner.

Children learn to solve problems the same way they learn everything else. They watch others, they practice and experiment, and eventually they master the skill. Some children master the skill very easily, while others require more direct instruction, scaffolding, or support to become proficient.

Teachers are especially fast and efficient problem solvers. As they multitask throughout their days, they solve dozens of children's problems, large and small: "Let me tie those for you," "There's an extra pencil on my desk; go get it," "Scoot over and make room for DeAndre."

The irony is that the skilled adult who least needs practice gets all the practice. Less-skilled children, who most need practice, get fewer opportunities to practice solving daily problems.

> "Clean up, clean up, everybody everywhere. Clean up, clean up, everybody do your share," the teacher chanted.
>
> Celina ignored the signal and continued to work with the blocks.
>
> "Time to clean up," the teacher reminded her as she walked by.
>
> When the teacher looked a few moments later, Celina still hadn't begun to pick up.
>
> "Celina, did you hear me? Cleanup time," the teacher said as she walked over to the child.

Now what? It's not always easy to think of solutions for problems. Many of us are in the habit of thinking that if a child does something inappropriate, we should give consequences or punishments instead of using a problem-solving approach. Sometimes we think of offering rewards, but they're not solutions either. They are just the flip side of punishments.

Figuring out the difference between punishment and solution is not always easy when we are thinking of working with children's problems. It may help you to clarify your thoughts if we shift for a moment to the adult world.

Imagine that the gas gauge is broken in your car. You have already been late for work twice because you have run out of gas. Come up with three ways you could solve this problem.

1. _____

2. _____

3. _____

Look at your answers. Did you put yourself in time-out or take away TV for a week? Probably not. Neither of those strategies would have solved the problem of running out of gas and being late for work.

The things you listed were probably genuine solutions to the problem. Maybe you thought to get the gas gauge fixed, take a bus to work, fill the tank up every night on the way home, or leave for work an hour earlier each day just in case. These solutions are ways to get done what needs to get done.

When we work toward solutions, we work toward ways to solve the problem and reach the intended goal. We don't look for ways to retaliate, punish, or blame someone for having a problem.

Let's take a moment to review what you already know about how best to teach young children. In the table below, list five or more typical discipline and guidance techniques in the left column.

Typical discipline and guidance techniques	Teaching rhyming words
_____	_____
_____	_____
_____	_____
_____	_____
_____	_____

Now imagine for a moment that you have decided to teach the children in your group about rhyming words. For two or three weeks you have used many of the strategies that you know from experience will help children learn the concept of rhymes. You read poems and did fingerplays. You read predictable rhyming books and played rhyming games. And after that time, most of the children in the class can tell you that *hat* rhymes with *cat*. But Bev and Jennifer are still in the dark. After another week of activities and songs, Bev catches on, but Jennifer still doesn't understand. In the column at the right, list at least five things you would do to help Jennifer.

Did your right column include most of the strategies you listed in the left column?

Probably not. Most of these are probably solutions to the problem. They are strategies intended to help the child overcome obstacles and learn the task at hand. These strategies are an attempt to work together in a supportive way to fix things.

"How can we solve this problem?" This sentence is one of the most magical things we can do for children to help them take responsibility for their own behavior. We don't need to write their name on the board, give checkmarks, or take away recess. What we need to do is help the child find a way to do what needs doing. We need to look for solutions rather than fall back on punishments. Some of these approaches are summarized on the following chart.

Punishment	Solution
Place blame	Take responsibility
Look back	Look forward
Pay for wrong	Fix things
Me against you	Support and mentor
Power and control	Cooperation

Supportive Interactions to Promote Problem Solving

Notice that the problem-solving process is very similar to the conflict-resolution process in chapter 5. As you probably remember, we use the conflict-resolution process to help children learn how to resolve disputes with other children over space and stuff. Although the methods are similar, here we will look at a process that can be used when a child comes to you with a problem, such as lost shoes, or when you go to a child because you have a problem with him or her, such as paper towels left on the bathroom floor.

Many children's problems don't need the full four-step process. Sometimes just a word of encouragement or a simple acknowledgment that a problem exists is all a child needs to regroup and move on. At times we have issues with families that need to be worked out as well. Using the problem-solving process can often help us find solutions that meet the needs of everyone involved.

The Four-Step Problem-Solving Process

1. Find out what is wanted or needed.
2. Define the problem.
3. Brainstorm and choose a solution to try.
4. Check in to see if the solution worked.

Let's use the four-step process now to revisit Celina and the blocks.

1. **Find out what is wanted or needed.** Before we can start thinking of solutions, we need more information about Celina. We know the problem from our point of view. It's cleanup time and she won't clean up. What we don't know yet is what Celina needs or wants. Seek first to understand.

   "Celina, you're still playing with the blocks. What is it that you want?" asked her teacher.

   "I didn't finish making the princess castle," Celina answered. "I still have to finish the top part here where she waves to the people."

2. **Define the problem.** Now that you know what Celina wants and why she is frustrated, how can you begin to more clearly define the problem?

   At first it might appear that Celina is being defiant or oppositional. Now you have more information and can understand that the problem is that Celina wasn't done with her work even though work time was over. Clarifying the problem opens the door to finding solutions.

3. **Brainstorm and choose a solution to try.** Look again at Celina's problem about the blocks. She wasn't done with her project, and it was time to clean up to go outside. Think about the right side of the rhyming chart. What might you suggest as solutions to the block problem? Did you think of things like leaving her structure out to work on after the class comes back inside? Or putting a sign on the structure so nobody else uses those blocks? Maybe letting her stay inside while one teacher does lunch setup so Celina can finish her work. Giving her five more minutes to finish up. Or letting her get a couple of friends to help her finish building before going outside. These would all be possible solutions to the problem.

4. **Check back to see if the solution worked.** If the solution worked, congratulate the child on having found a good solution to the problem. If the solution didn't work, say something like, "Uh-oh. That solution didn't seem to work. Let's figure out something else to try."

Problem-Solving Roadblocks

Sometimes we might encounter roadblocks to the problem-solving process. These are some common roadblocks:

- Roadblock: Children (or adults) are so emotionally charged that they can't engage in problem solving.
  Try: Wait a bit for everyone to cool down; STAR: Stop, Take a Deep Breath, Relax; or try other emotional-regulation strategies from chapter 4.

- Roadblock: Even when they are calmed down, some children can't tell you what they need or want.
  Try: Make your best guess and ask the child if that sounds right; give the child some thinking time.

- Roadblock: Children often don't have the skills to define the problem.
Try: It takes lots of coaching and practice for children (and often adults too) to be able to define the problem. Model a neutral problem statement, starting with the words "It looks like you wish (your best guess) and it's a problem because (what is getting in the way of the child getting what she wants)." For example, "It looks like you lost your keychain out in the playground, and it's a problem because it's time for us to go in for lunch. Is that right?"

- Roadblock: Children have very little experience at solving problems and might need help to learn how to think of and choose solutions.
Try: Just as it takes time to learn how to express a problem, it also takes time to learn to think of solutions. This is perhaps the most important piece of the whole process. Take time to model how you can brainstorm two or three possible solutions. In the example above, you might say, "Well, maybe we can come out and look for the keychain after lunch. Or Ms. Janet's class will be coming out now. We can ask her class to look for your keychain and bring it to our room. Or if nobody finds it today, we can all have a treasure hunt tomorrow morning to try to find it."

- Roadblock: Sometimes solutions don't work!
Try: Try, try again. Teach children how to persevere and overcome roadblocks when they are trying to reach a goal.

Help Children View Stumbling Blocks as Temporary

Sometimes children encounter obstacles in the way of them accomplishing what they set out to do. Children who don't see themselves as problem solvers may quit when the going gets hard. Help children identify stumbling blocks as problems that can be overcome, rather than dead ends.

"You are a smart person. You can figure this out."

"Let's think about what happened. I wonder what else a kid might try?"

"I know you'll find a way to do this."

"I know you can fix it."

"You sure have a big pile of work to do. What kind of help do you need?"

"Well, this choice didn't work so well. There must be some other way to do it. What could that be?"

That's a Problem

Give children opportunities to learn and practice problem solving on a three-year-old's problems to build the skills they'll need later for a five-year-old's problems, twelve-year-old's problems, teen's problems, and eventually an adult's problems. How do you do this? Start by acknowledging that the child has a problem and then turning it back to him to solve.

For example, when a child says she can't find a purple marker, acknowledge her dilemma by saying, "You want a purple marker and can't find one. That's a problem." And then wait. Resist the urge to say, "Just go fetch a purple marker from the writing table."

When you first introduce this strategy, children may be taken aback. They can become so used to us solving all the little, routine, daily problems that they become lazy problem solvers. At first you may have to do a little coaching. In the example of the purple marker, you might say something like, "Do you think there might be some purple markers someplace around here?"

When you first introduce "That's a problem," it is usually best to use it for very simple problems that children should be able to solve easily. But after children have had some successful practice, you can begin to scaffold up the difficulty of the problem solving. For example, if a child comes to you complaining that he wants a turn at the take-apart table, try saying something like, "That's a problem. Can you think of a way that kids can get turns at the take-apart table when they want one?" Again, you might give little prompts if children need them, but resist the urge to jump right in and solve the problem for the child.

Bad Timing

Problems can come up at inconvenient times. Sometimes you will be in the midst of other pressing issues and won't be able to help a child immediately.

That happens often in adult life. You may be at work and a friend calls in distress. Your break starts in fifteen minutes. What might you say? Perhaps, "I hear you're really upset. I can't get away right now, but I can spend some time with you in about fifteen minutes. I'm so sorry. Can you wait?" The language you would use to convey caring and respect for a friend while still setting limits is the same language you would use with a child. "I can see you are frustrated about something. It'll take me about ten more minutes to finish this lesson and then I'll come and help you. You can go over to the book corner or the aquarium if that would help you hang on until I can get to you."

Grown-Ups Have Problems Too

Do any of these situations sound familiar?

> "Triviana's mother doesn't want her to play in the sand anymore. She says it gets in her hair! For goodness' sake, can't she just wash the child's hair in the tub at night?"

> "Matthew is barely a year old and his grandma is insisting we sit him in the potty chair every hour! I gave her a flyer on appropriate potty training, but she still insists on starting now."

> "Shawna is dead tired after lunch, and her mama refuses to let her nap here. The child keeps falling asleep, even when I sit her at the puzzles to keep her up. What am I supposed to do, wake her? That's crazy."

We've all been there. Families want us to do something with their child that just doesn't fit into our program or philosophy. Often, these conflicts can erode our relationships with families to the point that they withdraw from the program.

When we focus on the practice instead of on the underlying need or want, we can easily lose sight of the fact that we and the parents most often have compatible goals for children.

- When Triviana's teacher asked her mother to share why the sand was such a problem, the teacher discovered that for some children, sand gets so embedded in braids or hair oil that it can be a day-long process to clean the child. Her teacher shared that Triviana loved playing in sand, and she learned science and math concepts in that area.

- Matthew's grandma said that in her culture children were expected to be toilet trained by a year old, and everyone in her family had done it that way for generations. His teacher said that the center didn't usually begin training children until two years old, and she didn't want to make him sit on the potty if he cried and struggled to get off.

- Shawna's mom said that Shawna had trouble sleeping at night if she took a long nap during the day. The teacher let the mom know that Shawna was falling asleep whether or not she was put down for a nap.

As the teachers and families worked together to share their goals, beliefs, and problems, they were able to come to mutually acceptable solutions that worked for everyone. Triviana's mother allowed her to play in the sand if the teachers made sure her head was covered with a scarf or cap. Matthew's teacher agreed to sit him on the potty as long as she could let Matthew up if he fussed or cried. Shawna's teacher and mother decided the child could sleep for up to half an hour and must be awake by three o'clock.

There may be times that families ask you to do something that is considered abuse or neglect by your state laws. Help the families understand the state laws and work to find another way to help families reach their goals for their children. If you suspect neglect or abuse in the home, follow your center guidelines and state laws for reporting the incident. Remember, as an early childhood educator, you are required by law to report suspected abuse.

Help Children Identify Their Importance to the Community

"Kaleen, I saw you teaching Sarah how to tie her shoes. That was very helpful." "Sumiko, we missed you so much while you were gone. We're all so happy that you are back." "Marcos, you're a fast runner. Would you fetch that bucket way over there real quick so we can water the pumpkin plant?"

While it's important to celebrate children's individual achievements, it's equally important to help children become aware of their potential to contribute to the well-being of their community.

Using Classroom Culture to Help Children Understand Their Importance to the Community

Help all of the children in your group appreciate the unique gifts they have to offer the community by emphasizing the importance of offering their skills and talents to others in the classroom who need their support. Develop a class-expert chart for children to record their skills and talents. Take pictures of cooperative activities and display them on the wall to visually reinforce the value of helpfulness in your classroom. And keep children striving to continually better themselves by helping them set goals for the future.

Class Experts

"I'm an expert at riding the big bike," volunteered AJ when the teacher led the children in making an expert chart.

"How about you, Lexi?" the teacher asked. "What are you an expert at? What can you do to help other children in our class?"

"I don't know," Lexi answered.

"Well, I know you like to draw pictures of your dog Max. Do you think you might be our class expert at drawing dogs?"

Lexi broke into a big smile. "I can draw the goodest dogs."

Children like AJ and Lexi are able to identify their own strengths and talents, sometimes independently and other times with adult support and guidance. They learn to recognize and take pride in their skills and accomplishments.

Everyone has a talent or skill they can contribute to benefit the classroom. Increase the richness of the classroom community by drawing on individuals and families. Help children appreciate their own strengths and talents as well as those of others in the class community with the class-expert chart.

1. On a big piece of chart paper, print the names of all community members down the left side of the paper. You can add small snapshots of the children and adults if you like.

2. Help each member identify a strength or talent, and print that talent on the right side of the chart. Enhance it with a photo of the child doing the behavior or clip art if you like. Some examples are: ties shoes, pumps on the swing, knows the day of the week, knows the names of dinosaurs, dances, can print letters, and so on.

3. As often as possible, call on children to contribute to the class using their unique skill. Also, get into the habit of referring children to each other for expertise. For example, if Lara asks you for help to draw a dog, help her refer to the expert chart to find that Lexi is the class dog-drawing expert, and have her ask Lexi for help.

4. Periodically redo the expert chart to reflect new skills or to find experts to fill a need in the classroom. For example, if many children are asking for help with zippers, try to find a child who is a zipper expert to help.

Each One Teach One

Nothing reinforces learning more than teaching. Help children gain confidence in their skills and knowledge by using them as teachers for other children in the classroom or for children in younger rooms.

- A child who has learned to recognize the names of classmates can teach a child who is still learning to set out name tags for an activity.

- A child who can count can teach other children at the snack table when the snack portion card says to take three crackers.

- A child who can tie shoes can teach another child how to tie.

- A child who can pump on the swing can teach a friend how to pump.

We All Have Goals

We all come with areas of strength and expertise. And we all come with areas of challenge. Part of the excitement of life is to use our talents and work on our more challenging areas. Help children identify their own personal goals and give them the practice and support they need to reach those goals.

1. Make a goal chart using the same directions as the expert chart. Make sure goals are stated in the positive.

2. Work with each child to find a way that the community can provide support with instruction, coaching, practice, or cheerleading.

3. Weave a reminder of goals into the daily schedule. At morning meeting or transition time, you might want to quickly go around the circle for children to state their goal. You can also do this at the lunch table or when patting children's backs at rest time. However it is done, it is important to help children focus on their goal every day.

4. Periodically, check in with each member to evaluate where they stand on reaching goals.

5. Goals are personal, and evaluation of goals should be an exercise in self-reflection, not a "grade" from others. One teacher meets with children

one-on-one periodically and says, "So, how are you doing with your goal?" Another checks in randomly during morning meeting.

All adults in the classroom should have goals as well. Make the goals challenging but realistic. Model for children the frustration of trying to meet goals, the persistence in pursuing goals, and the feeling of achievement when you have reached a goal.

Post Images of the Children Working and Playing with Others

One way to catch the attention of the children in your room is to use photos of your classroom community in place of commercially produced posters. In the same way that our talk to children becomes their self-talk, visual reminders of children engaged in cooperative behaviors reinforce children's image of themselves as cooperative beings.

- Take one or more pictures of children playing together, mount them on poster board, and label it "We Play Together" to replace a commercial poster.

- Photograph children in the classroom cleaning up the science area, and put it in a class-made book called "We Work Together."

- Mount pictures of classroom children engaged together in learning activities in each center. Label the display "We Help Each Other Learn."

- Make a poster of families and children reading books together to decorate your library center.

Activities to Help Children Understand Their Importance to the Community

Provide regular opportunities for children to be helpful to others, both within and beyond the school community. Recognize children's helpfulness in charts and photos. And don't forget the step of teaching children to recognize each other's helpfulness by offering sincere thanks.

Helping Hands Tree

Help children move from focusing only on themselves to focusing on the interactions of others in the classroom. When children are guided to focus on others' friendly behaviors, they begin to build up a repertoire of friendly behaviors that they can draw on in their own interactions.

1. Draw a large tree on bulletin-board paper or mount a real tree branch in a bucket of plaster of paris.

2. Cut out hand shapes from paper in various colors.

3. Have children identify when they have observed another child's helpful act, and record the event on the hand. For example, "Hazel helped Lola turn on the water in the bathroom."

4. Help the child who observed the act attach the hand to the tree.

5. Periodically read from the hands at a group meeting. Then pass out the hands for children to take home.

6. It is important that all children be represented on the tree. If some children are not represented, observe those children and find examples of their helpfulness to add to the collection.

Random Acts of Kindness Board

This is similar to the Helping Hands Tree above. Instead of just focusing on helpful acts, however, children are guided to recognize any kind act in the classroom community.

1. Have children observe each other for acts of kindness.

2. Record the acts on self-adhesive notes. For example, "Amity let Kiyoshi have the doll with the long hair."

3. Help the child who observed the act attach the note to a bulletin board.

4. Read the notes and distribute as in the previous activity.

5. Again, make sure every member of the community is represented on the board.

Shared Problems

Sometimes it takes more than one person to get a job done. Present children with these small groups situations so they are encouraged to work together toward a common goal. Make sure to give the children reflective feedback after the activity to reinforce the value of teamwork.

- Set up dramatic play scenarios to help children practice teamwork to reach a goal. Gather three to five children to play rescue squad or to chase a pretend tiger out of the classroom. At the end of the activity, say something like, "We all worked together to get the job done" or "I'm so glad we had so many helpers for this big job."

- Look for real-life opportunities during the day when many hands are better than one. Invite children to help move a heavy table or carry five or six balls out to the play yard. Make sure that your feedback encourages children to focus on the group and not on you. Instead of saying, "Thank you for helping me move the table" (teacher focused), say, "We all moved that table together. It's good to have so many hands."

Together We Are Better

Help children appreciate that it sometimes takes the talents of many people to achieve a goal or complete a task. Provide children with activities that depend on each child's skills and contributions to be successful.

- Come up with cooperative classroom activities, projects, and games.

- Act out a book.

- Put on a puppet show. Ask some children to be players and others to be the audience. Switch roles.

- Make a class garden. Rotate gardening chores such as watering and weeding. Make sure everyone plants and harvests. Take photos of all stages of the project, making sure that all children are represented in the pictures.

- Plan and execute a party or celebration. Help children make decisions about the decorations, food, and activities. Make sure each child has an important role in executing the plans. During the celebration, help children recognize that it took the efforts of everyone to make the vision a reality.

- Play "everybody wins" games such as modified versions of Musical Chairs and Farmer in the Dell from chapter 3.

Community Work

Community work is different from a group project. In a group project, the members work together for the benefit of the classroom. Community work is intended to benefit those outside the immediate classroom. Research has shown that children who participate in projects that benefit others are more successful in school and life than children who don't have those opportunities. Participation in community work helps children value "strength in numbers." Together, they are able to do far more than one child can do alone.

1. When doing community projects, it is important that every member play an essential role in getting the work done. Some ideas for community work include these:

   - Wash a staff member's car.

   - Pick up trash around the play yard.

   - Build a gingerbread house for a children's ward in a hospital or for a retirement village.

   - Put on a play for another class.

   - Paint a mural on an inside wall of the play yard.

   - Grow vegetables, then donate them to a children's shelter.

2. Reflection on community work after the project is completed is an important component of helping children visualize the process. Document the progress of the project with photos of the children participating in it, and if possible take photos of those who benefited from the work. Have the children dictate captions. Display the work on poster board or in a Big Book or scrapbook with a title such as "We Grew Vegetables for the Children's Shelter" or "We Made a Gingerbread House for the Senior Volunteers."

Thank-You Notes

Along with guiding children to view each other as valuable resources, teach children the courtesy of expressing thanks. A verbal thanks is one strategy to model and teach. Many teachers also find writing thank-you notes useful for this purpose, as well as being a valuable addition to their literacy program.

1. Keep a supply of note cards or small sheets of colored paper in the writing center, along with an illustrated list of class members.

2. Model and encourage writing thank-you notes for expressions of kindness. Adults should remember to write notes to individual children frequently.

Make sure to also write thank-you notes to guests and the school's support staff on a regular basis.

Help Children Recognize Fairness, Bias, and Injustice

Have you heard comments like these?

"Lola can't play with us, huh," Dewey said to the others at the sand table.

"She don't got no teeth in the front. She too ugly to play with us."

"Go 'way, Nicholas. Only girls can play with the dress-up," Ramona said.

The way we respond to children's comments like these sends important messages about justice and acceptance of diversity. Teaching children about fairness requires a multi-pronged approach over a long period of time. It's a way of life, not a two-week topic of study in October. Use the supportive interactions, classroom culture, and activity ideas that follow as your starting point for infusing the values of fairness, anti-bias, and justice into your classroom community.

Interactions to Help Children Recognize Fairness, Bias, and Injustice

Preschool-aged children naturally put things in categories. We've all seen children sit with a pile of rocks or a box of little cars and sort them into piles—big ones here, small ones there, or shiny ones here, dull ones there. By regularly using the labels "fair" and "unfair" in your classroom, you provide children with the vocabulary and awareness they need to begin to distinguish fairness and injustice on their own.

A special category of "unfairness" is a bias against the unfamiliar and those who are different from us. As children grow and mature, they begin to identify their own characteristics and the unique characteristics of those around them. They may develop fear or discomfort with differences and might avoid those who aren't like themselves. Acknowledge and model respect for diversity to reduce children's bias about differences and to guide them to appreciate the intrinsic value of each member of the community.

Make sure children who are themselves the target of bias or bullying have the language they need to assert their position as an equal member of the classroom community.

Fair and Unfair

Begin to regularly use the words "fair" and "unfair" in your daily interactions with kids. Understanding the concept of fairness is the beginning of understanding equity and bias. As children begin to recognize situations that are fair and unfair, they become excited and motivated to work to make a difference. Try to get into the habit of using the word "unfair" instead of the words "not fair" because young children find it easier to comprehend a word than a "not" word. To move children on to the next step of fixing wrongs, when they notice something unfair, guide them to think of how to fix the problem.

When a child says . . .	You might say . . .
"Me and Emily are sharing the stickers."	"You two found a fair way to make sure you both got to use what you need."
"Andrew took the computer and my name was the next one on the list."	"That sounds unfair. How can we fix it?"
"Juan took all the grapes at snack and now there's none left and I never got any."	"Hmm. That's unfair, isn't it? Let's go see what we can do to make it right."
"Look! Me and Dae and Ava are taking turns on the wagon."	"How fair! Now everybody gets a turn to be the rider and the puller."

People Are Different—And That Is Good

"What you wearin' that hat for, Hanif?" Ryker asked.

"Boys 'posed to wear it. My daddy say so," Hanif answered.

"My daddy don't say so," Ryker replied.

Their teacher, Samantha, heard the exchange and came over. "In Hanif's family, boys wear those kinds of hats. In Ryker's family, boys don't wear those kinds of hats. Each family decides what the boys will wear, and it's all right."

"Okay, I'm gonna wear the cowboy hat, and Hanif can wear his family hat," Ryker said, and the two boys ran off to play.

Preschool-aged children are likely to comment about differences in skin color, language spoken, hair texture, clothing styles, body fat, and the use of assistive technology such as wheelchairs or hearing aids. When you respond to children's observations with comments such as "That's not nice to talk about other people" or "Those things don't matter. All children are the same," you don't stop their observations. You just make them wonder what is so wrong that you are pretending to ignore it. If you are saying "it's not nice" or "everybody is the same" after the child says "Look how he can't walk right," a child picks up the unintended message that there actually *is* something wrong about differences. Instead, acknowledge the observation, explaining what the child has seen, helping the child begin to understand the diversity of the human race, and guiding the child, if needed, to understand how drawing attention to some differences can be hurtful to others. The table below provides some examples of how you might respond to children's observations or statements.

If a child says . . .	You might say . . .
"I don't want to play with Jesus. He can't talk right."	"Jesus talks in Spanish like his family does. You talk in English like your family does. How about we teach Jesus a few words in English, and he can teach us a few words in Spanish?"
"Why is Ella so fat? She's gonna break the chair if she sits on it."	"Ella *is* bigger than you. Some people are bigger and some people are smaller. And our chairs are made for all sizes of people. How do you think Ella might feel when she hears you talk about her size?"
"Berta, you can't play fire with us because only boys and mans can be firemans."	"Both men and women can be firefighters. And in our class, boys and girls can do all the same pretend play too."

Confronting Bias and Bullying Behavior

Be particularly aware of "doing for" when it comes to social and emotional skills. When one child uses name-calling or exclusionary behavior toward another, instead of jumping in to defend the child who was bullied, teach and coach that child to use assertive language to defend himself. Stand with the child while he practices assertive language with the child who offended him to lend your support.

If children who are victimized by bullying behaviors don't learn how to use assertive language to defend themselves, they will continue to be targets of bullying, even if they move to a new classroom or a new school. It is as important to support the targets of bullying behavior as it is to address the bullying behavior itself.

Instead of solving . . .	Try teaching and coaching . . .
"Nakita, don't hit Faith. Hitting hurts. She doesn't like that."	"Faith, you can tell Nakita you want her to stop hitting you. Say, 'Stop hitting me.' I'll stand by you to help."
"Zola, you need to let Kiana play babies too."	"Come, Kiana. I'll go back with you, and you can tell Zola that you can play babies if you want to."
"Caleb, I don't want you calling names here."	"David, let's go back and you can say, 'Don't call me dummy. I don't like that.'"
"Kelsey, boys can play in home living too."	"Jose, I'll come with you so you can tell Kelsey that boys and girls can play with everything at school."

Use the Classroom Culture to Support Children's Awareness of Fairness, Bias, and Injustice

Classroom norms and expectations are important for sending children messages about what kind of behaviors you value and expect. Make sure your classroom norms meet the needs of all the children in the group, not just the needs of the majority. Send a message that it's the responsibility of all of us to look out for the welfare of others and to report instances of bias and injustice to someone in authority who can intervene. Help children begin to distinguish when it is appropriate to march to the beat of their own drummer and when it's appropriate to temper their individuality to meld in with the group.

Consensus

Majority voting is not the best decision-making strategy to teach young children. Preschool is an opportunity to help children move from being egocentric toward being fair and sensitive to the needs of all, including the minority opinion. What happens when we use majority voting? "Raise your hand if you want to eat outside. Raise your hand if you want to eat inside. Okay. Everybody except Louisa and Brandon voted to eat outside so we're all eating outside." What have we just taught the children about the needs and feelings of the minority? How did this process help children practice inclusion of those who see the world in a different way? How does it support our problem-solving process, in which we teach children that for a solution to work, it has to meet everyone's needs?

Instead of using a majority vote to make class decisions, try using a process of consensus building. Consensus takes more time than majority voting, but the payoff is that the process of consensus building promotes mutual respect, problem-solving skills, and inclusion. Help children in your care learn that might doesn't necessarily make right.

How could that outside/inside decision be handled with consensus instead of majority voting?

> Sarah said to the children, "Raise your hand if you want to eat outside. Okay, now raise your hand if you want to eat inside. Uh-oh, not everybody agrees. Some people want to eat outside and some want to eat inside. How can we work it so everybody feels okay? Who has some ideas?"
>
> "I know," volunteered Gloria. "We can eat outside today and inside tomorrow."
>
> The teacher posed this solution to the group. "Let's see if this will work for everyone. The idea is to eat outside today and inside tomorrow. Raise your hand if that's okay. William, I see you don't agree with this. Do you have another idea that might work?"
>
> "Maybe some of us can eat outside with you and some of us can eat inside with Miss Laura," suggested William.
>
> "That would work for me. Miss Laura, would that work for you too? Oh good. Let's see if the kids are okay with that. William suggested that some of you can eat outside with me, and some can stay inside with Miss Laura. Raise your hand if that will work for you. Okay, I think we found a solution that works for everybody."

What did this process teach the children about the needs and feelings of the minority? How did this process help children to practice inclusion of those who see the world in a different way? Working toward consensus reinforces that it is possible to resolve differences of opinion and that everyone's needs are met.

Equality and Equity

"Why does Gabriel get to sit on a ball during circle time and I can't?" "How come me and Sam can't play at rest time and you let Deena play?" "Why does Shadha get to bring her lunch from home and we don't?"

As children become increasingly focused on fairness, questions about what they may perceive as bias may come up. Children may interpret fair as equal and may equate unequal with unfair. The truth is that we *shouldn't* treat all children "equally." Gabriel sits on a ball because his physical therapist recommended it. Deena plays quietly at naptime because of an understanding between the teacher and her mother. Shadha brings her lunch from home on the request from her family because of special dietary restrictions. Every child in the group gets what he or she needs as an individual.

Help children understand the concepts of "equal" and "equitable" with the following Bunny and the Goldfish activity that was shared with me by a generous teacher at a training many years ago.

1. Invite the children to pretend with you that your class will be getting a goldfish. Ask them to brainstorm what supplies you will have to get for the fish. They will probably suggest things such as a bowl, water, pebbles, fish toys, fish food, and so forth. Record these on chart paper as they make their suggestions.

2. When they are done, tell them that the class will also be getting a pretend bunny rabbit. Say something like, "So let's get another big bowl for our bunny to live in. We can fill it with water and rocks and fish toys (and whatever else might be on the list that the children generated) and we can buy more fish food for it." As you are saying this, the children will probably be laughing and protesting that bunnies don't live in water, they don't eat fish food, and so forth. Say something like, "Oh! What would we need for our bunny then?" and record their ideas on the chart paper. End the activity by saying something like, "I see. The fish needs fish things, and the bunny needs bunny things. Each one gets what they need."

3. After that activity, when a child poses a question such as "Why does Gabriel get to sit on a ball during circle time and I can't?" answer "Because Gabriel is a bunny and you are a goldfish. And in this classroom everyone gets what they need."

Equality versus equity. An important life lesson.

Encourage Children to Look Out for the Welfare of Others

Looking out for the welfare of others is sometimes called "tattling" in a preschool classroom. Tattling is a tricky topic. We work hard to form a classroom community in which everyone looks out for the welfare of each other. And yet we call it tattling when they warn us that another child is not following community guidelines.

If a child alerts you that Makayla has left the playground and is walking on the city street, is that tattling or looking out for the welfare of others? If a child comes to tell you that Kwan is filling the toilet with toilet tissue, is that tattling or helping to take care of the classroom? While teachers may need to hear that Makayla has escaped the school grounds, they may be far more reluctant to hear that that Sophia used the whole bottle of gold glitter. To get a better grip on tattling, shift for a moment to the adult world.

- You're at a stoplight and somebody rams into your car from behind. What do you do?

- You're at work and someone persists in making inappropriate comments to you even after you have told him to stop. What do you do?

- A child in your room is still biting other children, even after you have done everything you know how to do to help her stop. What do you do?

- You witness a mother beating her child with a belt in the parking lot. What do you do?

Help children distinguish between trying to get somebody in trouble and trying to aide somebody in need through your response to reporting. Ask the reporting child, "Are you telling me this to hurt someone or help someone?" Most children who are reporting incidents to hurt someone will say, "Nevermind," and walk away. If the child is trying to help someone, offer to go with him to see what the two of you can do.

An important life skill we develop is to know when we can handle a situation alone and when to seek help and support from others. When you call a police officer, talk to a supervisor about harassment, set up a conference with a child's family, or call child protective services, you are demonstrating wisdom in seeking support. Allow children to develop the same trust and interdependence by supporting their efforts to seek help when they feel unable to handle a situation themselves.

Young children lack the wisdom and life experience to distinguish dangerous from nondangerous behavior. Encourage children to report incidents that trouble them, whether they are participants, victims, or witnesses.

If a child reports . . .	Try saying . . .
An incident in which she is involved—for example, "He said I can't play in the block area because I'm not his friend."	"It's unfair when somebody stops a kid from using things in our room. Do you need help solving this?" If the child says yes, you can move into problem solving or conflict resolution.
An incident involving other children—for example, "Marcel is holding Anthony down and won't let him up, and Anthony is crying."	"Thank you for letting me know that somebody needs help. Let's go see what we can do."

Cooperation and Competition

Focus children on the delicate task of balancing the needs of self with the needs of the community. As you guide children in the art of cooperation, stay aware that part of the job of being a preschool child is to explore personal power. Provide many opportunities for children to personally strive and shine.

For cooperative activities, explain to the children, "You win the game by playing the same." This is a new concept for some very competitive children who are used to winning by standing out from the crowd. Think, for example, of when you are all singing the "Alphabet Song" at large group. While the group is happily singing away in unison, there's Martha, singing the song as fast as she can. "I finished first!" she says while the rest of you are still at "L-M-N-O-P." Or maybe you're playing a parachute game outside and Tyrone is flipping his part of the parachute up and down as fast as he can while the rest of you are working in unison to make the parachute billow and fill with air.

Try using this singsong reminder: "Not louder, not lower, not faster, not slower. You win this game by playing the same." Because most children are drawn to chants and rhymes, this little reminder seems to resonate with kids.

Give clear cues when it is time to match the others. Think, for example, when the group is doing scarf dancing. Most of the children are moving along with the music, waving their scarves in the air. And there is Benji, running around the room as fast as he can, calling out, "I'm the fastest one. Nobody can catch me." Motivate children to match others by letting them know that matching others is a very tricky skill. These children already know that faster is tricky. They know climbing higher is tricky. And it helps them when we reframe cooperation as being equally tricky, which in reality it is. You might say to Benji, "I know you're a fast runner. But scarf dancing is very, very tricky. The trick is to dance the same as the other children. I know you're a tricky runner. I wonder if you can be a tricky dancer too." It *is* very tricky to curb one's own impulses to conform to group norms. Sometimes the trick is to be the same; the trick is not to be different.

Discussion/Reflection Questions

1. How might you respond to support children in the development of their talents and skills in the following situations?

    - When a child asks if you like the way she cleaned up the table-toy area.

    _____

    _____

    - When a child says he can't put on his shoes.

    _____

    _____

- When a child asks you to draw a tree for her because she doesn't know how to do it.

_____

_____

2. Think about when it might be more appropriate to encourage children to do things by themselves and when it might be more appropriate for them to seek help and support from others. What guidelines do you use to decide which approach to use?

_____

_____

_____

3. How might you respond to each of these comments from children to acknowledge differences and generalize sameness?

- Boys can't play dolls with girls.

_____

_____

- Rudy is soooooo fat. We don't like her, huh?

_____

_____

- Xiaozheng talks funny words. He don't know how to talk regular.

_____

_____

Exercises

1. Make one of the hope books or a "My Life" book with the children in your classroom. How did that work for the children?

_____

_____

_____

_____

2. Develop a list of ten ways that children in your class can contribute to the well-being of the classroom community, the school as a whole, and those outside the school family.

    _____

    _____

    _____

    _____

    _____

    _____

    _____

    _____

    _____

3. For a week, record instances of bias that you observe in your classroom. Do you notice a common theme? Identify one or two strategies to try over the next few weeks to counter the biases. Do you notice changes in your classroom after using these interventions?

    _____

    _____

    _____

    _____

    _____

Reflection/Journal Assignment

Begin a "How I Am Growing" journal for yourself. Start it by recording ways you have grown and changed personally and professionally since beginning this study. Add to your journal weekly.

_____

_____

_____

_____

_____

_____

_____

_____

_____

_____

_____

_____

_____

_____

_____

_____

_____

_____

_____

Teaching Children about Helpfulness

According to researcher Dr. Marty Rossman, preschoolers who contributed to the household by helping out with chores were more successful as they grew up than children who did not contribute to the running of the household. We all know that it's usually faster and easier to do household tasks ourselves, but researchers are finding that the earlier we get children involved in contributing to the good of the community, the better off they will be in the long run.

Think About It

Were you required to do chores or community service as you grew up? How do you feel about asking your own children to contribute on a regular basis to the running of the household? If regular chores don't work for your family, try some of the other suggestions for ways to help children contribute.

Some Ideas

- **Assign chores**—Think about assigning one or more child-friendly chores to your child, such as filling a pet's water bowl every evening, helping to make the bed, or putting the clean spoons and forks away after washing. Make sure to keep eager children away from knives and chemical cleaners that might harm them. Fill spray bottles with water for children to use for cleaning.

- **Family projects**—Have your child help with family projects such as planting flowers or vegetables, shopping for groceries, putting away the clean laundry, or cooking supper.

- **Donating**—When it is time to receive gifts, such as at holiday time or on birthdays, help your child select an older toy to donate to a children's shelter.

Chapter 6 Resources

Bailey, Becky. 2000. *Conscious Discipline: 7 Basic Skills for Brain Smart Classroom Management.* Oviedo, FL: Loving Guidance.

Brooks, Robert, and Sam Goldstein. 2001. *Raising Resilient Children: Fostering Strength, Hope, and Optimism in Your Child.* Lincolnwood, IL: Contemporary Books.

Curtis, Deb, and Margie Carter. 2008. *Learning Together with Young Children: A Curriculum Framework for Reflective Teachers.* St. Paul, MN: Redleaf Press.

Derman-Sparks, Louise, and the ABC Task Force. 1989. *Anti-Bias Curriculum: Tools for Empowering Young Children.* Washington, DC: National Association for the Education of Young Children.

Dinkmeyer, Don, and Gary D. McKay. 1973. *Raising a Responsible Child: Practical Steps to Successful Family Relationships.* New York: Simon and Schuster.

Hewitt, Deborah, and Sandra Heidemann. 1998. *The Optimistic Classroom: Creative Ways to Give Children Hope.* St. Paul, MN: Redleaf Press.

Katz, Lilian G., and Sylvia C. Chard. 2000. *Engaging Children's Minds: The Project Approach.* 2nd ed. Westport, CT: Praeger Publishers.

Lake, Vickie E., and Ithel Jones. 2012. *Service Learning in the PreK–3 Classroom: The What, Why, and How-To Guide for Every Teacher.* Minneapolis: Free Spirit Publishing.

Pelo, Ann, and Fran Davidson. 2000. *That's Not Fair: A Teacher's Guide to Activism with Young Children.* St. Paul, MN: Redleaf Press.

US Department of Health and Human Services. 2011. "Building Blocks: Preschool Bullying." Updated January 21. http://bblocks.samhsa.gov/Family/time/bullying.aspx.

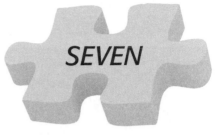

Adaptability

I am learning that there are different rules for different places.

Adaptability is the ability to move smoothly from situation to situation, adjusting language and behavior to conform to differing norms. Early childhood researchers, such as Samuel J. Meisels from Erikson Institute, have found that a child's ability to adapt to the behavioral expectations of school in the early years is one of the predictors of success later on in high school. Doing well in school depends in large part on the ability to develop school-related behaviors. The examples below from standards in Alaska, Kansas, Oregon, and Massachusetts outline many of the same adaptation skills you will find in your own state standards. This chapter will help you meet those standards.

- "Children adapt to diverse settings." *State of Alaska, Early Learning Guidelines*
- "Adapts behavior appropriate to different environments." *The Kansas Early Learning Standards*
- "Follows simple rules and participates in routines." *Oregon's Early Childhood Foundations Birth through Five*
- "Discuss why there may be different rules in different places (e.g., school rules may be different from rules at home)." *Massachusetts Guidelines for Preschool Learning Experiences*

Sam had just recently moved to town and already he was starting to adapt to the routines and expectations of his new school.

"At my old school," he said as the teacher guided him at the self-serve snack table, "the teacher gave us snack. This is funner."

When the teacher called the children to circle time, he eagerly sat down next to his new friend, Alex.

"You can't sit here," Alex told him. "This is Tara's space. Can't you see her sit-upon?"

Sam got up and looked anxiously at the teacher. "It's okay, Sam," she said. "At this school, kids have sit-upons at circle time. This blue one is yours. See your name on it? S-A-M. Sam."

Sam was reluctant to leave his new friend, but moved over to the place the teacher pointed out to him. When his mother came to get him at the end of the day, Sam ran over to her and told her all about his new friend Alex.

What Does Adaptability Look Like?

Although some of the rules and routines at this school were very different from what he was used to, Sam had little difficulty adapting to the new setting. Whether he liked the changes, such as self-serve snack, or didn't like the new guidelines, such as sit-upons at circle, he adjusted his behavior to be successful in the new setting. Adaptable children, like Sam, go with the flow of changing events and figure out how to act appropriately in various situations.

Adaptable children are also able to cope with the inevitable changes that occur in life. For example, they may have to adjust to a new sibling, a new school, and a new home. Children who come to school speaking a language other than English in their homes will have to learn English. Routines at school will be different than routines at home, and routines in kindergarten will be different from routines in preschool. Help all of the children in your group develop the skills they need to adapt and thrive in the face of change and adjust their behavior to fit changing situations.

When Things Go Wrong

Alvin couldn't wait to get to school Monday morning. He loved his classroom and loved his teachers. When he walked in the door, he knew right away that nothing was right. The block area was where the books were supposed to be and the take-apart table was pushed against the wrong wall.

"Look at our new classroom!" Ms. Maria said as she greeted him at the door. "Now we have more room to build. See?"

"Make it right again," Alvin said as he began to cry. "Make it the same like it was." He fetched his blanket from his cubby and hid under a table, not even coming out to play with the new cars the teachers had brought in.

◆   ◆   ◆

"Hailey, at school we don't hit kids. We use our words," reminded the teacher as she helped the two girls resolve a dispute.

"But she called me 'ugly girl,'" replied Hailey.

"We still don't hit people here, Hailey. That's not okay at school."

"My daddy said I need to hit kids who call me names," Hailey said. "And that Frannie girl called me names."

"Not at school, Hailey. No hitting at school."

"If girls call me names, they gonna get hit," Hailey said defiantly, slapping at the weeping Frannie one more time before running off.

Some children, like Alvin, struggle to adapt when anything deviates from their normal routines and expectations. A new teacher, a field trip, or even a new room arrangement can be overwhelming for children like Alvin. Whereas other children may embrace special events and novelty with excitement, children like Alvin may respond by withdrawing or having meltdowns.

According to past NAEYC president Barbara Bowman, by the time children are five years old they have learned the norms and rules of their homes and communities. Children like Hailey have trouble adapting to school rules when they differ from expectations and behaviors they have been taught at home and in their communities. Early childhood expert Samuel J. Meisels calls this a "social mismatch." Like Hailey, these children may struggle to go along with the daily routine or follow classroom guidelines that are different than those that have been successful for them in other settings. While some may react like Alvin by withdrawing or having meltdowns, others may respond with defiance the way Hailey did.

Children with temperaments like Alvin and Hailey are less adaptable by nature. They need a lot of adult support to manage changes and new situations successfully. You can help children like Alvin adapt to change and children like Hailey learn "how to do school" to prepare them to succeed both academically and socially.

Supportive Interactions to Promote Adaptability

Help children develop self-awareness by providing reflective feedback when they show evidence of adapting to a new situation. Establish and teach school expectations such as social scripts and classroom rules. Help children stay on track with prompting and supportive feedback. Make sure to clearly distinguish between those things that children must do and those things that are children's choice.

Acknowledge Adaptability

Include the vocabulary in your feedback to help children become aware of when they are exhibiting adaptability. For example, you might say:

"I heard you all using your whisper voices in the library instead of your outside voices. You're so adaptable."

"You guys did so well when the police officer came in to visit with his police dog. You're very adaptable."

"Elizabeth, I saw that you followed all the new rules for how to take care of the hamster. You're quite adaptable."

Help Children Learn the Social Scripts of School

People use social scripts to interact with one another as they move through the day. These social scripts grease the wheels of human interactions. For example, as you pass a colleague in the hallway, he might say, "Hi! How are you?" What would be your answer to this? If you are like most folks, you might answer something like "Fine. How are you?" This exchange is an example of a "greeting script" that many of us have learned for the workplace. The underlying meaning of this script is "Hello. I know and acknowledge you but I really don't want to begin a lengthy conversation with you. I merely want to acknowledge our relationship." What happens when you attempt this social script with somebody who doesn't know her lines? Imagine how you feel if the response to your greeting is something like this: "Oh my. You wouldn't believe what's going on in my life. My car is broken down and James is coming down with something. I think it might be the flu." This is an example of one person using a social script that is not understood by the other. The misunderstanding can lead to annoyance or hurt feelings, even when adults are involved. Imagine how much harder it is for children, who are just learning the appropriate social scripts to use in all the different settings they find themselves in.

Successful adults and children constantly adjust their language to fit the social norms. Children who know and use the "second language of school" use socially appropriate language as they navigate their school day. School is a microculture with its own very specific language, norms, traditions, and guidelines. For example, teachers want kids to use their words, to behave and speak in friendly ways, and to refrain from profanity and name-calling. These language customs are the social scripting we have established as the standard for classroom culture.

Children bring the social scripts they learn from home and from their neighborhoods with them to school. Perhaps their family has taught them to say thank you when they are given something. Maybe older children from the home and neighborhood model the use of profanity. Or maybe a child has learned from her family that when someone gets hurt you should ask, "Are you okay?"

You may ask children to use language and behavior at school that is different from what families model and teach at home. This "second language of school" is the words you teach children to use to connect, relate, and function within the classroom. Part of your challenge is to help children become fluent in the language of school so they can shift seamlessly between the culture at home and the culture at school.

Knowledge of and skill in the social scripts used by peer groups is essential to the smooth relationships among group members. Help children learn some standard social scripts used by their peers in the school setting. It is useful for children to have scripts for situations such as greetings and good-byes, apologies, entering play, rejecting play invitations kindly, and setting boundaries. You can find many typical scripts for these situations in chapters 3 and 4 and appendix B (beginning on page 293).

Use "At School We . . ."

The South Carolina Early Learning Standards state it this way: "Because young children have learned behaviors, language, and values through their families' lifestyle and modeling, they will bring these practices to school. Teachers must show respect for the child's family and culture while helping him/her to learn those skills and attitudes which have demonstrated to underlie school success" (2007, 27).

It is helpful to remember that rules and expectations at school are not the same as rules and expectations for everyone, everywhere. For example, when you are at the beach with your friends or family, you dress, talk, and behave differently than you do at work. When children are at a basketball game they are expected to follow different norms than when they are visiting the library. Socially savvy people ask themselves questions like this one (perhaps unconsciously): "Where am I and how are other people behaving?" As a teacher, you expect children to "use their walking feet" indoors, listen quietly during story time, and sit at the table when they are eating. Even though you may believe that guidelines such as "wash your hands before you eat" or "we don't use that kind of language" or "no hitting" are the same for everyone, don't assume that all families or all cultures would agree.

When you think about a child's behavior, remember that the child is coming to school with a set of social norms established in the home environment. The norms at home may be very different from the norms at school.

- At school, boys and girls often use different bathrooms. At home, family members probably use the same bathroom.

- At school, children might be discouraged from roughhousing. At home, sibling wrestling may be condoned or even encouraged by families.

- At school, a teacher might view eye contact as a sign of respect when reprimanding a child. At home, that same child might be taught to lower her eyes when an adult is redirecting her.

Sometimes, the way problems are solved at home might be different from the way problems are solved in the classroom.

- At home, siblings may be encouraged to "fight it out" when they have conflicts.

- At home, some family members may throw or break things when they are angry or frustrated.

- In some homes, family members might find it hard to tolerate children's sadness, and they may bend their rules in an effort to get children to stop crying.

Children do best when you are able to support home expectations while at the same time enforcing school expectations. How then can you avoid statements that start with "But my mommy said . . ."? (But my mommy said . . . I should hit him, I don't need to wash my hands, I can go outside without my shoes, and so on.)

Remind children of school guidelines by consistently using the phrase "At school we . . ." When you preface a statement with "At school we . . ." you help children identify immediately that what will follow is an expectation of behavior at school.

When . . .	"At school . . ."
Children physically fight over a bike.	"At school we use words, not hands, to solve problems."
Children cry in order to get adults to bend the rules.	"At school the rules stay the same, even when children cry."
Children behave as if they are helpless to get adults to do tasks for them.	"At school (zipping, flushing, drawing, pouring, and so on) is a child's job."

If a child responds with, "But my mommy said I don't need to throw away my own trash," simply respond, "It's okay that your mommy told you that rule for your house. At school we throw away our own snack trash." The "at school we" phrase is even more important when guiding about sensitive issues such as nudity, touching, hitting, profanity, and inclusion.

You will find this phrase is also useful when talking with parents. If a parent is worried because you won't let a child defend himself with physical aggression, avoid moral debates on violence as a means to resolve conflict. Instead, you can say something such as, "I understand you don't want Nathanial to be bullied. I don't want him to be bullied either. At school, we will find other ways to deal with bullying besides hitting back." Notice that this response also follows the template of "validate feelings before guiding behavior."

Ask "Where Are You?"

"At school we" is one way to introduce the concept of behavior changing based on the context. However, children can easily forget to monitor where they are so they can successfully adjust their behavior to match the environment. Are they at home? At school? At grandma's?

Many children are visual learners instead of auditory learners. Help children use their vision as a guideline for appropriate behavior. Use a phrase such as, "Look around you. Where are you right now?" This prompt often works to help children switch back to their "school persona."

- When Shea gets up during circle time and starts twirling around and bumping into others, say, "Shea, stop a minute. Look around. Where are you right now?"

- When Santo is on the loft, tossing baby dolls over the railing, say, "Santo. Look around. Where are you right now?"

Establish and Define Guiding Principles of Behavior

The core element of limits and expectations are the classroom's guiding principles of behavior. Children use these guidelines and expectations to help them organize themselves and make positive choices. As you think of what kinds of rules might be most useful in your classroom, keep the following questions in mind:

1. Does the rule teach an important life skill? If it doesn't, can it be reworded so that it does? For example, "no running" isn't a very good life skill. There are many times in life when running is not only appropriate but essential, such as running from a burning building. If the no-running rule was created to prevent accidents, perhaps the rule might be better worded as "keep yourself and others safe."

2. Is the rule or guideline stated in the positive? Developmentally, children are not generally able to flip a negative to a positive until they are in first or second grade. For young children, "bite" and "no biting" can sound like the same thing. Children have a much easier time doing something than not doing something. If the true meaning of "don't bite" is to treat each other gently, the rule might be worded "treat each other gently."

3. Is the rule a guiding principle of behavior? A guiding principle is a general statement that can be applied in many circumstances over a long period.

Try the following exercise to get a deeper understanding of the concept of guiding principles of behavior. Think of someone whom you greatly admire. This can be someone you know personally, such as your grandmother, or it can be a famous person, such as Abraham Lincoln. Now imagine that the person you admire has one rule she or he uses to guide decisions, large and small. What would that rule be? Write the rule in the following box.

Did you write something like "always be your best" or "do unto others" or "be kind and work hard" or "follow your beliefs"? These are all examples of guiding principles of behavior. They are all general guidelines that can be applied in many circumstances over a long period of time.

Establish the same kinds of broad guidelines for members of your classroom community. Here is a sample set of three guiding principles of behavior for an early childhood classroom:

1. We take care of ourselves.

2. We take care of others.

3. We take care of things.

Notice how broad these guiding principles are. Instead of five or six detailed rules like "no running" and "keep your hands to yourself," the three guidelines help children develop an internal compass or measuring stick to evaluate thousands of different possible behaviors. The guidelines are timeless life skills that will be useful long after preschool.

Maybe you are thinking that these rules are too vague for very young children who are still such concrete thinkers. You may be wondering how a child can get from "treat each other gently" to "don't hit Ralph just because you want his paintbrush." Children understand abstract concepts over time with many hands-on, immediate, concrete examples. Teach these global concepts with the same kinds of strategies you use to introduce children to any new concept. When you teach the concept of red, you talk about red paint during painting, tell kids who are wearing red that they may wash for lunch, or gather a basket of all the red things the children can find in the room.

One way to help children learn what the guiding principles mean is to use the principle when you are explaining a school rule. Use variations of the template: "At school we (rule) because (principle)." Here are some examples:

- At school we wash our hands to get all the germs off after we pet the goat, because we take care of ourselves.

- At school we keep the sand on the ground so it doesn't get into anyone's eyes, because we take care of each other.

- At school we put our smocks back on the hook when we are done painting, because we take care of things in the Rainbow class.

Provide Reflective Feedback

One of the most powerful tools we have to help children learn the guiding principles of behavior is to give them reflective feedback when they are acting in accordance with the principles. When you use reflective feedback instead of saying "Good job" or "I like the way you . . . ," you are helping children build intrinsic motivation and a deeper understanding of the expectations. Children begin to internalize the guiding principles and start to construct an internal compass that they can use to inform their behavior choices. Recognition invites repetition—the behavior that gets our positive response is most likely to be repeated again in the future.

One reflective-feedback template that you might find useful is: "You (action) because (principle)."

"You washed your hands before you ate because we take care of ourselves."

"You waited for a turn at the slide because we take care of each other."

"You put all the blocks back on the shelf because we take care of our stuff."

Use the Guiding Principles for Guiding and Redirection

Use guiding principles when you are asking children to comply with a direction or when children are off task and you are redirecting them to get back on track.

Give the direction . . .	Because . . . (guiding principle or behavior)
"Akio, we need to keep our shoes on outside . . .	. . . because we take care of ourselves."
"Tito, Miguel isn't done at the drinking fountain yet. You need to wait for a turn . . .	. . . because we need to take care of each other."
"When you're done with snack, please put your banana peel in the trash . . .	. . . because we take care of our stuff."

When a child has done something that requires redirection, weave in the guiding principles to guide the child to select a more appropriate behavior.

When the child . . .	Weave the guiding principle into the redirection
Wants to grab a bike from another child.	"You wish you had that bike. At school, we can't just grab things because we take care of others. Let's find another way to solve this."
"Borrows" things from school without asking.	"You would love to take this toy to your house. We take care of our stuff at school, so we'll leave it here to play with tomorrow. Let's find something that you can take home with you."
Hits a child to get what she wants.	"We take care of others at school. If the kids won't listen to your words, come get me and I'll help you."
Throws markers on the floor because he's frustrated by not being able to draw a car.	"You're having trouble drawing that car. At school, we keep markers on the table because we take care of our stuff. Let's see if there is some way to help you."

Mandatory and Optional

Young children have a fascination with new and unusual words. Make the most of this natural interest to introduce the concepts of *mandatory* and *optional* to the children in your group. When you label certain activities as mandatory or optional, you help children distinguish between what they *must* do from what they *may choose* to do. In a classroom where everything is new and where customs and expectations are all new to the child, clarifying this distinction makes life easier for everyone.

Consistency is key to help children form useful definitions of these words. The meaning of the word *mandatory* is "nonnegotiable." It must happen. For children to clearly understand this meaning, make sure to follow up when an activity is labeled mandatory. If an activity is mandatory and the child does not do it and slips through the cracks, she will have trouble forming the correct definition of the word. Make the word familiar to children by announcing one activity each morning that will be mandatory. Then make clear some other choices that are optional.

> "There is new smelly fingerpaint out on the round table. That is an optional activity today. Remember, though, that doing your job from the job board is mandatory."

> "I want everyone to do some work on the fish mural today. That is mandatory. All the other center activities are optional."

After the word has been in use in the classroom for a while, begin to use it for things such as cleaning up, hand washing before snack, or coming in from outside. Help children begin to internally organize the concept that sometimes there are mandatory and nonnegotiable tasks that must get done whether they want to do them or not. Use the label "mandatory" for these activities to remove it from debate. When a child whines, "But I don't want to wash my hands," instead of rationalization and debate you can simply reply, "I understand you don't feel like washing. Washing hands is mandatory, though. Come, let's go together." By setting yourself up as an empathetic support for the child and one who reminds the child of mandatory events, you can pull yourself out of personal power struggles. Children quickly learn these terms and use them to make sense of the world. One teacher who implemented these words in her classroom reported on how fluent the children became with the terms.

> "Is the gingerbread house project mandatory or optional?" asked four-year-old Ahbre.
> "Optional," Samantha answered. "But remember that choosing a book to take home this weekend is mandatory, so you might want to get that done now so you don't forget."
> "Okay, I'll go get a book and put it in my cubby."

Support Adaptability through the Classroom Culture

When children have a safe and predictable environment, they are more able to adjust to occasional changes. Help children adapt when there are changes by creating special rituals and routines to support them as they adjust.

Provide a Safe and Predictable Environment

Kids have trouble organizing their space, time, and actions when things change all the time. When children don't have to expend a lot of energy figuring out the system, they can relax and use that energy to learn, explore, and make positive connections with others. Children who have a safe and predictable base are more apt to be adaptable.

- Establish and stick to a classroom schedule and daily routine. While adults might find a regular schedule boring, children find predictability reassuring and safe. This doesn't mean you can never have special events. Just make sure that novelty is embedded in a foundation of predictability.

- Resist the urge to make frequent changes to the room arrangement. When you do rearrange the room, think of involving the children in the process. To understand how disorienting this can be for children, imagine what it would feel like if every few weeks you arrived home from work to find that someone had come in and moved everything around in your house.

- Make sure all the adults in the classroom are guiding children with the same set of rules. Hearing different messages from different teachers makes it difficult for children to figure out and follow classroom expectations. Think, for example, of rules such as whether or not children may take toys or books with them to their rest mats, whether or not children need to wait for everyone to be served food before they can begin eating, or whether everything in the room needs to be put back in place before transitioning outside. Make sure everyone who works with the children is on the same page.

Help Children Adapt to Changes

As much as you might try to provide consistency for the children in your care, things change. Staff members and children come and go, special events come up, and you might decide to rearrange the room to meet the changing needs of the children. Create classroom rituals and routines to help children prepare for and adjust to the inevitable changes such as these that happen in life.

Preview Changes

Help children adapt to change by preparing for new events, new people, and other unusual activities. Even small changes can throw off some young children and cause them to become anxious. Anxious children will either externalize their anxiety by hitting, running around, acting the fool, or being defiant, or they may internalize by withdrawing from activities, weeping, whining, or acting helpless and pathetic.

Prepare children for a field trip to the fire station, for a grandmother who will come in to read a story, or for moving the classroom furniture around. Help children focus on what will be the same and what will be different.

When talking about rearranging furniture, one class made the following discoveries.

What will be the same?	What will be different?
We will have the same toys.	The blocks will be in a different place.
We will have the same kids.	We will read books in the other corner.
We will have the same teachers.	The water table will be on the other side.
We will still have snack.	I don't know where dress-up will be.
We will still have a window.	
My friends will be here.	
We still go home to sleep at night.	

Rituals for Major Transitions

Teachers spend a lot of time at the beginning of the year helping children develop friendships and a sense of community. But often, too little time is spent at the *end* of the year learning how to say good-bye. Just as young children often need help learning how to form friendships and community bonds, they also need help to say good-bye at the end of the school year. Even in programs that don't close for the summer, children may transition into new classrooms as a group or perhaps around their birthdays.

Good-byes can be painful and scary. When children become aware that they will be moving on, they might begin to worry. Children who don't know how to say good-bye might behave much like the children who had trouble forming friendships at the beginning of the school year. They might hit or name-call or hide under the table. They might act younger in the hopes that they won't be old enough to move on. Often children will sabotage friendships and connections with peers and adults to ease the pain of parting.

Forming strong bonds and learning to say good-bye as we move on to new adventures is an emotional skill that will serve children for life. Saying good-bye at the end of the classroom year or when moving or transitioning to a new classroom is a beginning step to saying good-bye to an old house or a disintegrating blanket. Learning parting skills also prepares children for a dying pet, a move, a divorce, or the death of a loved one.

Like other social and emotional skills, learning to say good-bye doesn't happen from one activity or one project. Plan on introducing good-bye lessons at least a month before the end of the school year or even earlier if children are beginning to show symptoms of "good-bye anxiety."

The better the job we have done to form a cohesive community, the more the members need closure when the members of the community part ways.

- Have children draw a picture about what they think will be the same next year or what they think will be different. Bind these pictures into a "Same and Different" book to keep in the classroom collection. Read and reread the story as needed for the group and for individual children.

- Distribute class-made Big Books to children if you have enough to give one to each child.

- If only one child is leaving the group, help the children make a "We Will Miss You" book with drawings, photos, and dictated messages for the child to take with her. Make sure to also post a picture of the child who is leaving on a "We Will Remember You" poster that you keep on the wall to remind the group of members who have moved on.

Help Children Learn How to Say Good-Bye

Help children adapt by establishing rituals and routines for saying good-bye to staff or children who leave the group during the year. Remember that children are very egocentric, and they interpret life through a "how will this affect me?" lens. If a child should leave your group without a farewell ceremony of some sort, many children will feel uneasy and might make up all sorts of wild fantasies about why the child is no longer with the group, and they may worry that one day they, too, will disappear to who knows where. Increased anxiety might show up as clingy behavior, aggression, destruction, or contrary behavior.

Work as a class to make a good-bye ritual for members who have to leave during the year. Here are some ideas:

- Have a simple good-bye party for a departing member.

- Set up a writing center with paper and markers so children can "write" good-bye notes.

- Put together a blank book for the child who is leaving. Let the child paste in extra pictures you have of the class and then dictate captions for the photos. Invite children to "sign" the memory book if they like.

- Make up a good-bye and wish-you-well ceremony to do as a large-group activity. This might include a song or a chant. Maybe each child can share a good memory of the parting child.

- Have the class present the child or adult who is leaving with one of the Big Books that they have made during the year.

- If you know the last day in advance, make a countdown calendar and mark off the days at the morning meeting.

- Sometimes members leave without notice. Explain to the group what you know about the departure and include a memory activity. For example, at center time that day you might set up a "We Remember (name)" table. Put a photo of the child or adult on a large piece of paper. Invite children to dictate their memory or sign their name on the poster. Mount the finished work on the wall.

Activities to Support Adaptability

Help children think about change and explore guiding principles in playful ways with some of the following activities.

"What If"

Play "what if" games to help children think about changes in playful and non-threatening ways. Think of questions like these:

- What would happen if cars could fly?
- What if we went to school at night and slept in the day?
- What would happen if everybody had to walk upside down?
- What would happen if dogs could talk?
- What would happen if kids could fly airplanes to school?

Kindergarten Orientation

If you are a prekindergarten teacher, you have probably experienced children starting to act out in late spring. One reason this happens is because of a general increase in anxiety about moving on to kindergarten. Some children have heard stories from older siblings about school that may have scared them. Other children, who may have been in your program since they were toddlers, worry about leaving the familiarity of your program and moving on to the unknown.

In fact, kindergarten *will* probably be very different from preschool. There will probably be new rituals such as the morning pledge, raising your hand, restrooms down the hallway, and special teachers for art, music, and physical education. Children may wear uniforms, and there will probably be no more naptime. They may be moving from a part-day program to a full-day program or vice versa. Supplement the transition strategies above with the following ideas.

Panel Discussion

One teacher invited a few kindergarten children who had previously attended the preschool to come in for a "panel discussion." She set up a "speaker table" for the kindergartners at the front of the room, and sat the preschoolers on the floor. She began the discussion by asking the kindergarten children questions such as these:

- Do you take naps in kindergarten?
- Where do you eat lunch when you are in kindergarten?
- Do you have special school uniforms that all the kids wear?
- What is your favorite thing about going to kindergarten?
- Do you have toys in your classroom?

Then she asked the preschoolers if they had any questions to ask the kindergartners. She ended the activity by telling the preschoolers that next year, when *they* were in kindergarten, they could come back to visit and talk to the preschoolers just like these kids did.

Kindergarten Boot Camp

Another teacher conducted what she called "Kindergarten Boot Camp." To prepare, she visited a few of the kindergarten classrooms that some of her preschoolers would be going to in the fall to figure out some rules and rituals that might be new to her kids. For the last month or so of preschool, she included an activity called Let's Play Kindergarten, where she introduced these new rituals to the children. Let's Play Kindergarten might look something like this:

- "When I went to visit kindergarten, I saw that in the morning, all the children stood up and talked to a flag just like this one. (Show the children the American flag.) This is the flag for our country. Let's learn the little poem we say." (Help the children learn the pledge and how to stand with their hand over their heart.)
- "When I went to visit kindergarten, I saw that children put their hands up in the air when they wanted to say something at circle. And then the teacher saw their hand and said, 'What do you want to say?' Let's play 'Raise Your Hand' at circle this morning, okay? Remember, if I don't say, 'What do you want to say?' you need to be very, very quiet. Do you think you can do that? Let's try."
- "When I went to visit kindergarten, I saw that there was a chair in the room that the teacher called a 'Time-Out Chair.' This was a special place for children to sit if they forgot one of the rules in the class. Let me show you how that works. (Put a chair in the back of the room and sit in it). See how this works? Then the child sits there for a little while

until the teacher says it's okay to get up. Who would like to pretend they forgot a rule? Okay. Francisco, you can be first. I'll say, 'Go sit in time-out,' and you can go sit in the chair. Remember, you need to stay there till I say, 'Okay. You can come out now.' Ready?"

It is especially important to do activities such as these for children who have trouble adapting and react with anxiety when things are unfamiliar. Give children as many tools as you can to help them feel confident when they move into new situations.

Supporting Adaptability through Dramatic Play

Children can learn social skills, such as the ability to adapt to different situations, through the relatively risk-free environment of pretend play. Try these ideas for starters:

- Act out a storybook you have just read.

- Pretend to be animals who just escaped from the zoo.

- Switch roles and have the children be the teachers and the teachers be the children.

- Add new themes to the dramatic play area such as grocery store, hospital, or pet shop.

At Home . . . At School Book

Help children make "At Home . . . At School" books from some of the most universal differences between home and school. Create one page for each difference, and invite children to illustrate the pages. Below are some ideas of differences you might talk about.

- We stay in our house at night. We never stay at school at night.

- We sleep in beds at home. We rest on mats at school.

- We don't raise our hand at home. We raise our hand at school.

- We take a bath at home. We don't take a bath at school.

- We watch TV at home. We don't watch TV at school.

- We don't have fire drills at home. We have fire drills at school.

- We wear pajamas at home. We don't wear pajamas at school.

- We don't do circle time at home. We do circle time at school.

- We don't have centers at home. We have centers at school.

- We can have a snack when we want at home. We have snack at snack-time at school.

Guiding Principles Book

Children need concrete visual reminders and much repetition in order to learn guiding principles of behavior. Help the children in your class to make a Big Book that uses practical examples of the guiding principles.

1. Use one guiding principle for each Big Book. For example, "We take care of each other."

    - Give each child one blank page.

    - Help each child come up with an example of how he can help to take care of others. Some children have an easier time with this task if you have them complete the sentence: "I take care of other people when I _____." Print their words on the bottom of the page.

2. Have each child draw an illustration for their example.

3. Add a page where parents can write responses.

4. Bind the pages and add a cover.

5. Read the book to the children and allow them to take it home overnight to share with their families.

Looks Like/Sounds Like Charts

This is a variation of making guiding-principle Big Books. Instead of putting together books, work together with the children to make a chart for each guiding principle. Hang these charts on the wall at the children's eye level so they can see the pictures often during the day. The process of creating the chart is as much a teaching strategy as the resulting chart itself. For example, make a "Looks Like/Sounds Like" chart for "We take care of our stuff."

1. Divide the chart down the middle. Label the left-hand column "Looks Like" and the right-hand column "Sounds Like."

2. Work with the children to fill in the chart. For example, title a chart "We take care of our stuff" and brainstorm with the children what "taking care of our stuff" might look and sound like.

3. Have the children describe it, act it out, and see what it looks like and sounds like.

4. Take pictures of the children "taking care of stuff" and post these pictures on the chart. Since visual cues work much better for many young children than verbal cues, these pictures are invaluable.

5. As children act out what taking care "looks like," ask them to tell you what they are doing. For example, "Use the markers on the table" or

"I'm gonna wipe the water up." Take dictation of these words for the "sounds like" side of the chart.

Who should be the models for the "looks like" pictures? Choose the child who is least proficient at the skill. Ask the child if she would like to pose for "taking care of stuff." Now you have a picture of appropriate behavior that includes a picture of your struggling child doing the activity successfully. Each time that child sees that picture, she sees herself as successful at that task. Seeing this message over and over starts to reprogram her self-concept: "Yes, I'm a kid who can take care of stuff. There's the proof right up there on the wall. That's me taking care of things."

Story Time and Puppetry

Children need to see guiding principles in many different contexts if they are to internalize them as their own standards. Use your normal story time to reinforce these principles as one way to weave the guiding principles of behavior into your daily curriculum.

As you read books to children, take notice of examples of characters who demonstrate your guiding principles of behavior. For example, if the children in the story wash the dog, it could be used as an example of "we take care of each other."

You might say something like, "Look. They gave him a bath. The kids were following our guideline . . . they were taking care of each other."

Use puppets to act out other examples of your guiding principles and have children figure out which principle you are demonstrating.

Have the puppet(s)	Ask . . .
Wash his hands before snack.	"Is he taking care of himself, taking care of others, or taking care of his things? What do you think?"
Put a bandage on his friend's nose.	"Is he taking care of himself, taking care of others, or taking care of his things? What do you think?"
Put the puzzle pieces back in the box.	"Is he taking care of himself, taking care of others, or taking care of his things? What do you think?"

Poster Children

Similar to the Looks Like/Sounds Like chart, help a child who might have trouble adapting to a classroom expectation such as standing in line by posting a picture of the child doing the skill. For example, include a "standing in line at school" poster with a photo of the struggling child modeling the skill. This visual proof begins to change the child's self-talk and self-image. When children see visual reminders that they can do something, it encourages them to continue that behavior.

Who Can I Match?

Matching others is a life skill. I don't go to the opera very often. But when I do, I make sure to match others in the audience so I know when to applaud and when not to applaud. When I attend religious services in an unfamiliar house of worship, I need to match others to figure out what I should be doing.

Don't be afraid to use "child experts" in the classroom as visual models for children who are still learning limits and guidelines. When a child is struggling to figure out what to do in certain social situations, invite him to "match" somebody who does know.

1. Chat with the challenged child and brainstorm with that child to decide who in the class might know the expected behavior for the problem situation. For example, say to the child, "Who in our class seems to know how to do 'Music Special' really well?" "Who seems to know how to do lining up?" "Who in our class seems to know circle time?" Help the child find somebody who demonstrates the expected behavior in a skilled way.

2. Talk a bit about what it is that the skilled child does that lets us know she is doing it well.

3. Help the child who is still learning the skill use the more skilled child as a cuing system. Say, "Remember, you can take a look at Adam or Bethany if you forget what to do at circle. Usually they know what they are doing and then you can match them and get back on track."

4. Avoid saying, "Do like the other children," because often the child will choose someone who is equally challenged and off task. You want them to pick someone who is competent at the skill.

Discussion/Reflection Questions

1. What are the guiding principles of behavior that you use to guide your own behavior choices? Are they similar to the ones discussed in this chapter?

_____

_____

_____

_____

2. To what extent should we require that children change behaviors and expectations taught at home to adapt to school guidelines? Can you think of times that the school should adapt to home expectations?

_____

_____

_____

_____

Exercises

1. Take a look at your classroom rules. Try to develop two or three guiding principles that include the most important rules.

_____

_____

_____

_____

2. Create a class-made book with the children in your group with photos and dictation to illustrate your classroom's guiding principles of behavior. Read the created book to the children over the next few weeks. Do you notice any change in the children's behavior?

_____

_____

_____

_____

3. Think of a child who acts inappropriately at school. Might the issue be that the child is acting with behaviors and expectations from home? What two strategies might you use to help the child adapt to school expectations?

_____

_____

_____

_____

Reflection/Journal Assignment

What are some major changes you have had to adapt to in your life? What was the experience like for you? How do you respond to unexpected or unwelcome changes? Do you dig in your heels? Withdraw? Fall apart emotionally? Seek support from family or a trusted friend?

_____

_____

_____

_____

_____

_____

_____

_____

_____

_____

_____

_____

_____

_____

_____

_____

_____

_____

_____

Helping Your Child Adapt to School

As the Japanese author Kakuzo Okakura noted, "The art of life lies in a constant readjustment to our surroundings." We dress one way for the beach and another when going to a formal wedding. We talk one way to friends at a football game and another way with our boss at work. It is no different for children. At home they use the bathroom whenever they want. At school they may have to ask the teacher for permission. At home they may be able to run around barefoot, while at school they may be required to keep their shoes on all day.

Think About It

As children begin to experience life outside the home, they will find that some rules are the same and some rules are different. Maybe at school children are permitted to tell another child they don't want to play with them, but at home you expect your child to let anyone join their play. You might find that they try out their new school rules at home. Help children learn which home rules are rules for everywhere, such as "no playing with matches or fire." Let children know what other rules depend on where they are, such as "at home we say grace before we eat, but at school it's okay not to say grace."

Some Ideas

- Before going somewhere outside the home, remind children of the new rules they will need to follow. For example, "Remember, when we are in the store, you may not touch anything on the shelves" or "Remember, when we are at the movies, you need to talk in your whisper voice."

- Be clear with children when home rules are different than rules they might have outside of home. "I know at Grandma's you can eat cookies before supper. That's what you do at Grandma's. At home, we don't do that."

- Remind children of the rules you want them to follow no matter where they are. "We don't call people stupid, even if they call you that first."

Chapter 7 Resources

Bowman, Barbara. 1994. "Cultural Diversity and Academic Achievement." Oak Brook, IL: North Central Regional Educational Laboratory.

Cesarone, Bernard, ed. 1999. "Resilience Guide: A Collection of Resources on Resilience in Children and Families." ERIC Publications. ED 436307. http://www.eric.ed.gov:80/PDFS/ED436307.pdf.

Meisels, Samuel, J. Dorfman, and D. Steele. 1992. *Contrasting Approaches to Assessing Young Children's School Readiness and Achievement.* Washington, DC: National Center for Educational Statistics, US Department of Education.

Meisels, Samuel, Donna DiPrima Bickel, Julie Nicholson, Yange Xue, and Sally Atkins-Burnett. 2001. "Trusting Teachers' Judgments: A Validity Study of Curriculum-Embedded Performance Assessment in Kindergarten to Grade 3." *American Educational Research Journal* 38 (1): 73–95.

Ziegler, Robert G. 1992. *Homemade Books to Help Kids Cope: An Easy-to-Learn Technique for Parents and Professionals.* New York: Magination Press.

EIGHT

Children Who Need Extra Support

The six life skills, along with all their strategies, can be looked at as kind of "universal precautions" for all children. They are the basic building blocks needed for all children to succeed in school and in life. In order to support children's social and emotional development, infuse strategies such as those outlined in the life-skill chapters into the typical program, day in and day out, throughout the year.

As we know, though, children don't enter our programs with the same backgrounds, experiences, strengths, or challenges. While the six life-skill strategies will help all children, some children will still require additional support.

Review the rhyming exercise on page 198 in chapter 6. If you haven't already done this exercise, do it now before you go any further.

As I wrote about in that exercise, when one or two children require extra support to learn how to rhyme, you can try to figure out some additional strategies to help them develop those skills. You might try playing some extra rhyming games with them during transition time, sending some rhyming books home for parents to read to their children, or singing rhyming chants to them as you push them on the swings.

It is no different with social and emotional skills. Using the strategies in the six life-skills chapters will help most of the children reach a level of proficiency. Sometimes, even when you have implemented all the best practices you can think of to help children build the resiliency skills they need to thrive socially and emotionally, one kid still struggles through the day. There will always be a small number of children who need extra support. This chapter gives you a systematic way of looking at those kids to figure out additional strategies to use to teach them the skills.

Remember, when you taught rhyming and some kids didn't quite catch on, you didn't put those children in time-out or take away privileges. You didn't make them lose outside time. You figured out new ways to teach the skills. The remedial approach you use for language and literacy or number learning is the same approach that you can use for social and emotional development. Don't punish children for not having the skills they need—figure out what you can do to help them learn the skills they need. Children who have poor self-regulation don't "do it on purpose" any more than a child who has trouble rhyming does that on purpose. Children want to be happy and have a nice day. Some children just don't know how.

When things don't go right with a child, when he or she is still having problems even after there has been a good effort to build the six life skills, it is important to take a closer look. Look at how the child relates to adults and other children. Try to evaluate the child's level of social skills, emotional self-regulation, ability to problem solve, and general feelings of hopefulness and hopelessness. Plan to target building those basic resiliency skills since we know that children who have those skills generally move through life in a peaceful way. Another thing we know about "naughty" children is that they are actually good most of the time. Take a look at when the child does well and build on those strengths.

The trick is to figure out what the real issue(s) is/are and work from there. Typically, children, like everyone else, want to have a nice life. They want love, recognition, a feeling of belonging, a feeling of competence, a feeling of empowerment. They will do what they need to do to get it. Some people do screwy things to get those feelings. And when we have a child who does that, it's our job as the adults in his life to figure out where the glitch is and help him move through it.

So what do you do to help children learn how to develop the six life skills? Observe them carefully to see if you can find just what might be getting in the way of their success. Then target your interactions, rituals and routines, and special activities to give these children additional experiences they need to be successful. To help kids who need more support, take these steps:

1. Observe children closely using the "Getting to Know You" form (in appendix A) as a guide.
2. Develop an action plan.
3. Avoid the unintended side effects of punishment.
4. Use strength-based redirection strategies.

Teaching the six life skills is a preventative strategy. It is something that you would do for all children, just as you would teach all children literacy and math skills. Some children will need additional help in learning literacy or math skills, even when you have a solid literacy or math curriculum. Some children will need additional help in learning social and emotional skills.

Observe Children Closely

At training sessions, I often am asked questions like "What do I do about a kid who bites?" or "What do I do about a kid who runs away when I call him?" My answer is always the same: "I don't have any idea."

If there were a one-size-fits-all answer to questions like these, there would be no need for a book like this. The real answer is, "To know how to answer these kinds of questions, I would need to know a whole lot more about the child and what's going on in his/her life both inside and outside school." How do you find out this information? Systematically observe the children.

The "Getting to Know You" form is one way to go about recording observations so you can make an appropriate plan to help children if they are still struggling after all the universal strategies have been used. I designed this "Getting to Know You" form as a job aid for myself to focus my observations. I wanted to make sure that I looked at what I consider to be key indicators of what might be standing in the way of this child thriving in school. You can find a copy of the complete form in appendix A. Once I figure out where the problem areas are, I can target some specific interventions to help move the child along.

This observation begins with at least one uninterrupted hour of sitting on the side and observing. When doing an observation, there is so much going on in an early childhood classroom that the observer needs to know what she is looking for. I call this a "focused observation." The "Getting to Know You" form helps organize the collection of data from observations while focusing on seven key indicators that help you figure out what is going on, and provides clues as to how you can best support this child.

1. The six life skills.
2. What are this child's interests and areas of expertise? What does this child choose to play with?
3. What is the child's play level?
4. What is the child's preferred learning style?
5. When do things work?
6. When do things fall apart?
7. What are the child's family culture, hopes, and dreams?

Even though doing an observation like this requires a dedicated observer for an hour or two, most programs find that the time is well invested. An outside observer can see things that are invisible to a classroom teacher who is immersed in the action.

There are advantages and disadvantages to having the classroom teacher do the observation. One advantage is that the teacher knows the child and the classroom dynamics best, and might be able to more accurately interpret what is seen. However, a disadvantage is that the classroom atmosphere would not be quite the same with an assistant running the class while the teacher observes. Another disadvantage is that the teacher might have preconceptions about the child. An advantage to having an outside observer is that the observation is done in a typical setting with the regular teacher in charge. The outside observer also comes into the situation with no preconceptions. The disadvantage is that the outside observer doesn't know the child, the family, or the classroom, and might be less able to interpret what she's seeing as a result. Six of one, half a dozen of the other.

The task of the observer is to create a running record of what she or he sees and hears during an hour. The notes should be objective, with any guesses or interpretations set off by parentheses. Don't worry about full sentences, just get down the information.

Here is an example of five minutes of observation notes.

8:30 J goes to snack table. 4 other kids there already. L reminds wash hands. J sits. L reminds. J ignores. L takes hand and tries to walk to bathroom. J holds chair, chair falls, J laughs. Hooks feet in chair. L tries to free from chair, J kicks her. L picks up, takes to beanbag. Tells "No kicking. That hurt." J laughs.

8:35 J goes to other snack table. Eat, no wash. Talk, laugh with other kids. L busy, doesn't see him come back.

So here's how the observation process works, using an actual example from our program. The teacher reports that child "D" strikes out suddenly and for no reason, randomly hurting other children. Other children are becoming scared of D, and the teacher is afraid that D might severely hurt somebody. Nothing she has tried so far seems to work. The observer's challenge is to see if by looking at the situation from the outside she can see something that the teacher is missing by being in the action.

The task for the observer is to watch the child and jot down everything he or she sees and hears, noting the larger context as much as possible. For example, a fifteen-minute note talking about child "D" might look like this.

D in block area building structure. G joins. Work together on same structure. M joins. D leaves. Wanders. Knocks pegboard off shelf. Nobody sees. Goes to cubby. Gets small car and puts in pocket. Goes back to block area. Starts new structure alone. G/M talk to him. D gets up, kicks some blocks. Leaves again. Easel. Scribble paint for a minute (no smock), drips paint on floor, leaves. Brush falls on floor. Splash paint. Teacher sees. Calls back. D says happened by self. Teacher says clean. D paper towel, one swipe. Leaves. Teacher doesn't see.

So now the question is, what does this mean? What are we seeing? What questions might you be asking yourself about D's resiliency skill levels? When you are done recording your observations, sit down and work through the pieces of the "Getting to Know You" form to make sense of what you have seen. The full form can be found in appendix A.

The Six Life Skills

The first thing you will look for, of course, is evidence of the six life skills. How is the child relating to the adults in the room? Does the child participate in classroom activities and have friends? Does the child fall apart when things don't go as the child wants? What happens when there is a problem, such as when this child and another both want the same thing? What happens when the child tries to do something but is having trouble doing it? Does this child seem to know the routines and how to "do school"?

Use the continuums on the "Getting to Know You" form to help you see an overview of the child's level of the six life skills. For each skill, you will see one or more indicator behaviors. As you observe the child, make note of where on the continuum the child is performing, but don't mark the continuum at this time. After a few days of observation, review your notes and mark on the continuum the level of proficiency the child displays *most* of the time.

Careful observation might identify that even with all our work, the child still lacks one or two of the skills needed to move peacefully through the day. See the Six Life Skills section of the form.

Child's name _____ Date _____

Getting to Know You Form

Strengths and Challenges

Use the following list as a starting point to identify a child's strengths and challenges. Put a mark along the continuum for each item set. The mark can be anywhere along the range.

Attachment

Has little use for the adults in his/her world   Seeks out adults for love, comfort, company
◄───►

Belonging

Only plays alone   Seeks play with others
◄───►

Stands off to the side   Gets involved in classroom activities
◄───►

Self-Regulation

Uses behavior to communicate emotions ←——————————→ Uses words to communicate emotions

Falls apart when frustrated, disappointed, or hurt ←——————————→ Manages frustration, disappointment, or hurt

Impatient and impulsive ←——————————→ Thinks before acting, patient

Is oblivious to the emotions of others ←——————————→ Responds to the feelings of others

Collaboration

Can't wait, take turns, or share ←——————————→ Waits, takes turns, and shares

Uses aggression to get what s/he wants ←——————————→ Resolves conflicts with words or seeks help

Disrupts play when s/he tries to join in ←——————————→ Enters ongoing play smoothly

Contribution

Acts unable and hopeless ←——————————→ Optimistic and hopeful

Quits when things get challenging ←——————————→ Persists to achieve goals

Reluctant to help others ←——————————→ Seeks to help others

Teases, bullies, and excludes others ←——————————→ Is compassionate and fair with others

Adaptability

Has trouble adapting to changes ←——————————→ Usually adapts easily to changes

Ignores situation cues to modify behavior ←——————————→ Adapts behavior for the situation

Interests and Talents

The second thing to look for is a child's interests and talents. We can use this information as the theme on which we base our supports. Look at the table below for how we might use a child's interest in bugs to support the development of the six life skills.

Life skill	Possible action to improve skill
Attachment	Work with the child to plan a bug terrarium.
Belonging	Do a class study on bugs.
Self-Regulation	Construct the bug habitat over a period of days, focusing attention on the needs of the bugs.

(continued on next page)

Life skill	Possible action to improve skill
Collaboration	Facilitate taking turns and sharing; the child works with others to create the habitat.
Contribution	Encourage the child to persist in the construction even when there are challenges.
Adaptability	Work with the class to make a set of rules about caring for the bugs in the habitat.

Looking at a challenging child's areas of interest and expertise is also useful to remind ourselves that the child is a complex person with both gifts and challenges. The struggles we might be having with him are only one piece of his being. The second section of the "Getting to Know You" form asks about the child's gifts and talents.

1. What are this child's interests and areas of expertise?

_____

_____

_____

2. What does this child choose to play with?

_____

_____

_____

Play Level

The third thing to look for is what I call "level of play." Does the child seem to choose playing alone or with others? How many others? What happens when the child is playing happily and more children join in the play or come to share the space?

Sometimes what we find when we observe a child closely is that she seems to do well playing alone or with one other child but falls apart when she is in small or large groups. This is very important information to help us develop both learning strategies and strategies to help avoid meltdowns while she is learning how to get along well with groups of children.

Look at the image below from the "Getting to Know You" form for examples you might see at each play level.

Figure Out the Child's Highest Level of Independent Play

Observe the child to identify which of the five levels below describes the highest level of play the child can participate in without adult intervention or support. Circle the one highest level in the left-hand column that seems to describe this child.

Level of play	Looks like . . .
Solo	Child plays alone. For example, Patrice builds a block tower in the block area.
Parallel	Child plays next to another child with similar materials and themes, but does not interact with the other child. For example, Paley and Quentin play side by side at the water table, but don't play *with* each other.
Dyad	Looks a lot like parallel play, but in dyad play the children interact with each other. For example, Davon and Rebecca are dressing up in the dramatic play area. Davon hands a hat to Rebecca and says, "Here, you can wear this hat, and I will wear the green one." Rebecca says, "Okay, and I will be the grandma and you have to sit at the table and eat your lunch."
Small group	Looks a lot like dyad play, but instead of just two children, there are three to five children in the play.
Large group	Looks a lot like small group, but there are more than five children in the play.

Let's look now at how information on a child's play level might give us a clue to problem behavior.

I was asked to go into a first-grade class to figure out why a seven-year-old girl wasn't doing her work, even though the teachers knew she could do it. In the middle of work time, she would often start acting out, hitting, or throwing things at other children and then running off to hide someplace in the classroom. Teachers had tried making her stay in during recess to catch up on her work, and sending unfinished work home for her to do as homework. But that wasn't solving the problem of her hitting or throwing things.

When I went in to observe, this child seemed fine to me. She was friendly, happy, had a best friend who she stayed close to, and seemed to like her teacher. The classroom was set up in centers, and the children went from center to center to do individual work while the teacher pulled aside small groups of children for some guided work. I watched as this child went to the math table and began to do the task. Another child joined her and they worked together, relaxed and chatting. A third child joined them, and suddenly I could see this child tense up. She stopped talking and moved away from the other two children. When they tried to engage her, she brushed her arm over the table, knocking everything to the floor, left the table, and hid under a table on the other side of the room.

A few minutes later, she went to a writing table that was unoccupied. Again, the scene replayed itself. A first child joined her and all was well. A second child joined the table, and she tore up her work, threw it on the floor, and went again to be alone on the other side of the room.

Was it possible that her play level was still at dyad play and she didn't have the skills to function well yet in groups over two without adult facilitation? I mentioned my thoughts to the teacher, who said she had observed some of those behaviors herself. Our plan? We set up a few two-person tables around the room and explained to this child that we thought she would be happy working at them instead of at the bigger tables. We also set up some times for the teacher to join with her at the larger tables and coach her through the dynamics of working with more than one child at a time. The plan worked and the problem was solved!

Preferred Learning Style

The fourth thing I look for is how this child seems to learn best—his preferred style of learning. Does the child like to watch somebody else doing something before trying himself? Does he ask the teacher a million questions before trying something? Does the child like to go off by himself and look through books? Does the child seem to chat aloud most of the time, both to himself and others? Are his hands everywhere, constantly touching, manipulating, and feeling things?

Different children have different learning styles, and most children have two or three preferred ways that they learn best. Some kids can sit for an hour looking at a book about construction vehicles. Others have their hands all over things on the science table. Still others are constantly in motion. Observe children over a period of time to identify their preferred ways of learning.

The "Getting to Know You" form contains a section that can help you identify a child's learning style.

Preferred Learning Style

Most children will use a combination of many styles. Observe the child during the day and focus in on the two most preferred styles. A "preferred" style is the way a child learns when she has a free choice. For example, a child who is cooperative in large-group instruction may be compliant but prefers to work alone. Another child might eagerly look forward to large-group activities and tend to drift toward large groups even when it isn't a mandatory activity.

Learning style	Looks like . . .
Seeing	Learns best when he can see what he is learning. Likes photos, pictures, posters, books, and watching puppet shows and dramatic plays. Loses interest when activities are "talk heavy," but focuses in when there is something to look at.
Doing	Learns best from hands-on activities, play acting, opportunities to practice, journal writing, experience charts, and field trips. Enjoys getting actively involved in special projects.
Touching	Learns best by touching things such as artifacts and books. Likes to make things. Finds it hard to "look with no touching."
Moving	Learns best through dramatic play, puppets, dance and movement, and learning centers. Doesn't sit still for more than a few minutes.
Chatting	Learns best with discussions, buddy work, group work, and scripts. Finds it hard to keep quiet.
Working with others	Learns best working with a partner, in a small group, or in larger groups. Most often finds others to work with.
Exploring alone	Learns best when she can explore by herself or with an adult partner. Goes off often to work alone.
Individual cultures, interests, and challenges	Consider culture, family, language, individual abilities, interests, or challenges that influence the best learning situations for children.

Others have developed different ways to look at learning styles. Dawna Markova and Anne R. Powell, for example, offer a way to look at children's learning styles in their book *How Your Child Is Smart*. They identify six learning patterns that children might exhibit:

1. Show-and-Tellers
2. Seer/Feelers
3. Leaders of the Pack
4. Verbal Gymnasts
5. Wandering Wonderers
6. Movers and Groovers

Psychologist Howard Gardner from Harvard talks about what he calls "multiple intelligences." Gardner's nine intelligences include: mathematical, musical, kinesthetic, and linguistic, among others.

Regardless of which of these frameworks you use, just as with play levels, you might find that a child does just fine when engaged in an activity that takes advantage of her preferred learning style. This same child might be totally disruptive when the class is doing an activity that is *not* her style. For example, a child might do really well when the learning activity is kinesthetic, such as pretending to be the dragon from the story or counting how many times she can hop on one foot. This same child might be quite disruptive when asked to sit quietly to listen to a story at circle time. Knowing this about a child can help you make sure to provide her with many opportunities to employ her favored style.

When you design lessons and activities, make sure that they are accessible to all children in your class. Most children will have two or three preferred ways that they learn. Some learn best by seeing, others by doing. Some kids have to touch things or use their hands in some way in order to learn. You might see these children fiddling with things while you read them a story. Some children need to be able to move their entire body. They might rock or bounce about during story time. Some children don't process new information unless they can chat aloud about it. Some kids learn best with others, some best alone. In addition, you may have a child who is allergic to feathers, a child who can't touch anything sticky, a child who only understands Russian, or a child who lives in a homeless shelter. Regardless of what knowledge you are presenting to kids, whether it is learning to read, learning about animals, or learning appropriate behavior, help children explore the concept by providing a broad range of activities for all learning styles and individual needs.

If your target child learns by moving, for example, you might help her attend to large-group story time by periodically asking the children to act out a part of the story or by asking her to sit by you and turn the pages of the book. If the child learns best by seeing, you might want to have the child sit where he has a clear view of the book and draw his attention to the illustrations as you read. If your child is a social learner, make sure to stop reading at a critical point to invite the children to share their own personal stories that relate to the story being read. For example, when reading *The Kissing Hand*, say, "Was anybody else here scared to go to school like the little raccoon in our story?"

One teacher uses the study planning form that follows to make sure she has addressed the many learning styles of children in her group as she plans her units of study.

Learning style	Addressing learning style
Seeing	Include photos, pictures, posters, books, watching puppet shows and dramatic plays.
Doing	Include hands-on activities, play acting, opportunities to practice, journal writing, experience charts, field trips, and play sequences.
Using their hands	Include artifacts, books, and American Sign Language (ASL).
Moving	Include dramatic play, puppets, dance, and learning centers.
Chatting	Include discussions, buddy work, group work, and scripts.
Working with others	Include dyad, small-group, and large-group opportunities.
Exploring alone	Include opportunities for children to explore by themselves or with adult guidance.
Individual cultures, interests, and challenges	Be aware of family, culture, language, differing abilities, and challenges.

See how another teacher decided to use this planning form to teach the children in her class to share and take turns.

Learning style	Addressing learning style
Seeing	Take photos of children who are sharing. Use the puppets to illustrate asking for a turn. Read picture books that highlight children sharing and taking turns.
Doing	Have children act out asking for a turn at circle time. When children grab, use guidance and coaching to redo the situation and have them ask for a turn.
Using their hands	Teach all the children ASL for "turn" and have them use the sign at the same time they use the words.
Moving	Have children act out situations of asking to use something. Have them roll a ball back and forth to each other at circle.

(continued on next page)

Learning style	Addressing learning style
Chatting	Teach a "use your words" script to the kids. "Can I use that?" with a response of either "Okay" or "Not now, maybe later." Have kids practice the script at circle time. Have them do an experience chart on what they can do if they want something that somebody else is using. Have children notice when others have asked for a turn, and take dictation for leaves on the "I Can Do It" tree.
Working with others	Buddy children up to ask each other for a turn with a toy. Do a transition game from group to center time in which each child in turn asks another child for a turn with the "Talking Bunny." (The child who gives up the bunny transitions to the next activity—the child left holding the bunny is asked next for a turn by another child. Be aware that an adult must ask the last child for a turn!)
Exploring alone	Read picture books of children sharing and taking turns. Practice sessions with teachers on asking to use something.
Individual cultures, interests, and challenges	Maya's family feels it is too forward to ask for something that others are using. They want her to stand by quietly and wait a turn. Teach the children to be aware of others who stand by watching. Have them say, "Did you want a turn?" or "I'll give you a turn when I am done."

What Is Going on When It's Working?

When you have a child who disrupts plans and interferes with the experience of other children in the group, your view of the problem can become skewed. Evidence for this can be seen in some of the reports teachers might give to parents at the end of the day, such as, "Mario had a bad day today." What does that mean? Is the teacher saying that for all eight hours that Mario was in the program, there were problems? When we say, "He tantrums all day long," are we really saying that he had tantrums for eight hours straight? In all likelihood, what we mean is that there were many relatively short episodes during the day and Mario struggled to move peacefully through the day. Even if he had a total, full-blown tantrum for thirty minutes straight, it means that for the other seven and a half hours he did *not* have a tantrum.

The key here is to *very carefully* begin to document when things seem to go well. What does the child do when given a choice? When does the child have the most peaceful, successful time in the classroom? What makes this kid happy? Use this section of the "Getting to Know You" form to record your observations.

What Is Going On When It's Working?

In the space below, jot down what is going on during the times that the child is doing fine. Is it outdoor time? After lunch? When her best friend is there? Jot down as much information as you can to help you narrow down the environment in which the child works at her best.

_____

_____

_____

_____

_____

_____

_____

What Is Going on When It's Falling Apart?

When things fall apart, record what was happening, who was around, and where the child was. This might turn out to be the most important information you gather.

For example, Sarah was starting to physically attack other children, seemingly at random. Children were getting hurt and were beginning to avoid being near Sarah, and the attacks seemed to get worse and worse. The teachers finally asked the director to ask the parents to remove the child from the program before anything serious happened. Instead, the director spent a half a day observing the child in the classroom. What she discovered was that Sarah did just fine almost all of the time. But the four times the class transitioned between activities, Sarah got agitated and became physically aggressive with other children, causing them to cry or strike back. Once it was discovered that transitions were the trigger for the behavior, Sarah was assigned the job of teacher helper during transitions to keep her and the other children safe. As soon as the strategy was implemented, the problem was resolved. Teachers were then able to work with Sarah on strategies to remain calm during transitions without endangering the other children.

Use this portion of the form to record your observations.

What Is Going On When It's Falling Apart?

In the space below, jot down what is going on during the times that the child is struggling. Is it when his mother is class helper? Right before nap? During transitions? During large-group activities? Jot down as much information as you can to help you figure out what might be going on that is overwhelming this child.

_____

_____

_____

_____

_____

_____

_____

Seeing the Child through the Eyes of the Family

Finally, and sometimes the hardest piece to discover, is who is this child in the context of the family? What is the child's life like at home? Who does he live with? What are the expectations of behavior, and what happens when the child misbehaves? Does the child have frequent opportunities to interact with other children, or is that rare? Is there anything significant in the child's history that would give you insight into the child's behavior now?

Think of using the following portion of the "Getting to Know You" form sometime early in the school year. It's best to fill in this form through a conversation with the elders in the family rather than give them the form to fill out.

Seeing the Child through the Eyes of the Family

Use these questions to help obtain information from the child's family.

1. Who are the members of your family?

_____

_____

2. Who else cares for your child?

_____

_____

3. Who does your child sleep with? When does your child sleep?

_____

_____

4. Who does your child eat with? Does your child feed himself/herself or is your child fed by an adult?

_____

_____

5. What are some of the rules for children at home?

   _____

   _____

6. What do you do when your child misbehaves?

   _____

   _____

7. What do you do at home if your child is crying or having a tantrum when he/she doesn't get what he/she wants?

   _____

   _____

8. Does your child have any jobs to do at home?

   _____

   _____

9. Who does your child play with?

   _____

   _____

10. Does your child have to share his/her things with others?

    _____

    _____

11. What do you tell your child to do if somebody calls him/her names? Hits him/her?

    _____

    _____

12. What do you want for him/her from the program?

    _____

    _____

13. Is it okay with you if your child calls the teachers by (their first name, Ms. Alice, Mrs. Johnson)?

    _____

    _____

14. How do you feel about your child coming home from school with dirt or paint on his/her clothing?

    _____

    _____

15. Is there anything about the child's history that might be helpful for us to know? (For example, hospitalization, history of abuse, recent death in the family, or a traumatizing event in his/her past.)

    _____

    _____

What you might find is that expectations parents have for their children at home might not be the same as expectations you have in the classroom. What you might be seeing as a problem might actually be a matter of differing expectations at home and school. For example, at home Matthew's mother reports that she solves disputes between her children with the "find a way to share with your brother" rule. However, Matthew's teacher uses the "who had it first" rule. Maybe that's why when Matthew tries to use the blocks that Dana is using, he can't understand when the teacher tells him to play someplace else.

Here's another example of how knowing the child in the context of the family might give you insight into classroom behavior. A kindergarten teacher asked me to come in to troubleshoot the behavior of one of the five-year-old boys. The problem was that he stole food from other children's lunch boxes in their cubbies and from a drawer in the teacher's desk where she kept extra snacks. They had tried time-outs, keeping him inside during outdoor time, sending notes home to his mother, and explaining that stealing was wrong.

If this teacher had come to you asking what to try next, what might you have suggested if you've never seen the child? Think about this for a moment and jot down a few thoughts before reading on.

I went into the classroom expecting to see a heavy child who had poor social skills with peers, maybe some bullying-type behaviors, and maybe ignoring teacher requests. Instead I found a small, slim child who played and got along very well with his peers and who seemed to be quite affectionate with the teacher. I found this to be totally unexpected. Why would this child—who seemed to be attached to his teacher, connected to his peers, and have pretty good self-regulation—be stealing food on a regular basis? It just didn't make any sense to me.

During break time, I sat down to chat with the teacher to get more information and maybe find some clues to understand what was going on. She agreed that he was otherwise well behaved and liked school. He had friends and followed directions. The only problem he had was this stealing thing. I asked about his family life, wondering if there might be some suspicion of abuse or neglect. His teacher replied, "Oh no, they are great parents and they adore him. In fact, he was adopted at two years old from a Central American orphanage. He had been a street baby there, surviving on his own until the orphanage picked him up at two years old. When he was adopted, he was severely underweight and malnourished. But he's totally recovered now, is fluent in English, and is doing great according to his doctors."

Does this information give you any clues to why the child might be stealing food, even though he brings his own lunch every day? Do you want to revise the intervention you thought about earlier?

What we did, in fact, was keep snacks for this child in the teacher's desk. He was repeatedly reminded, "If you are ever hungry, ask me and we will get you a snack." When he took food from others, he was guided to give it back and was reminded to ask the teacher for more food instead. Within a couple of weeks, the stealing food behavior stopped.

Develop an Action Plan

The next step is to summarize what you have learned about the child on the "Develop an Action Plan" form and create concrete plans about how you will begin to support the child. When you first look at this plan you might wonder how you can possibly find time to do everything. But as you can see from the plan that follows, you can often select one activity, such as the basketball activity, and build other strategies around it. In the example, the teacher uses shooting baskets to build attachment, to scaffold friendship skills, and to build on the child's interests and learning style.

What follows is a sample of the completed plan. Notice how each section refers back to information you have gathered from your observations and have put in the "Getting to Know You" form.

Develop an Action Plan

This child needs more support on (circle the most basic one needed):
Attachment   Belonging   (Self-Regulation)
Collaboration   Contribution   Adaptability

The interaction strategy I will use to help the child develop this skill is:
I'll use the "what's your plan" strategy.

The classroom culture strategy I will use to help the child develop this skill is:
I will create a one-person area in the shelf under the window.

The activity I will use to help the child develop this skill is:
I will have the children make a chart on what they will do to calm down when they are angry.

I will strengthen my bond with this child by:
Spending 5 minutes a day playing with him.

This child is interested in/good at:
Outdoor activities . . . climbing, shooting baskets, and soccer.

I will work this into the upcoming lesson plan by:
Planning my 5 minutes a day with him either shooting baskets or kicking the soccer ball.

This child's highest independent level of play is:
dyad

I will scaffold this child to the next level by:
Gathering him and a small group of children during outside time and take turns shooting baskets with them.

This child's two preferred styles of learning are:
Moving; using his hands.

I will include activities for this learning style each day in next week's lesson plan as follows:

We will spend time outside shooting baskets every day.

Things seem to work well for this child when:

He is outside, at the take-apart table, during snack and lunch, in the science area. I will make sure to give the child positive reflective feedback during these times.

Things seem to fall apart for this child when:

We have large-group time and rest time.

Our plan to avoid meltdowns during those times is to:

Give him small toys to play with on his mat at rest time. At group time, I'll have him sit by me to hand me things we'll be using, like the book.

Family factors that may be significant (refer to the information you gathered on the form):

They live in a small apartment. He doesn't get to play with other children except for at school.

The last section of the form refers to "Daily Reflective Notes." Many parents and teachers feel a need to send home daily reports from school, especially when a child is struggling with behavior issues. Notes such as "Veronica hit three times again today" or "Elliot refused to come inside again when he was called" are not useful tools to help children develop the skills they need to be more successful the next day. While notes such as these can act as a report card of behavior, they neither serve as plans for improving the future nor do they help children see themselves as people who have the potential to do better the next day. Instead, use daily reports that help everyone maintain a healthy vision of the child as a complex individual with strengths, challenges, and plans for future improvement.

For example, one report might say, "Today I was proud that I helped set the table for lunch. Tomorrow I will work hard to ask for a turn with words instead of hands."

1. Help children reflect on their own behavior by involving them in completing the daily report. Say something like, "Powell, let's do your note to take home to your auntie Nicole."

2. Plan a meeting time each day when you and the child can reflect on the successes and challenges of the day and select one of each to report on.

3. Begin first with a success. Say, "Okay, first we need to write down a wonderful thing you did today." If the child can't think of something, gently remind him of two or three things from which to choose. "Let me think. Oh, I remember seeing you set the table for lunch. And I saw you reading a book quietly on your rest mat today. And what else? Didn't you and Saffron play Mr. Potato Head together at center time?" Record the child's successes for him.

4. Next, address one challenge of the day. Ask the child to recall one and then prompt him to switch from the problem itself to how he will address the problem tomorrow. For example, if a child says the biggest challenge was that he and Luke threw sand in the play yard, ask the child what he will try to do tomorrow instead of throwing sand.

   This step is very important. Help the child envision what a better choice might have been. Often at this point, the child will say, "I'll play nice." That isn't going to help the child tomorrow. Coach the child to be more specific. For example, say, "What will you do tomorrow with the sand that will keep everyone safe? Will you build tunnels with the sand? Will you keep the sand on the ground? Will you put water in the sand to make a river? How will you be safe with the sand?" Record the child's choice on the note.

5. If the child can't remember a challenge, prompt him in a similar way as you did for the success. Tactfully suggest, "Hmm. Let me think. Wasn't there some kind of problem out in the sandbox today? Something with Luke? And sand?" Keep slowly, tactfully, and respectfully adding bits of detail until the child can "remember" the incident.

6. It's at least as important to recognize success each day as it is to report problems. Initially, you will have to do a lot of coaching and asking guided questions to help the child remember successes and to reword challenges as plans for tomorrow. After a few weeks, however, most children can begin to construct these answers with less help from adults.

I will keep families informed about their child's progress using Daily Reflective Notes such as the following.

- Today I was proud that:

  _____

  _____

  _____

- Tomorrow I will work hard to:

  _____

  _____

  _____

Avoid the Unintended Side Effects of Punishment

We have looked at punishment versus solution a number of times in this book. But now I'd like for us to look at it from a child's point of view. What might be some of the unintended side effects of using punishment as a strategy?

- Punishment might be rewarding.

- Punishment sends a message that you can misbehave if you are willing to pay the price.

- Punishment discourages kids from developing self-regulation.

- Being sent away (home, to another classroom, to the office) sends a message that the teacher doesn't have the ability to help the kid control her behaviors.

Punishment Might Be Rewarding

We assume that consequences such as time-out or being sent to the office will change children's behavior. Let's look at those strategies from a child's point of view.

I'll start with a story about my own daughter when she was four years old. She came home from preschool complaining one day that she never got a chance to sit in the "special kid" chair. The next morning I asked her teacher what was going on, and he had no idea what I was talking about. My daughter pointed to the little chair in the back of the classroom, the time-out chair. I explained to her that kids went there when they misbehaved to think about what they did wrong. She didn't care. She wanted her turn. So I told her to disobey her teacher the next day. And sure enough, she came home beaming ear to ear. "I got to sit in the special chair! Mike held my hand, and we walked there together. And then I kicked on the wall like you're supposed to do and everybody looked at me." She couldn't have been more delighted at the attention she received.

Here's another example. I was asked to come in to help with a kindergarten child who was misbehaving. "We send him to the office probably four days out of the week," the teacher told me. During my observation, the children were all at their seats filling out math worksheets. I could see this child becoming restless, and before long he made a ball out of his paper and tried to toss it into the wastebasket from his seat. The teacher sent him to the office and I watched him from the hallway mirror. The office ladies all greeted him by name and had a long conversation with him about why he was there again. The UPS man came in with a delivery and a child was brought in with a bleeding nose. Phones rang and interesting people came in and out. No wonder this child acted out. He'd figured out the system: "be bad and get tons of attention" and "be bored and get sent to the principal's office where it's a heck of a lot more interesting." At some of my meetings, I often wish that somebody would open the escape hatch and send me to the principal's office! Revisit the strategies you are using to discourage bad behavior and see if perhaps you are rewarding it instead.

Pay the Price, and You Can Misbehave

Maybe you are thinking now that if we don't punish children then we are allowing them to get away with things. However, when we punish a child, such as keeping her inside during outdoor time, we are essentially saying to the child, "You have a choice not to comply if you are willing to pay the consequence." Seen in this light, perhaps it's when we do punish children that we let them get away with things. It's when we say, "How are you going to solve this problem?" that they take ownership of their behavior.

This willingness to pay the price of punishment differentiates our difficult kids from our easy kids. Typical children will understand the threat to mean "don't do that." Challenging kids hear us giving them a choice. They can either comply, or they can pay a price. They weigh whether the price we have put on hitting is a price they are willing to pay and often purposefully choose the consequence over being socially appropriate. Is that the message we intend to send with our threat?

Someone told me recently of a friend who loves to drive fast. Every year or so he gets a speeding ticket, which he refers to as his "license to speed." He's more than willing to pay this price to drive the way he wants to drive. Many corporations use the same reasoning, preferring to pay high fines as the price for violating environmental or labor laws. When they look at the bottom line, it's more cost effective to ignore guidelines and pay the fine than it is to comply. Many children view punishment in a similar way.

Punishment Discourages Kids from Developing Self-Regulation

Being punished can be experienced by the child as an easy way out. "I messed up. I sit in a chair for ten minutes, and that's that." The problem-solving approach comes from a different perspective. Instead of asking if the child is willing to pay the price for making poor choices, problem solving says, "This needs doing. Let's figure out how to get it done." The problem-solving approach doesn't even entertain the notion that something mandatory might not be done, because once we do that, we have told the child it is optional.

Using a problem-solving approach, we might say to a child, "It looks like you're having trouble staying quiet at rest time. How do you think you can get that job done?"

The problem-solving method is much more challenging for a child than sitting in time-out. It involves thinking, reflection, identifying needs, and finding solutions. We don't want to raise a generation of adults who are willing to be antisocial and pay the price for it. We want a generation of adults who can figure out how to take care of business even when it's not a convenient or pleasurable choice. Examine your own life for a moment. Is there a dry-erase board in the break room at work where you write your name when you mess up? Probably not. Do you have someone following you around to reward you with stickers when you hang the towel back on the rack? I doubt it.

Successful adults have figured out the more demanding process of "it's a challenge, but how am I gonna get it done?" We have alarm clocks to wake us up. We close the office door when we have a report due. We get an exercise buddy to encourage us to work out regularly. These are all "how are you gonna get it done" strategies—life skills. Begin now to build that same attitude in the kids you teach. Instill in children the belief that all problems can be resolved, and teach them the skills they need to make that belief a reality.

Don't Send a Message That the Teacher Can't Help the Kid

When kids have taken us to the breaking point, we might be tempted to send them to another classroom or to the office. The problem is that challenging children sometimes interpret this as meaning that you don't have the skills or strength to handle them when they are out of control. That can scare a little kid to death. When a child is out of control, she is looking for someone who says through actions, "Look, kid. I'm the grown-up and you are the child. I love you to death, and I am going to help you figure out how to do school. You do *not* scare me with your antics. I'm an adult who doesn't get scared by little kids."

If you have ever calmly and confidently supported a child through a tantrum, you have probably experienced how the child feels emotionally closer to you after the incident. This is because you have sent a message to the child that you are strong enough to take the worst she has to dish out without falling apart or getting angry. Children who have behavior challenges often search for such an adult to use as their anchor. Be that adult.

Redirect Children

Most children will learn to do what they need to do whether or not we use specific strategies to help and redirect them. But I have found that there is very little leeway when working with challenging children. These children respond best when we are exquisitely careful to use affectionate and hopeful language as we guide their behaviors. They learn best when we remain calm and in control and gently guide and support them to do their best. The strategies below are my "go to" strategies that I use day in and day out with children—not just with challenging children, but all the children in my care. At first the words and approaches may feel unfamiliar and stilted. But with practice they will become second nature—your "second language of guidance," so to speak.

Model Cooperative Language

When children are uncooperative, perhaps it's because parents and teachers have failed to create an environment in which children are truly involved in creating plans, making choices, and brainstorming solutions. Many children have more practice protecting their sense of self through resistance and rebellion than through self-control and cooperation. Model cooperation rather than aggression, bribery, threats, or control in your own interactions with children throughout the day.

Instead of saying . . .	Try saying . . .
"Do it because I said so."	"Let's figure this out together."
"Whoever cleans up fastest gets to be line leader."	"Let's see how fast we can work together to get the room cleaned up."
"You took them out, so you put them back, or you don't get to use them again."	"Let's help Bianca put the blocks away. She needed to use so many for the airport she made, and she needs some help."

Approach Problems as Opportunities

Problems, challenges, and mistakes are a part of life. Children who do well accept this fact and focus their energies on fixing or solving issues instead of looking for excuses or the opportunity to place blame. The language we use with children when there are problems sets them up to look back or to look forward. Approach problems and misbehavior as opportunities for future growth and development. Help children look forward to solutions rather than dwelling on the problem.

Instead of focusing on the problem . . .	Try to focus on what happens next
"Do you want to stay in from recess?"	"How can we solve the problem?"
"I warned you about that, didn't I?"	"Let's figure out a way to fix this."
"You should know not to do that. Go pull a color card."	"Everyone makes mistakes. Let's figure out a way to fix this."
"Why did you do that?"	"What can you do differently next time?"

Validate Feelings, Then Guide Behavior

Help children distinguish between feelings and actions. Children are not in control of their emotional responses to things that happen, but they do need to learn to take responsibility for their behavior choices. If someone grabs their toy, they might feel angry. Feeling angry is fine. However, they're the ones to make the decision to either grab the toy back, use assertive words to get the toy back, find adult help, or walk away. Their reaction to their feelings is their responsibility. Our role is to guide children to handle that anger with control and make a purposeful decision.

To validate a child's feelings, make your best guess of what the child is feeling. One way to start out is to use the words "you wish" or "you want." Other phrases that might work are: "You look frustrated," "I wonder if you are afraid," "Are you disappointed?" or "Are you hurt?"

Only after you have helped the child identify the feeling do you limit and guide behavior. By doing this, you validate for the child that the feeling is acceptable and that the action needs some thought and channeling.

Practice validating feelings and then guiding behavior until it becomes second nature. Try to use it on a regular basis whenever you approach a child to redirect his behavior. It's one of the most important techniques to use with young children to help them understand and manage their powerful feelings.

Instead of saying . . .	Validate feeling by . . .	Guide behavior by saying . . .
"Stop grabbing that doll. Arsenio is using it."	"Do you want to use that doll?"	"You can ask Arsenio for a turn or I will help you find another one."
"Quit kicking Jarvis's block tower."	"Do you want to play with Jarvis?"	"At school we don't kick blocks. You can ask Jarvis if you can play with him."
"Move away from the sink. Sophia has been waiting a long time."	"It looks like you are having fun in the water."	"This sink is for washing. Let's find a different place to play in water."
"No throwing shoes."	"Are you frustrated with those shoes?"	"We need to keep kids safe, so no throwing. I can help you tie if you like."

Use a Solution-Based Redirection Script

Use this very simple, three-step script when redirecting children. The goal is that when all is said and done, the child does what needs doing.

1. Identify the child's needs or wants.
2. Define the problem.
3. Help the child find a solution.

Let's look at this script in closer detail.

Identify a Child's Needs or Wants

Reflect your understanding of the child's point of view. When the child hears that you understand his perspective, you have put yourself in the role of an understanding mentor instead of an arbitrary dictator. An easy way to word this step is to begin with "You wish" or "You want." For example:

"You want to use the magnifier."

"You were in a hurry."

"You wish we didn't have rest time at school."

Define the Problem

Clarify the conflict between the child's behavior, want, or need and the existing situation. Keep the message short, sweet, and clear. Use the word *and* to connect the two parts of the sentence. For example:

"You want to use the magnifier and Blossom is using it."

"You were in a hurry and you knocked the chair over."

"You wish we didn't have rest time at school and that's what's next on our picture schedule."

Notice how the examples used the word *and* instead of *but*. For instance, "You wanted to choose our story book and I let Harold choose one today" instead of "You wanted to choose our story book but I let Harold choose one today." The use of *and* is intentional. When we use the word *but*, we are trivializing or negating the first part of the sentence. In this case, that would be the child's feelings. The use of the word *and* conveys the message that the child's feelings are as important as the limit or expectation.

Help the Child Find a Solution

Try saying something like:

"What can you do now?"

"What's your plan to solve this?"

Some children will need prompts to help them find solutions. Over time, they will need less help.

- Give a choice: "Would you like to ask Blossom for a turn or do you want to get another magnifier from the science shelf?"

- Guide the child to undo the harm: "Uh-oh. Do you think you can pick that chair up all by yourself?"

- Redirect: "Come, I'll help you find a book and we'll bring it to your rest mat" or "Let's go to the water table now, and I'll come get you when there is a magnifier to use."

Using the Three Steps

Fortunately, the three steps are much simpler to use in practice than to read on a page. Here are some examples of how it might look in your classroom. Each of the three steps are indicated:

- "(1) Bruce, you're so hungry you rushed to snack and (2) you forgot to wash your hands. (3) How can you fix that?"

- "(1) You wanted to get a swing and (2) you pushed Barbie down while you were running. (3) Come help me see if she's okay."

- "(1) You're having fun throwing the foam blocks and (2) those blocks are just for building. (3) Would you like to toss beanbags into the clown mouth with Diana, or do you want to wait to throw balls when we go outside?"

Acknowledge Positive Intent

Everyone's days are a mix of successful and not so successful experiences. One of the tricks of life is to figure out how to work through the hard stuff and continue to move forward. Help children develop this forward-looking attitude with words that convey your trust and belief that at her core, the child has a positive intent.

When a child . . .	Say . . .
Has been working on being quiet at story time but had a hard time today.	"I know you are working hard to stay quiet during story time."
Has been working to come inside at the signal but continued to play today instead.	"Pretty soon you'll be a kid who can come inside when the chime rings."
Is learning to share supplies and refuses to share the markers today.	"Pretty soon your brain will be strong enough to tell your body to share the markers."
Is learning to stop using profanity and slips.	"It takes a long time to learn how to use new strong words."

Encourage Children to Strive Up Instead of Belly Up

Most young children love to challenge themselves and "be big." They love the fact that every day they gain more skills. For a preschooler, tomorrow is an opportunity to be even better than today! Because they are asserting their independence, it is very difficult for them to "belly up" and do something "just because I said so."

Use this knowledge of typical child development when you are faced with children who chronically or stubbornly won't comply because they need to be big. Learn strive-up language instead of belly-up strategies to motivate children to do what needs doing. Reframe a task for them as something tricky or challenging and most children will put their energies toward achieving the goal. Turn compliance into a sign of strength rather than a sign of weakness.

Instead of saying . . .	Try . . .
"Get out from under that table right now."	"I wonder if you're a kid who knows how to get out from under the table all by herself."
"I'm counting to three and you had better get yourself inside this door."	"I wonder if you can get all the way into the classroom by the time I reach blastoff. Here I go: five-four-three-two-one-blastoff."
"You took all those puzzles out, so you need to put them all back on the shelf."	"Do you think you're a kid who can put all seven puzzles back on the shelf with no help?"
"Why do I have to keep reminding you to put your shoes in your cubby?"	"Pretty soon you'll be a kid who can put his shoes in his cubby all by himself."

(I learned this strategy in a therapeutic preschool from the psychologist I had the privilege to work with when I was first learning how to help challenging children. My thanks to Susan L.)

Use First/Then

Working and playing in the school community sometimes requires doing things kids don't feel like doing. Maybe they are involved with clay work when it is time to clean up for lunch, or they're feeling full of energy and ready to go when it is time to sit quietly and listen to a story. Threats, punishments, or bribes might get the child to comply, but this keeps the burden of responsibility with us. Our ultimate goal is that children learn to do undesirable but necessary tasks without this external motivation.

Help children develop the understanding that sometimes we need to do a less desirable action before we do actions that are more desirable by using the first/then technique.

Instead of saying . . .	Try . . .
"If you don't pick up the blocks, you won't go outside."	"First pick up the blocks, then you can go outside."
"You're not going to get snack if you don't come inside right now."	"First come inside, then you can have snack."
"If you finish your job, I'll let you have a turn at the cooking table."	"First finish your job, then you can cook."
"If you lie quietly at rest for ten minutes, I'll give you a sticker."	"First rest quietly for ten minutes, then you can get up and play."

Teach "I Don't Want To and I'll Do It Anyway"

Young children love predictable books, rhymes, and rhythm. Use this natural attraction to help children do things they would rather not do. Teach children the singsong mantra "I don't want to and I'll do it anyway."

1. Begin by modeling the sentence yourself when you do something you'd rather not do. For example, when you need to clean up spilled flour, say, "I don't want to and I'll do it anyway."

2. Use puppets and dramatic play with the children to rehearse and practice the skill.

3. After children have learned the chant, help them put it into practice in real-life situations. When a child is resistant, try saying "I don't want to and . . ." and hesitate to allow the child to finish the sentence. For most children, once they have said the words "I'll do it anyway," they find it easier to comply.

Help Children Take Responsibility

Tooth fairies, Easter bunnies, cartoon characters, and wishes on birthday candles—the lines of reality and fantasy are still blurred for preschool-age children. "If I say it is so, and I wish it were so, then it becomes so" is truth for children at this age. Yes, Deanna hit Brady on the head with a shovel. But when she is asked, she can say, "No, I didn't hit him," and mean it. She believes that if she said she didn't hit him, then she can rewrite the past. When you know a child was responsible for a particular event, instead of asking whether she was responsible, begin with the mutual assumption that she was.

Instead of saying . . .	Try . . .
"Did you grab that toy from Connie?"	"Tell me what happened about the toy."
"Did you spill that water?"	"Uh-oh. I see the water spilled. Let's find the paper towels to clean it up."
"Did you finish cleaning the home-living area?"	"Let's go to the home-living area to check it out."
"Did you knock over the bookshelf?"	"I see you knocked over the bookshelf. You must have been pretty upset."

Avoid False Praise

What about using the phrase "I like the way JuJu is behaving" as a way to motivate Alvin to act like JuJu? Before trying this strategy, reflect on what values you might be teaching to Alvin and the rest of the group. You are modeling that it is okay to give false praise to someone (in this case JuJu) and to take advantage of her without her knowledge and consent. Of course, there is nothing wrong with giving JuJu positive, reflective feedback for her own growth and development. But praising JuJu as a roundabout way to motivate Alvin is manipulative and disrespectful.

Try talking directly to Alvin about your concerns and brainstorm with him how to resolve the problem. This is a much more respectful and honest approach. Instead of using false praise, you might say, "Alvin, let's find somebody to match. JuJu knows what to do. How about matching JuJu right now?"

Responding to Profanity

Children may use profanity for a variety of reasons. Some are simply using the language used in their home when people have strong feelings. Others have discovered that profanity can be a powerful way to get a reaction from adults.

And still others are just testing out some new and interesting vocabulary they have learned. Regardless of the reason, for children to be successful in their school careers, they will have to refrain from using profanity at school.

The most important advice I can give about profanity is to avoid giving the words or the person speaking the words any power. The way you react to swearing in your room can either empower the words or can make those words useless to use in the classroom.

I Don't Understand

My first "reaction" when children use profanity in the classroom is to not understand what the speaker is saying. Here's an example of a typical conversation I might have with a child who calls me a vile name in response to redirection.

Child: You are a ####.

Me: I don't get it.

Child: I said, you are a ####.

Me: I don't understand what you are saying. (In my head I pretend the child is speaking a foreign language that I don't understand.)

Child: You don't know what #### means? It means ####.

Me: Sorry. Still don't get it.

Child: It means I'm mad at you. It means I don't like you anymore.

Me: Ohhh. That I understand. You're mad at me because I told you to go back and wipe up the spill.

I avoid saying things like "We don't use that language here" or "Those words are nasty." Challenging children hear that as "Ohhh . . . so now I can have power and control by saying ####. Isn't *that* interesting."

Avoiding Copy-Cat Profanity

Teachers are often concerned that if they don't punish or reprimand children for using profanity, other children in the group will feel free to swear as well. Sometimes you might actually have another child test the waters with a swear word. When this happens I say, "Gabriel, you know better than that. You're being silly. Hillary is still learning how to use other words when she is angry. You already know the school words to say. The best way we can help Hillary learn how to talk at school is for us to keep using the right words." I say this very lightly and casually, not as a reprimand. Again, this "un-powers" profanity and sends a message that the classroom community values other ways to express oneself.

Give Children Powerful Vocabulary

Children love powerful words and powerful language. Instead of letting profanity have power, introduce sophisticated language into the culture of the classroom. For example, I wrote earlier in the book that in our class we introduced the words *mandatory* and *optional*. We used these words every day at the end of morning meeting to describe what activities were available that day. For example, we might say, "There are some new hats in the dramatic play area. That activity is optional. But remember to sign in when you eat snack. That's mandatory." Children loved when we introduced sophisticated and powerful words like that, and they integrated them into their own vocabulary. Shortly after we introduced this language, one of the parents came in to talk to me, asking about some words her child had learned at school. The mother said, "I told her it was bath time last night, and she looked up at me and asked me if that was mandatory or optional!"

Chapter 8 Resources

Covey, Stephen R. 1997. *The 7 Habits of Highly Effective Families: Building a Beautiful Family Culture in a Turbulent World.* New York: Golden Books.

Divinyi, Joyce E. 1997. *Good Kids, Difficult Behavior: A Guide to What Works and What Doesn't.* Peachtree City, GA: The Wellness Connection.

Dreikurs, Rudolf, and Vicki Solz. 1964. *Children: The Challenge.* New York: Duell, Sloane, and Pearce.

Gardner, Howard. 1999. *Intelligence Reframed: Multiple Intelligences for the 21st Century.* New York: Basic Books.

Gestwicki, Carol. 2011. *Developmentally Appropriate Practice: Curriculum and Development in Early Education.* Belmont, CA.: Wadsworth Cengage Learning.

Greenspan, Stanley I., and Serena Wieder. 1998. *The Child with Special Needs: Encouraging Intellectual and Emotional Growth.* Reading, MA: Addison-Wesley Publishing.

Kaiser, Barbara, and Judy Sklar Rasminsky. 2012. *Challenging Behavior in Young Children: Understanding, Preventing, and Responding Effectively.* 3rd ed. Boston: Pearson.

Levin, Diane E. 2003. *Teaching Young Children in Violent Times: Building a Peaceable Classroom.* 2nd ed. Cambridge, MA: Educators for Social Responsibility.

Markova, Dawna, and Anne R. Powell. 1992. *How Your Child Is Smart: A Life-Changing Approach to Learning.* Emeryville, CA: Conari Press.

Marston, Stephanie. 1990. *The Magic of Encouragement: Nurturing Your Child's Self-Esteem.* New York: William Morrow.

Tobin, Larry. 1991. *What Do You Do with a Child Like This? Inside the Lives of Troubled Children.* Duluth, MN: Whole Person Associates

York, Stacey. 2003. *Roots and Wings: Affirming Culture in Early Childhood Programs.* Rev. ed. St. Paul, MN: Redleaf Press.

A Few Last Words

"Change has a considerable psychological impact on the human mind. To the fearful it is threatening because it means that things may get worse. To the hopeful it is encouraging because things may get better. To the confident it is inspiring because the challenge exists to make things better."
—King Whitney Jr.

Now that you have a bag full of new tricks and ideas, I hope you feel ready to go try them out. Remember, this information is just a starting point; it is not a cure-all. Some children are going to be a challenge. They'll make you cry and break your heart. They'll make you want to just give up. Keep in mind, though, that growth and healing may be going on so far under the surface that any progress may be invisible to you.

Domingo brought this lesson home to me many years ago. Socially and emotionally, he had so far to go. At five years old, he had been "asked to leave" his previous four preschools. For months it seemed that Domingo resisted all our attempts to build nurturing relationships and mutual respect. Establishing even the most rudimentary level of trust with him seemed impossible.

And then a new boy joined our group—a child with a similar history and similar challenges. Fear washed over me as I saw those two conspiring that first day at the lunch table. I edged over close enough to hear the conversation, certain that Domingo was coaching Christopher on how to make my life miserable. But I couldn't have been more wrong.

I got there just in time to see Domingo gently pat Christopher's hand. "Don't worry," he said quietly as he leaned in. "The teachers here won't kick you out. They're here to teach you how to be good and how to do good at school."

Remember why you picked up this book and what is at stake. There is nothing to lose, but there is oh so much to be gained.

—Jenna
www.kidsfromtheinsideout.com

Appendix A: Forms

Child's name _____ Date _____

Getting to Know You Form

Strengths and Challenges

Use the following list as a starting point to identify a child's strengths and challenges. Put a mark along the continuum for each item set. The mark can be anywhere along the range.

Attachment

Has little use for the adults in his/her world ←——————→ Seeks out adults for love, comfort, company

Belonging

Only plays alone ←——————→ Seeks play with others

Stands off to the side ←——————→ Gets involved in classroom activities

Self-Regulation

Uses behavior to communicate emotions ←——————→ Uses words to communicate emotions

Falls apart when frustrated, disappointed, or hurt ←——————→ Manages frustration, disappointment, or hurt

Impatient and impulsive ←——————→ Thinks before acting, patient

Is oblivious to the emotions of others ←——————→ Responds to the feelings of others

Collaboration

Can't wait, take turns, or share ←——————→ Waits, takes turns, and shares

Uses aggression to get what s/he wants ←——————→ Resolves conflicts with words or seeks help

Disrupts play when s/he tries to join in ←——————→ Enters ongoing play smoothly

Child's name _____ **Date** _____

Contribution

Acts unable and hopeless   Optimistic and hopeful
⟵————————————————————————————⟶

Quits when things get challenging   Persists to achieve goals
⟵————————————————————————————⟶

Reluctant to help others   Seeks to help others
⟵————————————————————————————⟶

Teases, bullies, and excludes others   Is compassionate and fair with others
⟵————————————————————————————⟶

Adaptability

Has trouble adapting to changes   Usually adapts easily to changes
⟵————————————————————————————⟶

Ignores situation cues to modify behavior   Adapts behavior for the situation
⟵————————————————————————————⟶

Interests and Talents

1. What are this child's interests and areas of expertise?

   _____

   _____

   _____

2. What does this child choose to play with?

   _____

   _____

   _____

Child's name _____ Date _____

Figure Out the Child's Highest Level of Independent Play

Observe the child to identify which of the five levels below describes the highest level of play the child can participate in without adult intervention or support. Circle the one highest level in the left-hand column that seems to describe this child.

Level of play	Looks like . . .
Solo	Child plays alone. For example, Patrice builds a block tower in the block area.
Parallel	Child plays next to another child with similar materials and themes, but does not interact with the other child. For example, Paley and Quentin play side by side at the water table, but don't play *with* each other.
Dyad	Looks a lot like parallel play, but in dyad play the children interact with each other. For example, Davon and Rebecca are dressing up in the dramatic play area. Davon hands a hat to Rebecca and says, "Here, you can wear this hat, and I will wear the green one." Rebecca says, "Okay, and I will be the grandma and you have to sit at the table and eat your lunch."
Small group	Looks a lot like dyad play, but instead of just two children, there are three to five children in the play.
Large group	Looks a lot like small group, but there are more than five children in the play.

Preferred Learning Style

Most children will use a combination of many styles. Observe the child during the day and focus in on the two most preferred styles. A "preferred" style is the way a child learns when she has a free choice. For example, a child who is cooperative in large-group instruction may be compliant but prefers to work alone. Another child might eagerly look forward to large-group activities and tend to drift toward large groups even when it isn't a mandatory activity.

Learning style	Looks like . . .
Seeing	Learns best when he can see what he is learning. Likes photos, pictures, posters, books, and watching puppet shows and dramatic plays. Loses interest when activities are "talk heavy," but focuses in when there is something to look at.
Doing	Learns best from hands-on activities, play acting, opportunities to practice, journal writing, experience charts, and field trips. Enjoys getting actively involved in special projects.

(continued on next page)

Child's name _____ **Date** _____

Learning style	Looks like . . .
Touching	Learns best by touching things such as artifacts and books. Likes to make things. Finds it hard to "look with no touching."
Moving	Learns best through dramatic play, puppets, dance and movement, and learning centers. Doesn't sit still for more than a few minutes.
Chatting	Learns best with discussions, buddy work, group work, and scripts. Finds it hard to keep quiet.
Working with others	Learns best working with a partner, in a small group, or in larger groups. Most often finds others to work with.
Exploring alone	Learns best when she can explore by herself or with an adult partner. Goes off often to work alone.
Individual cultures, interests, and challenges	Consider culture, family, language, individual abilities, interests, or challenges that influence the best learning situations for children.

What Is Going On When It's Working?

In the space below, jot down what is going on during the times that the child is doing fine. Is it outdoor time? After lunch? When her best friend is there? Jot down as much information as you can to help you narrow down the environment in which the child works at her best.

_____

_____

_____

_____

_____

_____

_____

Child's name _____ **Date** _____

What Is Going On When It's Falling Apart?

In the space below, jot down what is going on during the times that the child is struggling. Is it when his mother is class helper? Right before nap? During transitions? During large-group activities? Jot down as much information as you can to help you figure out what might be going on that is overwhelming this child.

_____

_____

_____

_____

_____

_____

_____

Seeing the Child through the Eyes of the Family

Use these questions to help obtain information from the child's family.

1. Who are the members of your family?

   _____

   _____

2. Who else cares for your child?

   _____

   _____

3. Who does your child sleep with? When does your child sleep?

   _____

   _____

4. Who does your child eat with? Does your child feed himself/herself or is your child fed by an adult?

   _____

   _____

Child's name _____ **Date** _____

5. What are some of the rules for children at home?

   _____

   _____

6. What do you do when your child misbehaves?

   _____

   _____

7. What do you do at home if your child is crying or having a tantrum when he/she doesn't get what he/she wants?

   _____

   _____

8. Does your child have any jobs to do at home?

   _____

   _____

9. Who does your child play with?

   _____

   _____

10. Does your child have to share his/her things with others?

    _____

    _____

11. What do you tell your child to do if somebody calls him/her names? Hits him/her?

    _____

    _____

12. What do you want for him/her from the program?

    _____

    _____

13. Is it okay with you if your child calls the teachers by (their first name, Ms. Alice, Mrs. Johnson)?

    _____

    _____

Child's name _____ **Date** _____

14. How do you feel about your child coming home from school with dirt or paint on his/her clothing?

   _____

   _____

15. Is there anything about the child's history that might be helpful for us to know? (For example, hospitalization, history of abuse, recent death in the family, or a traumatizing event in his/her past.)

   _____

   _____

Child's name _____ Date _____

Chronological age _____ Teacher _____

Develop an Action Plan Form

This child needs more support on (circle the most basic one needed):

Attachment   Belonging   Self-Regulation

Collaboration   Contribution   Adaptability

The interaction strategy I will use to help the child develop this skill is:

_____

_____

_____

The classroom culture strategy I will use to help the child develop this skill is:

_____

_____

_____

The activity I will use to help the child develop this skill is:

_____

_____

_____

I will strengthen my bond with this child by:

_____

_____

_____

This child is interested in/good at:

_____

_____

_____

From *Beyond Behavior Management: The Six Life Skills Children Need*, second edition, by Jenna Bilmes, © 2012.
Published by Redleaf Press, www.redleafpress.org. This page may be reproduced for individual or classroom use only.

Child's name _____ **Date** _____

I will work this into the upcoming lesson plan by:

_____

_____

_____

This child's highest independent level of play is:

_____

_____

_____

I will scaffold this child to the next level by:

_____

_____

_____

This child's two preferred styles of learning are:

_____

_____

_____

I will include activities for this learning style each day in next week's lesson plan as follows:

_____

_____

_____

Things seem to work well for this child when:

_____

_____

_____

Things seem to fall apart for this child when:

_____

_____

_____

Child's name _____ **Date** _____

Our plan to avoid meltdowns during those times is to:

_____

_____

_____

Family factors that may be significant (refer to the information you gathered on the form):

_____

_____

_____

When problems occur, I will reflect on these factors to see if they might play a part in what I am seeing.

_____

_____

_____

I will keep families informed about their child's progress using Daily Reflective Notes such as the following.

- Today I was proud that:

_____

_____

_____

- Tomorrow I will work hard to:

_____

_____

_____

Appendix B: Scripts

Scripts: Chapter 2, Attachment

Get to Know Children Well

You might say to a coworker . . .	When talking with a child . . .
"Hi, is Alvie over his cold yet?"	"Good morning. Is your nana still visiting you at your house?"
"I saw there was a gem show in town last week. Did you go?"	"You're such a good ball kicker. Do you play soccer with your cousins?"
"You know how to use this new computer program, don't you? Can you help me with a problem I'm having?"	"Your mom told me she is teaching you how to cook at your house. No wonder you are always first to sign up for a cooking project!"

Recognize "Insides"

Instead of saying . . .	Try saying . . .
"Good morning. I like your new tennis shoes."	"Good morning. I feel happy when I see your big smile."
"What pretty hair ribbons."	"Tell me about your visit with your grandma."
"Aren't you a handsome boy today."	"I'm so happy to see you this morning."

Be a Pillar of Safety

When . . .	Instead of saying . . .	Try . . .
Tyesha cries to you because Jaylyn hit her back.	"That's what happens when you hurt. You get hurt back. See?"	"This is a safe place. Let's find a way to keep you safe and a way to keep Jaylyn safe."
Mazen uses profanity and directs it toward you.	"Do you want to get kicked out of this school like you got kicked out of your last school?"	"Let's figure out words you can use here at school to tell me when you are angry with me."
Sovannary gets anxious during transitions and starts to toss things around the classroom.	"Go sit over there by yourself in the thinking chair. I'm tired of you breaking our things."	"Sovannary, come on over here with me so I can help you feel safe."
Matthew bites Amina.	"Nobody likes bad boys, Matthew."	"Let's get ice for Amina, and then you can stay by me so everyone stays safe here this morning."

From *Beyond Behavior Management: The Six Life Skills Children Need*, second edition, by Jenna Bilmes, © 2012. Published by Redleaf Press, www.redleafpress.org. This page may be reproduced for individual or classroom use only.

Use a Magic Word: Come

Instead of saying . . .	Approach the child, take her hand, and gently say . . .
"Go wash your hands."	"Come, let's wash hands."
"Go put on your shoes before we go out."	"Come, let's get your shoes."
"Sit down while you eat."	"Come, let's sit down."

Get Close

Instead of . . .	Try . . .
Calling across the room, "Lavone, is this your coat on the floor?"	Bringing the coat over to Lavone, squatting down, and gently saying, "Lavone, is this your coat? Put it in your cubby to keep it clean."
Calling across the room, "Frederick, did you wash your hands after you went potty?"	Walking over to Frederick, squatting down, taking his hands in yours, and gently saying, "Frederick, your hands are dry. I think you might have forgotten to wash. Scoot back in there and clean them up quickly."

Play with Children

Instead of saying . . .	Try . . .
"How many rectangles did you use to build that farm?"	"How can I play?"
"Let's match up the mommy animals and the baby animals."	"Here's some food for the cows. Eat, cows."
"Oh no. Elephants don't belong in a farm. Where do elephants go?"	"Oh no. My chicken is scared of the elephant. He's running to try to get under the fence."

Sportscasting

Instead of saying . . .	Try . . .
"What do you think will happen if you pour the water into the funnel?"	"Lulu is picking up the large bottle of water. It looks like she's going to pour it into the funnel."
"The boat is upside down. Turn it over and see how it works."	"Stephano has the boat upside down and is riding it in the water. He let go and the boat went right down to the bottom. Now he's picking it up. He turned it over. He let go. It is staying on top this time."
"What color is that water?"	"Tito has a pitcher of red water. He's filling little cups. Now he's filling the big cup."

Scripts: Chapter 3, Belonging

Supportive Interactions to Reinforce Family Belonging

Strategies to promote independence	Strategies to promote helpfulness
"Look at you! You got your shoes on all by yourself!"	"Arturo, thank you for helping David put his shoes on. Now we can all go outside."
Job board with tasks for each child.	Buddy jobs for children to do in pairs.
"Who was playing in the block area this morning? Please go back and put the blocks away so we can do story time."	"There are lots of blocks still out in the block area. Can we get some helpers to put them away so we can do story time?"

We Are Each Unique

When a child says . . .	Acknowledge the difference	Generalize the sameness
"Dharma's lunch looks yucky."	"Dharma's lunch is different than yours."	"But everybody's lunch is yummy food."
"Karen's skin is all pasty white."	"Karen has light skin, and you have dark skin."	"All people have skin on the outside of their bodies."
"Passion don't have no mama."	"Passion lives with her grandma, and you live with your mama."	"All kids live with grown-ups who take care of them."

Use Peers as Resources

When you say . . .	The child learns . . .
"_____ knows how to_____. Go ask him/her." For example, "Brandon knows how to open the jar. Go ask him for help."	Peers are valuable resources.
"That was a heavy table. It was good to have two kids work together to move it."	Sometimes it takes more than one person to reach a goal.
"I saw you guys playing catch outside. It's good to have another kid to play with."	Interacting with others can be fun.

Scripts: Chapter 4, Self-Regulation

Respond to Children's Emotions

You might want to . . .	Sounds like . . .
Ask how the child is feeling.	"Are you upset about that?"
Guess how the child is feeling.	"Your face and voice tell me you are very happy about your grandpa visiting you."
Mirror what you hear.	"I hear that you're angry that your shoe keeps falling off."
Validate feelings.	"I can see why you feel frustrated."
Empathize.	"You must feel so disappointed."
Let the child know that her feelings are a reaction to a trigger.	"You got scared when the fire alarm went off, huh?"
Reassure the child that his reaction is normal.	"A lot of kids are scared of loud noises."

Less Effective Ways of Responding to Children's Emotions

When you . . .	It . . .
Gush with sympathy—"Oh, you poor little thing. How mean of Allegra to say that to you."	Promotes victim mentality.
Give advice—"Here, let me show you how to put the bead on the string."	Sends the message that the solution is more important than the feeling.
Use humor—"You look like a volcano ready to explode. Ha, ha, ha! Is a bunch of hot lava going to come out of you?"	Makes light of the child's strong emotions.
Reassure—"Oh, don't feel like that. He didn't really mean it. He was just angry with you."	Sends the message that the child shouldn't feel the way she does.

Feeling or Information?

When a child says . . .	Feeling or information	Try saying . . .
"Nobody will play with me."	Feeling	"You sound lonely to me."
"Where does this block go?"	Information	"Look on the shelf and find the shapes that match."
"I can't draw a horse."	Feeling	"You aren't happy with how your horse looks?"
"How many crackers can we take?"	Information	"The sign shows that you can take two crackers."

From *Beyond Behavior Management: The Six Life Skills Children Need*, second edition, by Jenna Bilmes, © 2012. Published by Redleaf Press, www.redleafpress.org. This page may be reproduced for individual or classroom use only.

Name and Validate Feelings

Instead of saying . . .	Try . . .
"What's that face supposed to be all about?"	"I wonder if you are feeling frustrated (hurt, scared, disappointed)."
"Pouting isn't going to get you anywhere."	"It looks like you want to use the soccer ball first."
"There's no reason to be angry."	"You're angry, and that's okay."
"There's nothing to be upset about."	"I can see you're upset, and I understand."
"Don't feel that way."	"I'm sorry you feel that way."
"Go sit on the beanbag chair until you can come back with a smile on your face."	"What do you need? What do you want?"

Discover What's Underneath "Angry"

Instead of saying . . .	Try . . .
"You seem angry that you have to wait for a turn."	"You seem frustrated that you have to wait for a turn."
"I bet you're angry that it isn't your show-and-tell day."	"I bet you're disappointed that it isn't your show-and-tell day."
"When Emmaline said your shoes are ugly, you felt angry."	"When Emmaline said your shoes are ugly, you felt hurt."
"You're angry that we have a new teacher-helper today."	"You're scared about the new teacher-helper today.

Help Children Understand That Feelings Are Responses

When . . .	Template . . .	Example . . .
Outside events have an impact on their feelings	You feel (emotion) because (event).	"You feel excited because Josie is coming for supper" or "You feel tired because you worked so hard on the climber."
Other people's actions have an impact on their feelings	When (person) (action), you felt (emotion).	"When Margaret said you couldn't go to her birthday, you felt sad" or "David shared his blocks, and you felt happy."
Their actions have an impact on other people's feelings	When you (action), (other person) felt (emotion).	"When you pushed Denise, she felt hurt" or "Jose liked it when you asked him to sit by you at circle."

Change Children's Destructive Self-Talk

Instead of . . .	Suggest . . .
Nobody likes me.	I want somebody to play with.
This is too hard for me.	I need somebody to help.
I can't do this. I'm dumb.	I'm frustrated.

One More Thing

When you are playing with a child . . .	Try saying . . .
in blocks	"One more thing. Can we add three more blocks to the tower?"
in home living	"One more thing. Would you get me some pretend supper before you go?"
at the water table	"One more thing. Would you hold this funnel a minute so I can pour this big pitcher?"
at the writing table	"One more thing. Would you find me Orson's name card?"
in the book center	"One more thing. Before you go, would you find me a fun book from our bookshelf that I can read?"

Help Children Identify with Others

Morning meeting	"Who heard that big thunderstorm last night? Oh my goodness, I see a lot of you heard it. Look around at how many children heard that storm."
Story time	"Marcin, you ride the bus to school with your mommy just like the boy in our book. Angel, you ride the bus with your mama too, just like Marcin."
Mealtime	"Robert, look at MaryLynn's plate. I think she might like applesauce as much as you do. MaryLynn, are you an applesauce lover too?"
Outdoor time	Say to the children on the climber, "I see three kids who like to play on the climber—Akin, Steven, and Sunny. All three of you like to climb."

Model Perspective Taking

Describe what you see	Guess the emotion	Imagine the reason	Take action
"Mila has a big smile on her face."	"I think she might be happy . . ."	". . . because we have glitter and glue today."	"Mila, do you want to work at the art table this morning?"
"Jacob has tears in his eyes."	"He looks like he might be sad . . ."	". . . because he lost his lion keychain."	"Let's go help Jacob."
"Hannah's face is getting red and she's starting to talk very loud."	"She might be upset . . ."	". . . because Wagner crashed into her."	"Hannah, do you need help with something?"

From *Beyond Behavior Management: The Six Life Skills Children Need*, second edition, by Jenna Bilmes, © 2012. Published by Redleaf Press, www.redleafpress.org. This page may be reproduced for individual or classroom use only.

Recognize Helpfulness

Instead of . . .	Try . . .
"Give Amit some of the blocks."	"See if you can help Amit find a way to play blocks."
"Stacy needs a doll too. Paul, give her one of yours."	"Let's help Stacy be able to play babies with you."
"Stanley, move over so Albert can sit at circle."	"We need to help Albert find a place to sit." (Then just wait.)
"LeBron, Abby is crying because her mama just left. Can you paint with her at the easel, please?"	"Abby feels sad because her mama just left. How can we help her feel better?"

Behavior Affects Others

Instead of using the word *make* . . .	Try "When you _____, I feel _____."
"Tell Raymond how he made you feel."	"Tell Raymond that you don't like it when he calls you names."
"Don't make me call your mother."	"When I call and you don't come in, I feel very frustrated."
"Look at his face. How did you make him feel?"	"When you told Benjamin he couldn't play, he felt bad."

Scripts: Chapter 5, Collaboration

Help Children Calm Down

Neutral statement	Biased statement
"Wow, it sounds like two children are very upset about something. Let's stop for a minute so we can all hear what the conflict is all about."	"It sounds like you're upset that Benjamin took the stethoscope you were using."
"Whoa. It sounds like we have a conflict here. We'll fix this so it works for everyone. First, let's do some STAR breathing. Stop, Take a Deep Breath, and Relax."	"I see that Angel isn't letting you have any space to work."
"Uh-oh. It looks like we have a conflict about feeding Fishy. Let's all get a drink of water and then we can figure things out."	"Whoa. It sounds like it was Amie's turn to feed Fishy but Ricardo pulled the food away from her. Let's all get a drink of water and then we can figure things out."

Help Children Say What They Need and Want

What the child says . . .	How you reframe it . . .
"I want Pia to give me my book back."	"So you want the book, is that right?"
"I want Frederick to give me a turn at the computer."	"You want to use the computer, is that right?"
"I want to set the table all by myself. I don't want to do it with Leah."	"You want to set the table by yourself. Is that what you said?"

Help Define the Conflict

The clues	The conflict is . . .
Gabriel is arguing with Kyrha over who will use the wagon. Each one says that they want to use the wagon.	Two kids want to use the same wagon.
Tyreck and Caden jostle with each other so they can better see the new rat. Each one says they want to see the rat.	Two kids both want to see the rat.
Daniel is using the red beads and LaVita moves the beads to her side of the table. Each one says they want to use the beads.	Two kids want to use the same beads.

Help Children Find Resolutions

If . . .	Try . . .	Sounds like . . .
The child is very new at brainstorming solutions.	Suggest one or more solutions, such as sharing, taking turns, or finding duplicate items.	Instead of saying, "You can find more markers or put your name on a waiting list," think of saying, "Some children decide to find more markers on the shelf and some children like to put their name on a waiting list." Using this format helps children think of solutions without the teacher taking control of the process.
The child has had ample experience brainstorming solutions.	Encourage the child to find a peer to help.	"Would you like to find another friend to help you think?" "Who might know?" "Who can you ask?"
	Help the child break through his or her block.	"Pretend you're a kid who has an idea. What would you say?"

Demonstrate Conflict-Resolution Attitudes

Conflict-resolution attitude	How to model
Conflicts can be resolved.	"Uh-oh. The block area is so crowded it looks like you are having trouble working. Let's find a way to solve this conflict."
Nobody is all wrong or all right.	"Nobody is doing anything wrong. We just have a conflict we need to resolve."
Figure out what's going to happen next; don't assign responsibility for what already happened.	"Let's look at what we can do so everybody has room to work."
The solution needs to work for everyone.	"How about we move this shelf over so we can find room for everyone. Does that work for all of you?"

Invite Children to Come to You for Help with Conflicts

If a child reports . . .	Try saying . . .
An incident in which the child is personally involved—for example, "He won't let me get on the slide."	"Do you need help solving this?" If the child says yes, you can move into conflict resolution.
An incident involving other children—for example, "Kim won't let Dallas get on the slide."	"Thank you." If the child pushes for a greater response, you might say, "I'm taking it under consideration."

Avoid Naming the Child Who Reported an Incident

Instead of saying . . .	Try saying . . .
"Kim, Dow said you won't let Dallas use the slide."	"Dallas, it looks like you're trying to use the slide. Are you having a conflict?"

Help Children Learn Assertive Responses

When . . .	Children can say . . .
A child is allowing another child to interfere	"I don't want you to help. I'll do it myself."
A child is the object of name-calling or profanity	"I don't like those words. Stop it."
A child is being bullied	"I don't like that. I'm going to play with somebody else."
Someone is grabbing a toy from a child	"Stop it. Ask for a turn."

Break Down Assertive Language into Baby Steps

	Teach	Includes . . .	For example
First	"Stop" or "No."	A single word to set a boundary	"Stop."
Second	"I don't like that."	Expression of a feeling	"I don't like that."
Third	"I don't like it when you (behavior)."	Expression of feeling in response to the action of another	"I don't like it when you call me names."
Fourth	"I don't like it when you (behavior). I want you to (suggestion for change)," or "I don't like it when you (behavior). I'm going to (action)."	Expression of feelings, the action of another, and a suggestion for change or action	"I don't like when you call me names. I'm going to play with somebody else."

From *Beyond Behavior Management: The Six Life Skills Children Need*, second edition, by Jenna Bilmes, © 2012. Published by Redleaf Press, www.redleafpress.org. This page may be reproduced for individual or classroom use only.

Model Assertive Language

When a child . . .	Instead of . . .	Try saying . . .
Calls you a name	Sending the child to time-out	"I don't like those words. I'm going to walk away right now."
Talks while you are trying to read a story	Saying, "That's so rude to talk while I'm reading"	"When you talk I have trouble reading. I wish you could be more quiet."
Calls another child a rude name	Saying, "Be nice"	"When you call Paloma names, I wonder what you are trying to say. Let's see what's wrong and find another way to say that."
Grabs a toy from another child	Grabbing the toy back and returning it to the child	"I don't like it when you grab toys. We take care of people in our classroom. I want you to give the squirter back to Dana."

Scripts: Chapter 6, Contribution

Use Encouraging Language

Descriptive feedback	Focus on process	Encourage self-reflection
"I see you made it all swirly up here on top."	"Tell me how you made this swirly part up here."	"What's your favorite part of this painting?"
"Look how many different colors you used."	"How did you decide what colors to use in this?"	"Do you like the colors you used for this painting?"
"That tower is almost as high as you are."	"That must have been tricky to build a tower so high."	"What do you think of that tower?"
"You got all the way across the monkey bars."	"You worked hard to learn how to get across those monkey bars."	"How do you feel about getting all the way across the monkey bars?"

From *Beyond Behavior Management: The Six Life Skills Children Need*, second edition, by Jenna Bilmes, © 2012. Published by Redleaf Press, www.redleafpress.org. This page may be reproduced for individual or classroom use only.

Fair and Unfair

When a child says . . .	You might say . . .
"Me and Emily are sharing the stickers."	"You two found a fair way to make sure you both got to use what you need."
"Andrew took the computer and my name was the next one on the list."	"That sounds unfair. How can we fix it?"
"Juan took all the grapes at snack and now there's none left and I never got any."	"Hmm. That's unfair, isn't it? Let's go see what we can do to make it right."
"Look! Me and Dae and Ava are taking turns on the wagon."	"How fair! Now everybody gets a turn to be the rider and the puller."

People Are Different—And That Is Good

If a child says . . .	You might say . . .
"I don't want to play with Jesus. He can't talk right."	"Jesus talks in Spanish like his family does. You talk in English like your family does. How about we teach Jesus a few words in English, and he can teach us a few words in Spanish?"
"Why is Ella so fat? She's gonna break the chair if she sits on it."	"Ella *is* bigger than you. Some people are bigger and some people are smaller. And our chairs are made for all sizes of people. How do you think Ella might feel when she hears you talk about her size?"
"Berta, you can't play fire with us because only boys and mans can be firemans."	"Both men and women can be firefighters. And in our class, boys and girls can do all the same pretend play too."

Confronting Bias and Bullying Behavior

Instead of solving . . .	Try teaching and coaching . . .
"Nakita, don't hit Faith. Hitting hurts. She doesn't like that."	"Faith, you can tell Nakita you want her to stop hitting you. Say, 'Stop hitting me.' I'll stand by you to help."
"Zola, you need to let Kiana play babies too."	"Come, Kiana. I'll go back with you, and you can tell Zola that you can play babies if you want to."
"Caleb, I don't want you calling names here."	"David, let's go back and you can say, 'Don't call me dummy. I don't like that.'"
"Kelsey, boys can play in home living too."	"Jose, I'll come with you so you can tell Kelsey that boys and girls can play with everything at school."

Encourage Children to Look Out for the Welfare of Others

If a child reports . . .	Try saying . . .
An incident in which she is involved—for example, "He said I can't play in the block area because I'm not his friend."	"It's unfair when somebody stops a kid from using things in our room. Do you need help solving this?" If the child says yes, you can move into problem solving or conflict resolution.
An incident involving other children—for example, "Marcel is holding Anthony down and won't let him up, and Anthony is crying."	"Thank you for letting me know that somebody needs help. Let's go see what we can do."

Scripts: Chapter 7, Adaptability

Use "At School We . . ."

When . . .	"At school . . ."
Children physically fight over a bike.	"At school we use words, not hands, to solve problems."
Children cry in order to get adults to bend the rules.	"At school the rules stay the same, even when children cry."
Children behave as if they are helpless to get adults to do tasks for them.	"At school (zipping, flushing, drawing, pouring, and so on) is a child's job."

Use the Guiding Principles for Guiding and Redirection

Give the direction . . .	Because . . . (guiding principle or behavior)
"Akio, we need to keep our shoes on outside . . .	. . . because we take care of ourselves."
"Tito, Miguel isn't done at the drinking fountain yet. You need to wait for a turn . . .	. . . because we need to take care of each other."
"When you're done with snack, please put your banana peel in the trash . . .	. . . because we take care of our stuff."

Guide Children to Select More Appropriate Behaviors

When the child . . .	Weave the guiding principle into the redirection
Wants to grab a bike from another child.	"You wish you had that bike. At school, we can't just grab things because we take care of others. Let's find another way to solve this."
"Borrows" things from school without asking.	"You would love to take this toy to your house. We take care of our stuff at school, so we'll leave it here to play with tomorrow. Let's find something that you can take home with you."
Hits a child to get what she wants.	"We take care of others at school. If the kids won't listen to your words, come get me and I'll help you."
Throws markers on the floor because he's frustrated by not being able to draw a car.	"You're having trouble drawing that car. At school, we keep markers on the table because we take care of our stuff. Let's see if there is some way to help you."

Scripts: Chapter 8, Children Who Need Extra Support

Model Cooperative Language

Instead of saying . . .	Try saying . . .
"Do it because I said so."	"Let's figure this out together."
"Whoever cleans up fastest gets to be line leader."	"Let's see how fast we can work together to get the room cleaned up."
"You took them out, so you put them back, or you don't get to use them again."	"Let's help Bianca put the blocks away. She needed to use so many for the airport she made, and she needs some help."

Approach Problems as Opportunities

Instead of focusing on the problem . . .	Try to focus on what happens next
"Do you want to stay in from recess?"	"How can we solve the problem?"
"I warned you about that, didn't I?"	"Let's figure out a way to fix this."
"You should know not to do that. Go pull a color card."	"Everyone makes mistakes. Let's figure out a way to fix this."
"Why did you do that?"	"What can you do differently next time?"

Validate Feelings, Then Guide Behavior

Instead of saying . . .	Validate feeling by . . .	Guide behavior by saying . . .
"Stop grabbing that doll. Arsenio is using it."	"Do you want to use that doll?"	"You can ask Arsenio for a turn or I will help you find another one."
"Quit kicking Jarvis's block tower."	"Do you want to play with Jarvis?"	"At school we don't kick blocks. You can ask Jarvis if you can play with him."
"Move away from the sink. Sophia has been waiting a long time."	"It looks like you are having fun in the water."	"This sink is for washing. Let's find a different place to play in water."
"No throwing shoes."	"Are you frustrated with those shoes?"	"We need to keep kids safe, so no throwing. I can help you tie if you like."

Acknowledge Positive Intent

When a child . . .	Say . . .
Has been working on being quiet at story time but had a hard time today.	"I know you are working hard to stay quiet during story time."
Has been working to come inside at the signal but continued to play today instead.	"Pretty soon you'll be a kid who can come inside when the chime rings."
Is learning to share supplies and refuses to share the markers today.	"Pretty soon your brain will be strong enough to tell your body to share the markers."
Is learning to stop using profanity and slips.	"It takes a long time to learn how to use new strong words."

Encourage Children to Strive Up Instead of Belly Up

Instead of saying . . .	Try . . .
"Get out from under that table right now."	"I wonder if you're a kid who knows how to get out from under the table all by herself."
"I'm counting to three and you had better get yourself inside this door."	"I wonder if you can get all the way into the classroom by the time I reach blastoff. Here I go: five-four-three-two-one-blastoff."
"You took all those puzzles out, so you need to put them all back on the shelf."	"Do you think you're a kid who can put all seven puzzles back on the shelf with no help?"
"Why do I have to keep reminding you to put your shoes in your cubby?"	"Pretty soon you'll be a kid who can put his shoes in his cubby all by himself."

Use First/Then

Instead of saying . . .	Try . . .
"If you don't pick up the blocks, you won't go outside."	"First pick up the blocks, then you can go outside."
"You're not going to get snack if you don't come inside right now."	"First come inside, then you can have snack."
"If you finish your job, I'll let you have a turn at the cooking table."	"First finish your job, then you can cook."
"If you lie quietly at rest for ten minutes, I'll give you a sticker."	"First rest quietly for ten minutes, then you can get up and play."

Help Children Take Responsibility

Instead of saying . . .	Try . . .
"Did you grab that toy from Connie?"	"Tell me what happened about the toy."
"Did you spill that water?"	"Uh-oh. I see the water spilled. Let's find the paper towels to clean it up."
"Did you finish cleaning the home-living area?"	"Let's go to the home-living area to check it out."
"Did you knock over the bookshelf?"	"I see you knocked over the bookshelf. You must have been pretty upset."

From *Beyond Behavior Management: The Six Life Skills Children Need*, second edition, by Jenna Bilmes, © 2012. Published by Redleaf Press, www.redleafpress.org. This page may be reproduced for individual or classroom use only.

Index